Study Guide

to accompany

Zimbardo • Gerrig

PSYCHOLOGY AND LIFE

Fourteenth Edition

Prepared by

Richard J. Gerrig
State University of New York-Stony Brook

and

John Caruso
University of Massachusetts-Dartmouth

HarperCollins*CollegePublishers*

Study Guide to accompany Zimbardo/Gerrig *PSYCHOLOGY AND LIFE,*
FOURTEENTH EDITION

ISBN: 0-673-99385-X

96 97 98 99 00 9 8 7 6 5 4 3 2

TABLE OF CONTENTS

Preface

☙ Welcome to the Study Guide ☙

Why did you buy this Study Guide? There are probably several reasons, but we are confident that one of the reasons is that you want to do your very best in your course. Perhaps someone has suggested that using a Study Guide can improve your understanding and mastery of course material, and ultimately this will show in better test scores. Those were certainly the goals we had in mind as we wrote the Study Guide. We want to make sure you get your money's worth!

Let us introduce you to each of the features of this Guide (note that we have repeated much of this material in Chapter 1 as a reminder to you):

📖 Chapter Outline

We begin each chapter with a chapter outline so that you can think about how the chapter is structured. For each major topic, we also provide a question under the heading "What you need to know." You should be aware that the contents of introductory psychology books are sampled from a broad range of psychological inquiry. Authors of introductory textbooks have to choose which material to include in their texts. The authors of your book always chose material that they felt, for many reasons, students **need** to know. The questions under the "What you need to know" heading should help you study by allowing you to understand how your authors made their choices.

Guided Study ☞ ☞ ☞ ☞

For each section of the chapter, we will ask you a series of questions that are intended to guide your study. You should work your way through these questions at least twice: once, while you are reading the textbook, and a second time--without looking at the book--after you have studied the material. Note that the numbering is preserved from the chapter outline. Questions preceded by an * apply to material in the introduction to each section. We also give you page numbers for the start of the section.

Three important notes about the Guided Study sections. First, if we asked you a question for every fact or conclusion in your textbook this Study Guide could be a thousand pages long! Therefore, these questions and exercises are just intended to guide your study. Don't ignore other parts of the text. Second, sometimes the questions are very specific (they will have one precise answer) whereas other times they are somewhat broader (so they may have more than one good answer or you might have to find a way to summarize a section of the text). We introduced this variety to keep you from getting bored with the Study Guide. Third, the questions sometimes go a bit beyond what is in the textbook--to get you to think about the material more deeply or from a slightly different perspective. This should help you to learn the material more thoroughly.

For Group Study

One of the best ways to prepare for an exam is to study with your classmates. This study guide can help you do that in many ways. For example, you can try to answer each question yourself and then discuss your answers with your friends. Similarly, you can take each practice test and then talk through the answers with classmates before you look at the answer key. If you teach your friends and they teach you, you will end up with greater mastery of the material.

For each chapter, we will also make specific suggestions of extra activities you can carry out in group study. Some of the exercises you could carry out on your own, but doing them with friends will enhance the experience. We will number each idea according to the chapter outline.

Practice Tests

Each chapter includes two practice tests. You should use these tests to assess your knowledge. Don't take the tests until you're confident you have studied enough not to have to peek at the answers! If you take them too soon, you'll only make yourself nervous. If you feel like you still can't answer the questions after you've studied, you should consult with your professor or your classmates to improve your memory techniques.

We hope this Study Guide will add to your enjoyment and understanding of introductory psychology.

📖 Chapter 1

Probing the Mysteries of Mind and Behavior

We will take the opportunity in this first chapter to introduce each of the study guide features to you. We believe that if you understand why we have included each of these features, it will make the study guide even more useful.

📃 Chapter Outline

We begin each chapter with a chapter outline so that you can think about how the chapter is structured. For each major topic, we also provide a question under the heading "What you need to know." You should be aware that the contents of introductory psychology books are sampled from a broad range of psychological inquiry. Authors of introductory textbooks have to choose which material to include in their texts. The authors of your book always chose material that they felt, for many reasons, students **need** to know. The questions under the "What you need to know" heading should help you study by allowing you to understand how your authors made their choices.

Section	What you need to know
I. Psychology: Definitions and Goals	
A. Definitions	How is the field of psychology defined?
B. The Goals of Psychology	Why do psychologists do the things they do?
1. Describing what happens	
2. Explaining what happens	
3. Predicting what will happen	
4. Controlling what happens	
5. Improving the quality of life	

Section	What you need to know

II. The Evolution of Modern
Psychology

   A. Psychology's Historical   What issues and scholars gave rise
      Foundations   to modern psychology?

     1. Structuralism: The contents of
       the mind
     2. Functionalism: Minds with a
       purpose
     3. The legacy of these approaches

   B. Current Psychological   What ideas differentiate the six
      Perspectives   contemporary perspectives?

     1. Biological approach
     2. Psychodynamic approach
     3. Behavioristic approach
     4. Humanistic approach
     5. Cognitive approach
     6. Evolutionary approach
     7. Comparing perspectives: Focus on
       aggression

III. What Psychologists Do   Why is the field of psychology
divided into so many specialties? How are those
specialties defined?

IV. Looking Ahead

Close-up: Psychological Expertise in   Why do researchers seek
the Public Forum   to "give away" psychology?

Guided Study

For each section of the chapter, we will ask you a series of questions that are intended to guide your study. You should work your way through these questions at least twice: once, while you are reading the textbook, and a second time--without looking at the book--after you have studied the material. Note that the numbering is preserved from the chapter outline. Questions preceded by an ➣ apply to material in the introduction to each section. We also give you page numbers for the start of the section.

Three important notes about the Guided Study sections. First, if we asked you a question for every fact or conclusion in your textbook, this Study Guide could be a thousand pages long! Therefore, these questions and exercises are just intended to guide your study. Don't ignore other parts of the text. Second, sometimes the questions are very specific (they will have one precise answer) whereas other times they are somewhat broader (so they may have more than one good answer or you might have to find a way to summarize a section of the text). We introduced this variety to keep you from getting bored with the Study Guide. Third, the questions sometimes go a bit beyond what is in the textbook--to get you to think about the material more deeply or from a slightly different perspective. This should help you to learn the material more thoroughly.

I. A. Definitions (p. 3)

➣ What is the scientific method and how is it used?

➣ Give some examples of behavior.

➣ What types of individuals are studied by psychologists?

➣ Why is there a focus on mental processes?

➤ Why is psychology considered to be a unique field?

I. B. The Goals of Psychology (p. 5)

➤ Make sure that you understand how each of the goals is different from the others. Begin by listing the five goals:

_____   _____   _____

_____   _____

1. Suppose you want to describe behavior. What choices must you make?

2. What does an explanation add to a description?

For what sorts of explanatory patterns do psychologists look?
What is the role of *inference* in explanation?

3. What types of variables are used to make scientific predictions?

How do base rates allow predictions to be made?

What is the relationship between explanations and predictions?

4. Why is control such an important goal?

Why are there sometimes ethical problems with the goal of control?

5. Give some examples of how the findings of psychology can be used to solve human problems.

II. A. Psychology's Historical Foundations (p. 12)

➤ What sorts of psychological questions have been posed by thinkers since ancient times?

➤ Who were some of the figures that founded early psychological laboratories?

➤ What was the importance of the doctrine of *determinism*?

1. What was the main focus of *structuralism*? What scholars are associated with this perspective?

What role did *introspection* play in structuralist research?

What were some of the important objections to structuralism?

2. What was the main focus of *functionalism*? What scholars are associated with this perspective?

Make a list of early psychologists and what they wished to study (include topics and methods):

Scholars	What they wished to study

II. B. Current Psychological Perspectives (p. 15)

➤ List the six perspectives that dominate contemporary psychology.

_____   _____   _____

_____   _____   _____

➤ What dimensions help define the unique approach of each perspective?

1. At what levels do researchers who adopt the biological approach try to understand behavior? What are the assumptions of the approach?

2. What is the importance of instinctual, biological drives in the psychodynamic approach? What role did Freud play in the development of the psychodynamic approach?

3. Why do researchers in the behavioristic tradition emphasize observable behavior? What is the main objective of behaviorist analysis, and how do behaviorists collect their data?

4. Why do humanistic psychologists focus on individual lives?

5. What determines behavior according to the cognitive approach? Why does the cognitive approach present a challenge to behaviorism?

6. Why do researchers who adopt the evolutionary approach analyze environmental conditions in the Pleistocene era? How does evolutionary psychology differ from other perspectives?

7. Describe how each approach attempts to understand the nature of aggression and violence.

Biological approach:

Psychodynamic approach:

Behavioristic approach:

Humanistic approach:

Cognitive approach:

Evolutionary approach:

III. What Psychologists Do (p. 20)

➤ There are many different types of psychologists because there are so many different types of questions that can be asked about human experiences. To understand what each type of psychologist does, you should focus on the questions they address. This should enable you to figure out how each specialty got its name. For each specialty, write down a sentence to help you remember what those psychologists do.

Psychiatry

Clinical psychology

Counseling psychology

Community psychology

Biological psychology

Neuroscience

Psychopharmacology

Behavioral genetics

Experimental psychology

Cognitive psychology

Cognitive science

Personality psychology

Social psychology

Developmental psychology

8

Industrial psychology

Organizational behavior

Human factors psychology

Applied psychology

Educational psychology

School psychology

Environmental psychology

Health psychology

Forensic psychology

Sports psychology

Don't let yourself be intimidated by this long list! Again, just try to use the name of each specialty to help you remember the questions psychologists address.

⌒ Close-up: Psychological Expertise in the Public Forum (p. 25)

➤ In what circumstances do psychologists "give away" psychology?

➤ Why is it sometimes controversial?

For Group Study

One of the best ways to prepare for an exam is to study with your classmates. This study guide can help you do that in many ways. For example, you can try to answer each question yourself and then discuss your answers with your friends. Similarly, you can take each practice test and then talk through the answers with classmates before you look at the answer key. If you teach your friends and they teach you, you will end up with greater mastery of the material.

For each chapter, we will also make specific suggestions of extra activities you can carry out in group study. Some of the exercises you could carry out on your own, but doing them with friends will enhance the experience. We will number each idea according to the chapter outline.

II. B. 7. Current Psychological Perspectives

Your textbook describes how each of the different perspectives contributes to an analysis of aggressive behavior. Choose another aspect of human behavior that interests you, and discuss how each approach may apply. You might consider dating and loving relationships, sports and competition, or child rearing practices.

III. What Psychologists Do

Try to formulate questions from your own life and discuss what type of psychologist might try to answer them.

Close-up: Psychological Expertise in the Public Forum ⟨⟩ ⟨⟩ ⟨⟩

Read a newspaper together or watch the evening news. Do any of the stories quote or feature psychologists? Are there any stories for which psychological knowledge might have been relevant?

Practice Test ①

1. Vicky and Amelia are talking about whether Rahul will be on time for an important meeting. They both say "no." Vicky thinks Rahul will be late because he is not a very conscientious person. Amelia thinks he will be late because the room is hard to find. Vicky is using a(n) _____ variable; Amelia is using a(n) _____ variable.

a. dispositional; situational
b. dispositional; organismic
c. stimulus; response
d. environmental; stimulus

2. Psychologists are most likely to study _____ in _____.

a. the scientific method; natural habitats
b. mental processes; individuals
c. the scientific method; individuals
d. limitations; mental processes

3. To what domain did John Dewey apply his functionalist perspective?

a. Politics
b. Physics
c. Education
d. Philosophy

4. Dr. Grouper is a social psychologist. In her research, she is most likely to study

a. the type of environmental input children need to learn language.
b. whether shy people are more likely to experience job failures.
c. the kinds of brain damage that lead to memory loss.
d. whether people take greater risks when they are part of a group.

5. Imagine that you have become a rich and famous humanistic psychologist. One day, you are asked to represent the humanistic approach in a panel discussion on dreaming. The title of your talk is most likely to be

a. "The Effects of Birth Order on Dream Onset."
b. "Brain Activity During Dreaming."
c. "Dreaming and Creative Potential."
d. "Dreaming and Memory Enhancement."

6. To put your children through college, you have decided to take on some additional work. One day, while skimming the "help wanted" section of a newspaper, you see an item advertising for a human factors psychologist. The job is most likely to involve

a. devising tests of a new drug to combat depression.
b. comparing human and nonhuman animal responses to cancer treatments.
c. designing the cockpit of a new fighter airplane.
d. researching the political backgrounds of potential jurors.

7. Your teacher has asked whether anyone in the class knows Wilhelm Wundt's significance to modern psychology. You should answer that he

a. invented the scientific methods that ensure objectivity.
b. founded the first formal psychology laboratory.
c. was one of the professors who trained Sigmund Freud.
d. originated the idea that mental processes control behavior.

8. Psychologists can be characterized as "a rather optimistic group" because they believe that

a. virtually any undesired behavior can be modified with an appropriate intervention.
b. the legal system will always follow the conclusions drawn by researchers.
c. mental processes can be understood without the use of inference.
d. ethical issues never interfere with the goal of controlling behavior.

9. Researchers who adopt the evolutionary approach

a. focus on the environmental conditions in which the human brain was formed.
b. explore the mechanisms that allow human brains to acquire new information.
c. view antecedents and consequences as the most important forces in the environment.
d. study the instinctual forces that give rise to modern behavior.

10. Which of the following might have been a book written by Edward Titchener?

a. Introspection Reveals the Contents of the Mind
b. The Triumph of Functionalism
c. The Multiple Purposes of Behavioral Acts
d. The Dangers of Reductionism

11. The eternally observant Dr. Kildoor has noticed that his pet poodle arrives in the kitchen to be fed exactly at 6 p.m. He decides to study this interesting phenomenon at the micro level of analysis, so he

a. compares his poodle to other dogs in the neighborhood.
b. wakes the dog at different times each morning and looks for changes in body rhythms.
c. records how quickly his dog is running at 6 p.m.
d. monitors his poodle's brain activity as the time approaches 6 p.m.

12. On your way to visit the department secretary, you overhear two psychologists having a loud discussion about what can properly be studied in the laboratory. One insists that psychologists should stick to observable behaviors. The other believes that psychologists can also study mental processes. These psychologists most likely represent the _____ approaches.

a. behavioristic and cognitive
b. humanistic and psychodynamic
c. biological and cognitive
d. psychodynamic and biological

13. Do you always need to have an explanation for a behavior before you can make predictions about its occurrence?

a. Yes, because the explanation allows you to understand the importance of intervening variables.
b. Yes, because you can't make a prediction without using the scientific method.
c. No, because dispositional variables are equally as important as situational variables.
d. No, because base rates can be a good indicator of future behavior.

14. For three years, Samantha has worked as a psychologist in a day care center for underprivileged children. She has developed a teaching program that enhances each child's self-esteem. This program most clearly satisfies psychology's goal of

a. description.
b. explanation.
c. prediction.
d. control.

15. You are concerned because you think a good friend is having trouble coping with the stress in his life. You might recommend that he see a _____ psychologist.

a. community
b. social
c. clinical
d. human factors

16. The _____ approach to the study of psychology is most likely to include researchers who focus on behaviors that are motivated by inner drives.

a. behavioristic
b. psychodynamic
c. cognitive
d. evolutionary

17. Your psychology professor tells you that she carries out research on the genetic basis of individual differences in intelligence. She is most likely to endorse the _____ approach.

a. biological
b. psychodynamic
c. humanistic
d. cognitive

18. Structuralists and functionalists were all interested in the study of _____.

a. language
b. aggression
c. consciousness
d. scientific objectivity

19. Which of the following is more than just a description of behavior?

a. Karla dropped the ball so she had to bend to pick it up.
b. Karla was hungry so she ate a handful of cookies.
c. Karla chased another child around the playground.
d. Karla sat at her desk and sang along with the class.

20. While watching a televised trial one day, you notice that the American Psychological Association has filed a "friend of the court" brief. The television commentator says this is because

a. lawyers do not understand the scientific method.
b. psychological knowledge is often relevant to legal policy.
c. legal proceedings only involve situational variables.
d. individual psychologists are not allowed to testify in criminal cases.

1. Two housemates are arguing over the cause of a third housemate's poor social behavior. One attributes it to shyness, but the other believes it is due to a conceited personality. Researchers would probably judge which explanation is best by

a. measuring how strongly each housemate feels about his opinion.
b. attributing the social behavior to an intervening variable.
c. using informed imagination and inferences.
d. determining how well each explanation predicts behavior in new situations.

2. Who was the founder of the first formal experimental psychology laboratory, and probably the first person to refer to himself as a psychologist?

a. Wilhelm Wundt
b. John Hopkins
c. William James
d. Edward Titchener

3. In her Research Methods course, Amy is giving a short classroom presentation on the "scientific method." She is most likely to mention the

a. steps used by researchers to analyze and solve problems.
b. general inability of scientists to draw conclusions from their research.
c. importance of authority and personal beliefs in the determination of truth.
d. reliance of researchers on biased methods.

4. Dr. Fernandes is a professor at the state university. She is interested in developing methods to improve learning in various instructional environments, and occasionally does applied work involving teacher training. Dr. Fernandes is probably a(n) _____ psychologist.

a. educational
b. social
c. forensic
d. environmental

5. Andrea's mother returned to school and eventually received her doctorate in psychology. Now, she works in a community setting, delivering psychological services to the poor and homeless. In this role, she can best be classified as a

a. sociologist.
b. psychiatrist.
c. community psychologist.
d. clinical psychologist.

6. Which of the following would be an example of a relationship between responses?

a. Students who are punctual are also intelligent.
b. Most people who dream, do so in color.
c. When Kim has an itch, she scratches it.
d. More people have brown eyes than have blue eyes.

7. You are thinking about taking a course entitled "Cognitive Psychology" because it fits into your schedule. A friend has taken the course, so you ask her what it is about. She is most likely to tell you that it concerns

a. unconscious drives, motivations, and conflicts.
b. human thought and processes associated with knowing.
c. the achievement of human potential and personal fulfillment.
d. Charles Darwin's theory of evolution by natural selection.

8. What is the major focus of the Stanford Heart Disease Prevention Program for smokers?

a. Smokers should take self-directed control of their smoking behavior.
b. Non-smokers need to be taught that nicotine is psychologically addictive.
c. Friends and relatives of smokers need to be educated concerning their role in supporting a smoking habit.
d. Smoking is a manifestation of a "death wish" that can only be overcome by substituting a "life wish."

9. Imagine being transported back in time over 100 years to the days of Wundt, von Helmholtz and Fechner. If you could eavesdrop on their conversations, what would you most likely overhear them say?

a. "Natural laws are irrelevant to human behavior."
b. "We must rebel against the new notion of determinism."
c. "We can study human behavior using natural science techniques."
d. "It can be demonstrated that human organisms are special in the kingdom of animals."

10. Imagine being at an auction of rare manuscripts. Up for bid is a previously undiscovered early manuscript of Sigmund Freud. What would it most likely be entitled?

a. "You Are What You Eat"
b. "Evolution or Revolution?"
c. "Humans Are What Humans Do"
d. "Pushed and Pulled by Hidden Forces"

11. A man is convicted of being a serial killer. A psychologist who favors the biological approach would be most likely to look for the determinants of the killer's behavior in the

a. man's brain and nervous system processes.
b. man's unconscious drives and conflicts.
c. immediate stimulus environment.
d. adaptive behaviors of the man's ancestors.

12. Mike grew up in a home where his father and mother had terrible fights, often ending in violence. Now, married himself, Mike often explodes in anger and sometimes physically abuses his wife. Assuming that Mike learned to be abusive by watching his parents would be most consistent with the _____ approach.

a. biological
b. psychodynamic
c. behavioristic
d. evolutionary

18

13. Fred thinks of himself as shy and excitable, but his friends see him as reserved and enthusiastic. A(n) _____ psychologist could use psychological tests and inventories to assess and interpret Fred's identity.

a. personality
b. experimental
c. human factor
d. social

14. Imagine that you have decided to live your life based on the humanistic approach. Your main task will be to

a. identify the antecedent environmental conditions that lead to your behavior.
b. try to understand the inner and outer forces that control you.
c. simply realize that life is a biochemical process.
d. strive for growth and the development of your potential.

15. Imagine living in the time of the classical Greek philosophers Socrates, Plato, and Aristotle. If you were interested in explaining human nature at that time, your primary method of proof would have been

a. medicine.
b. witchcraft.
c. logic.
d. psychology.

16. Which of the following psychological researchers is using the biological approach in a clinical setting?

a. Dr. Audee is investigating the relationship between genes and intelligence.
b. Dr. Bentlee is studying how diet influences the maze-running ability of a group of laboratory rats.
c. Dr. Caddie is looking at the attentional deficits suffered by children who are taking medication.
d. Dr. Duzy is studying how brain chemicals affect sexual behavior.

17. Dr. Soose has decided to do research on reading behavior. If he were to approach this topic from a macro level of analysis, he would be most likely to study

a. whether there are cultural differences in attitudes toward reading.
b. the fixation points readers make while reading a page of text.
c. whether readers speak aloud while reading.
d. which parts of the brain are most active during the reading of a foreign language.

18. A central concept in the evolutionary approach to the study of psychology is

a. humanism.
b. determinism.
c. natural selection.
d. a phenomenological approach.

19. While making your annual trip around the world, you encounter many psychologists in Asian and African countries. Compared to Westerners, cross-cultural research indicates that psychologists in Asian and African countries are more likely to have the ultimate goal of

a. description.
b. understanding.
c. control.
d. improving the quality of life.

20. Which of the following questions would a cognitive psychologist be most interested in?

a. How do hormones affect sexual behavior?
b. Why are males more likely to be color blind?
c. Why do some people make poor decisions?
d. Why do crowds sometimes get out of control?

Answers, Practice Test ①

1. a (p. 9)

2. b (p. 3)

3. c (p. 14)

4. d (p. 22)

5. c (p. 17) The humanistic approach emphasizes the growth potential of each individual.

6. c (p. 22)

7. b (p. 13)

8. a (p. 10)

9. a (p. 18)

10. a (p. 14)

11. d (p. 6)

12. a (pp. 17-18)

13. d (p. 10) A base rate can allow you to make a prediction even when you don't have an explanation.

14. d (p. 10) If the program changes each child's self-esteem, it most clearly satisfies the goal of control.

15. c (p. 21)

16. b (p. 16)

17. a (p. 16)

18. c (p. 14)

19. b (p. 7) "Karla was hungry" is a possible explanation for why she ate the cookies.

20. b (p. 25)

Answers, Practice Test ②

1. d (p. 9)

2. a (p. 13)

3. a (p. 4) The scientific method consists of a set of orderly steps used to analyze and solve problems.

4. a (p. 23)

5. c (p. 21)

6. a (p. 8)

7. b (p. 18)

8. a (p. 10)

9. c (p. 13) All three researchers assumed that psychological processes could be studied objectively by using methods adapted from the natural sciences.

10. d (p. 16) Freud viewed a person as pulled and pushed by a complex network of inner and outer forces.

11. a (pp. 19-20)

12. c (pp. 19-20)

13. a (p. 22)

14. d (p. 17)

15. c (p. 12)

16. c (p. 16)

17. a (p. 6)

18. c (p. 8) The evolutionary approach assumes that animals' brains evolve just as other organs do.

19. b (p. 11)

20. c (p. 22) The research focus of the cognitive psychologist includes judgment and decision-making.

📖 Chapter 2

Psychological Research

▤ Chapter Outline

Section	What you need to know
I. The Context of Discovery	How do psychologists develop the ideas they test?
II. The Context of Justification: Safeguards for Objectivity	
A. Observer Biases and Operational Definitions	How can researchers prevent beliefs from biasing observations?
1. The challenge to objectivity 2. The remedy	
B. Experimental Methods: Alternative Explanations and the Need for Controls	How can experiments be designed to yield a unique casual explanation for a phenomenon?
1. The challenge to objectivity 2. The remedy	
C. Correlational Methods	Why do researchers use correlational designs? Why does correlation not imply causation?
D. Subliminal Influence?	How can experimental methods be used to address real-life claims?

Section	What you need to know
III. Psychological Measurement	
A. Achieving Reliability and Validity	Why must measures be reliable and valid?
B. Self-Report Measures	Under what circumstances do subjects provide information directly to researchers?
C. Behavioral Measures	What types of information do psychologists obtain by observing behavior?
D. Physiological Measures	How are physiological observations relevant to psychological questions?
IV. Ethical Issues in Human and Animal Research	How do researchers protect the rights of subjects from all species?

A. Informed Consent
   B. Risk/Gain Assessment
   C. Intentional Deception
   D. Debriefing
   E. Issues in Animal Research: Science, Ethics, Politics	

Close-up: Evaluating Drug Prevention	How can you design research to address important societal issues?
V. Becoming a Wiser Research Consumer	What critical thinking skills should you bring to the evaluation of research and real-world claims?

26

Guided Study

I. The Context of Discovery (p. 28)

➤ What is meant by the context of discovery?

➤ What is meant by determinism?

➤ What are hypotheses and their sources?

➤ What kind of attitude is needed for scientific research?

➤ Why is public verifiability important?

II. A. Observer Biases and Operational Definitions (p. 31)

1. Summarize an example from the book of the effects of observer biases.

Now try to think of a situation from your own life that was affected by observer biases.

2. Why is standardization important? What is an operational definition?

Consider an experiment in which a researcher examines the effects of mood on memory. She is going to use a hypnotic induction to place subjects in a happy, sad, or neutral mood, and then ask them to share childhood memories. The researcher wants to determine whether the emotional tone of the memories matches the mood in which the subjects have been placed.

What is/are the independent variable(s)?

What is/are the dependent variable(s)?

How might you operationalize the "emotional tone" of the memories. That is, how would you measure their "emotional tone?"

II. B. Experimental Methods: Alternative Explanations and the Need for Controls (p. 33)

1. You see a man running out of a building. What are some alternative explanations for this behavior? Suppose you wanted to test one explanation. What might some confounding variables be?

Why do researchers worry about expectancy and placebo effects?

2. A researcher wishes to show that people who are given chocolate to eat have an easier time memorizing lists of words. Which of these is a double-blind control? Which is a placebo control? Why?

a. The experimenter who gives each subject chocolate (or not) is different from the experimenter who administers the memory test.

b. One group of subjects is not given any food, but each subject in this group spends as much time in the experimental room before taking the memory test as do the "chocolate" subjects.

What problems in interpretation of the results do these two controls prevent?

Is this a between-subjects or within-subjects design? How could you change the experiment to transform it from one to the other? How could you make it an A-B-A design?

II. C. Correlational Methods (p. 37)

➤ Make sure you understand the difference between positive and negative correlations. Can you think of a real-world example in which high values on one dimension are generally matched by high values on a second dimension (a positive correlation)? Can you think of a real-world negative correlation?

➤ Summarize an example from the textbook of why correlation does not imply causation.

➤ Why does cross-cultural research require correlational methods? What differences have cross-cultural studies revealed?

II. D. Subliminal Influence? (p. 40)

➤ What was the result when researchers examined subliminal influence in the laboratory?

III. A. Achieving Reliability and Validity (p. 42)

➤ What are reliability and validity? (You may want to preview the section in Chapter 15.)

III. B. Self-Report Measures (p. 43)

➤ What types of information are gathered through self-report?

➤ What are common self-report methods?

III. C. Behavioral Measures (p. 44)

➤ What is meant by behavioral measures?

➤ What do observations focus on?

➤ What sets naturalistic observation apart from other behavioral measures?

➤ Why is Jane Goodall's research an example of naturalistic observation?

➤ What would be a self-report measure for sleepiness? What would be a behavioral measure? (Challenge yourself to provide more than one measure for other phenomena that interest you.)

III. D. Physiological Measures (p. 47)

➤ What are some physiological measures? To what uses do psychologists put them?

IV. Ethical Issues in Human and Animal Research

A. Informed Consent (p. 48)
B. Risk/Gain Assessment (p. 48)
C. Intentional Deception (p. 48)
D. Debriefing (p. 48)

➤ For these four brief sections, focus on the types of ethical issues researchers must consider before they set out to conduct a study.

➤ Why are informed consent and debriefing such crucial parts of ethical research?

IV. E. Issues in Animal Research: Science, Ethics, Politics (p. 48)

➤ Summarize the debate over the uses of nonhuman animals in psychological research.

Professor Yes (supports the use of nonhuman animals in restricted circumstances):

Professor No (believes all nonhuman research should be banned):

Close-up: Evaluating Drug Prevention (p. 51)

➤ Why is it often the case that people on both sides of an issue can produce statistics that support their points of view?

➤ What have evaluations of DARE shown?

➤ Make sure you understand what the authors mean by "becoming a wiser research consumer" and "critical thinking skills."

➤ Work your way through the list beginning on p. 53 and try to understand how each of the rules grows out of applications of an open-minded skepticism and the scientific method.

For Group Study

I. The Context of Discovery

Choose some real-life issues for which psychological data might be relevant (you may already have done this for Chapter 1). Discuss in what ways the current societal context might influence the hypotheses people would develop to explain important phenomena. You might consider, for example, the roots of criminal behavior or concerns about violence on television.

II. A. 2. Observer Biases and Operational Definitions

Challenge each other to operationalize abstract concepts. How would you measure equality? freedom? honesty? courage?

II. B. Experimental Methods: Alternative Explanations and the Need for Controls

Watch a television program with the sound off and try to come up with alternative explanations for the behavior you are seeing. Discuss what evidence you would need to decide among the alternative explanations. (If you don't have a television handy, try watching people who are far enough a way so that you can't hear them.)

III. B. Self-Report Measures

Find a recent newspaper or magazine that presents poll or survey data. Discuss the wording of the questions that were asked. Do you think the wording or type of question (for example, open-ended vs. fixed alternatives) influenced the answers that were given or the conclusions that were drawn?

III. C. Behavioral Measures

Look out the window at people walking by and try to describe as precisely as possible what they are doing. Discuss how you can reach agreement on judgments that are potentially subjective. Are the people happy? Are they angry? Are they in love? Are they having a fight?

Close-up: Evaluating Drug Prevention ⌒⌒ ⌒⌒ ⌒⌒

Choose an important societal problem. First discuss possible interventions for solving the problem. Then discuss how you would evaluate the effectiveness of your interventions. Try to apply the terminology you have learned in the chapter to your research design.

1. Ms. Gap does a study to determine the relationship between age and amount of money spent on new clothing. She discovers that the older an adult gets, the less money he or she generally spends on clothing. This is a

a. base rate estimate.
b. negative correlation.
c. dependent variable.
d. positive correlation.

2. A recent poll revealed that, among those who have an opinion, 63% of adults in North America prefer Mickey Mouse to Bugs Bunny. The margin of error for the poll is 3 percent. Why do reports of poll results almost always include margins of error?

a. Some people say they are "not sure" of their response.
b. The results are only based on a sample from a large population.
c. The error term factors in bias in the way the questions were asked.
d. The researchers don't want to be accused of misleading the public.

3. You heard a report on the news this morning that 72% of car owners drive over the speed limit because they don't believe they will get caught. The most likely source of this information is

a. A-B-A methodologies.
b. behavioral observations.
c. self-report questionnaires.
d. placebo biases.

4. Suppose you wanted to test the idea that you can get people to purchase more popcorn by briefly flashing "Buy Popcorn" during a movie. To conclude that "Buy Popcorn" was effective as a subliminal message, it would be necessary for you to use a control condition in which

a. some viewers would be warned that you're going to flash "Buy Pepsi" on the screen.
b. some viewers would be given free tickets to the movie.
c. all viewers would be given tests of perceptual ability.
d. some viewers would be warned that you're going to flash "Buy Popcorn" on the screen.

5. Which of the following is likely to be the conclusion from a study using a correlational method?

a. Children sleep better when they are read stories at bedtime.
b. Rats learn mazes best when they receive food as a reward.
c. People find horror movies less scary after they have viewed a television program that explains special effects.
d. Women are more likely than men to talk with friends about personal problems.

6. Your history professor catches you yawning during his lecture, and asks you how much sleep you got last night. When you say, "five hours," he concludes that you wouldn't be yawning if you got more sleep. One possible confounding variable that your professor may be overlooking is that

a. the professor was giving a boring lecture.
b. you get only five hours of sleep every night.
c. you got up early to come to history class.
d. the professor got eight hours of sleep.

7. While walking past an auditorium, you overhear, "There are no morally relevant differences between human and nonhuman animals." The debate is likely to be about the

a. ethics of using nonhuman animals as subjects in psychological research.
b. ethics of using deception without informed consent.
c. importance of studying basic psychological processes in a wide range of species.
d. importance of debriefing all experimental subjects.

8. Your faculty advisor is still talking on the telephone when she signals you into her office. You overhear her say, "I need a measure that yields comparable scores when I use it repeatedly with the same subject." It sounds like she is concerned about

a. validity.
b. placebo biases.
c. naturalistic observations.
d. reliability.

9. One day when you have nothing better to do, you decide to try out two new recipes for chocolate chip cookies. You want to determine which of them yields tastier cookies. You ask ten friends to try one cookie from each recipe and then tell you which one he or she prefers. This is a(n)

a. A-B-A design.
b. between-subjects design.
c. within-subjects design.
d. placebo control.

10. Binna claims that every time she goes jogging, bees come out to attack her. She takes this very personally. You've even heard her say, "The bees are out to get me." You might explain to her that

a. correlation does not imply causation.
b. bees are not appropriate research subjects.
c. she needs to operationalize her claim.
d. she needs a placebo control group to test her hypothesis.

11. Tommy claims that he doesn't believe in the assumption of determinism. Which of the following statement he's likely to make?

a. "Sometimes people fail no matter how determined they are to succeed."
b. "The scientific method is only appropriate for research with humans."
c. "You can test some hypotheses without using an independent variable."
d. "Some behaviors are not brought about by specific causal factors."

12. A critic of Professor Clark's research has suggested that all of his results can be explained in terms of expectancy effects. The strongest counter-argument that Professor Clark could offer would be to say that he

a. operationalized all of his variables.
b. used an A-B-A design.
c. used a double-blind control.
d. used a between-subjects design.

13. Mrs. Kim thought that her son was the best actor in his high school play. A psychologist might say that Mrs. Kim's judgment was influenced by

a. an ordeal of proof.
b. an observer bias.
c. standardization.
d. placebo effects.

14. You are looking at a friend's notes from a lecture on the scientific method. You discover that the only statement he got down correctly is that

a. independent variables must be operationalized.
b. some variables cannot be operationalized.
c. experiments must have more dependent variables than independent variables.
d. dependent variables are more valid than independent variables.

15. Evaluation of the DARE (Drug Abuse Resistance Education) program has shown that

a. drug abuse can be prevented through tough law enforcement.
b. young children cannot comprehend anti-drug abuse information.
c. it is easier to change attitudes than to change behaviors.
d. teenagers don't abuse drugs even when they say they do.

16. Prior to an experiment, subjects must give their informed consent. This means that they

a. have agreed that the risks of the experiment outweigh the benefits.
b. have been made aware of the risks and benefits of the experiment.
c. will try to recall all the information given to them during the experimental session.
d. will try to provide data in line with the experimenter's predictions.

17. Fillmore announces that he has collected convincing data that support the existence of extrasensory perception. As the next step in the research process, Fillmore should

a. carefully operationalize and standardize each of the variables in the study.
b. keep his methods secret to protect the anonymity of his subjects.
c. publicly verify that he is a trained experimentalist.
d. reveal his methods so that other researchers can attempt to replicate his findings.

18. You are in a subject in an experiment. The researcher asks you to answer questions such as "What is your happiest childhood memory?" and "What is your least happy childhood memory?" while monitoring your brain activity. This experiment combines _____ and _____ measures.

a. self-report; naturalistic
b. physiological; naturalistic
c. naturalistic; behavioral
d. self-report; physiological

19. A key feature of naturalistic observation is that the experimenter

a. uses only open-ended questions.
b. does not interfere with the behavior being studied.
c. observes the same subjects for several years.
d. attempts to recreate a natural behavior in a laboratory setting.

20. Imagine that you are a new teacher and that you want to study the effect of rewards on children's performance in school. You might choose as a dependent variable

a. each child's age at the beginning of the study.
b. the number of A's each child gets.
c. the number of brothers and sisters each child has.
d. each teacher's attitude toward rewards.

Practice Test ②

1. Missie has missed class again, and is copying her friend's notes. Unfortunately, she can't figure out which research design uses each subject as his or her own control. Which would you tell her?

a. within-subjects
b. between-subjects
c. double-blind
d. randomly assigned

2. A seafood distributor hires Dr. Klam to determine whether eating oysters makes one more passionate. Dr. Klam collects data which show that the more oysters people eat, the more active their love life is. What can he conclude from his research?

a. People with active love lives consume more oysters.
b. Eating oysters makes one passionate.
c. Being passionate causes a craving for oysters.
d. He can conclude nothing from this study.

3. Based on carefully controlled studies of the effectiveness of subliminal audiotapes that are designed to improve self-esteem and memory, what conclusion should you draw?

a. Other than what can be attributed to a placebo effect, subliminal tapes will not bring about improvement.
b. Subliminal tapes bring about improvement in self-esteem, but not in memory.
c. Subliminal tapes bring about improvement in memory, but not in self-esteem.
d. Only "non-believers" are likely to see improvement as a result of subliminal tapes.

4. A psychologist has tape-recorded the instructions he gives to his research participants, and their responses are recorded directly on a computer terminal. It appears the psychologist is being careful about the use of

a. alternative explanations.
b. standardization.
c. a placebo.
d. confounding variables.

5. Which of the following does not belong with the others?

a. behavioral measures
b. questionnaires
c. surveys
d. interviews

6. A researcher is interested in how best to prevent panic behavior. As part of his procedure, he plans on locking subjects in a room, pumping fake smoke under the door, and sounding the fire alarm. How should he handle the issue of deception?

a. He must tell the subjects everything he plans to do.
b. Once the subjects consent to participate, he can do whatever he wants.
c. It would be best if he said nothing to the subjects about the deception.
d. He should consider alternatives to deception and reduce potential risks.

7. A psychologist is doing research for a pharmaceutical company. The drugs he is testing are numbered so that he does not know what they are, nor does he know which subjects are receiving which drugs. The control that is being used in this study is called

a. a double-blind control condition.
b. random assignment by chance procedures.
c. an A-B-A design.
d. a correlational method.

8. Which correlation coefficient must be a mistake?

a. -0.7
b. 0.0
c. +1.0
d. +2.4

9. Ludwig believes that music affects a person's mood. He has some subjects listen to waltzes and other subjects listen to military marches, then measures each subject's mood with a paper-and-pencil test. What are the independent and dependent variables?

a. The waltz music is the independent variable; the military march music is the dependent variable.
b. The subject's mood is the independent variable; the scores on the paper-and-pencil test are the dependent variable.
c. The type of music is the independent variable; the subject's mood is the dependent variable.
d. The subject's mood is the independent variable; the type of music is the dependent variable.

10. Marvin strongly believes that teenagers are loud and rude. He goes to a shopping mall to watch a group of teenagers, and finds support for his viewpoint. Marvin's data collection may be subject to

a. independent variables.
b. dependent variables.
c. standardization.
d. observer bias.

11. An investigator is interested in whether ignoring a child's misbehavior will reduce its occurrence. In the first and third week of a study, a child's acts of misbehavior are recorded. In the second week, teachers are instructed to ignore such misbehavior, and the number of incidents is also recorded. What type of research design is being used?

a. between-subjects
b. A-B-A
c. placebo control
d. experimental and control group

12. Mr. Harris wants to build low-income housing in the city he lives in, but he is not sure how the other residents will react. He decides to do a sample survey of their opinions. Rather than trying to survey all of the city residents, Mr. Harris should send questionnaires to

a. his friends.
b. only people that he does not know.
c. a representative sample of residents.
d. residents with high incomes.

13. If a driver is given a ticket for speeding, he or she will be less likely to exceed the speed limit in the future. This statement is an example of a(n)

a. hypothesis.
b. paradigm.
c. operational definition.
d. expectancy effect.

14. Researchers must be careful that they do not give subtle cues to their subjects in an experiment, which might communicate expected behaviors. This is to control for

a. placebo effects.
b. expectancy effects.
c. control procedures.
d. randomly assigning subjects.

15. When Frank went to the hospital after his accident, the doctor attached a series of electrodes to different locations on his scalp. The graphical representation of Frank's brain activity is known as a(n)

a. electroencephalogram.
b. electrocardiogram.
c. electromyogram.
d. brain map.

16. Sonja would like to be a scientist, and she has taken a self-test in a magazine to determine whether she has a "scientific" personality. A high score on which of the following personality traits should cause her the most concern?

a. open-minded
b. biased
c. critical
d. skeptical

17. You are about to take your first test in an introductory psychology class. Much to your surprise, the instructor hands you a test that contains 10 analytical geometry problems. You would probably be able to argue that the test is not

a. reliable.
b. valid.
c. reliable or valid.
d. accurate.

18. At the start of an experiment, it is best to place subjects in the various groups

a. in a way that assures that the hypothesis will be supported.
b. in a way that makes the groups as different as possible.
c. using random assignment.
d. based on subject preferences.

19. A psychologist is using high-speed photographic equipment to capture subtle changes in the facial muscles of research participants who are acting out different emotions. The research procedure being used is _____ observation.

a. direct
b. indirect
c. unnatural
d. natural

20. Imagine that a researcher has just completed a study. During the study, subjects were partly deceived, and some were made to feel embarrassment. After collecting the data, the researcher met briefly with the subjects, thanking them for their participation, and paying them for their time. Should the researcher have done anything else after the study?

a. Since the subjects were paid, the researcher was under no obligation to do more than was done.
b. The subjects should have gone through a formal debriefing process.
c. The researcher should have helped the subjects deal with their embarrassment, but he should have avoided mentioning the deception.
d. The subjects should have been asked to give informed consent after the study was over.

Answers, Practice Test ①

1. b (p. 37) This is a negative correlation because high ages go with low spending.

2. b (p. 44; this is not a real result)

3. c (p. 43; this is not a real result)

4. a (p. 41) If you warn people that you're going to flash "Buy Pepsi" and then they still buy more popcorn (which is the intended effect of "Buy Popcorn"), you'd have very solid evidence that "Buy Popcorn" was working.

5. d (p. 37) You can't randomly assign people to be men and women, so research on sex differences almost always has a correlational component.

6. a (p. 33) The quality of the professor's lecture is a good alternative explanation for your yawning.

7. a (p. 49)

8. d (p. 42)

9. c (p. 36)

10. a (p. 38) You should help Binna think about real causal explanations for the bees' behavior--assuming that the bees do not, in fact, have a personal vendetta against her.

11. d (p. 29)

12. c (p. 35)

13. b (p. 31)

14. a (p. 32)

15. c (p. 51)

16. b (p. 48) Make sure that you understand the risks and benefits for any experiment in which you agree to participate.

17. d (p. 30) He should have operationalized and standardized his variables (answer a) before the study.

18. d (pp. 43, 47)

19. b (p. 45)

20. b (p. 33) Each of the other three answers could be independent variables. That is, you might examine the effects of the child's age, the teacher's attitude, and number of siblings on performance. The number of A's would be your dependent measure of performance. Can you think of a more sensitive measure?

Answers, Practice Test ②

1. a (p. 36)

2. a (pp. 38-39) A correlation could reflect any one of several cause and effect possibilities.

3. a (p. 41)

4. b (p. 32)

5. a (p. 43-44) Self-reports include questionnaires, surveys, and interviews.

6. d (pp. 48-49)

7. a (p. 35)

8. d (p. 37)

9. c (p. 33)

10. d (p. 31)

11. b (p. 36)

12. c (pp. 43-44)

13. a (p. 29)

14. b (p. 33) Expectancy effects occur when behaviors that are expected are subtly communicated to subjects, thereby producing the desired reaction in them.

15. a (p. 47)

16. b (p. 30) Science demands an open-minded, critical, and skeptical attitude until conclusions are duplicated repeatedly by independent investigators.

17. b (p. 43) A valid test measures what it is intended to measure.

18. c (p. 35)

19. a (p. 45)

20. b (p. 49)

◫ Chapter 3

The Biological Bases of Behavior

This is a chapter that often makes students nervous because it seems so technical. You should rest assured, however, that the material is worth mastering. Biological concepts will appear repeatedly in your textbook. This reflects psychologists' growing interest in understanding the brain mechanisms that underlie behavior. You have also probably noticed how often biological topics get discussed in the popular media. This chapter should give you a deeper understanding of those real-world discussions.

▤ Chapter Outline

Section	What you need to know
I. Heredity and Behavior	
A. Evolution	What forces shaped the diversity of life?
1. Natural selection	
2. Genotypes and phenotypes	
B. Human Evolution	What are the critical landmarks of human evolution?
C. Variation in the Human Genotype	How can genetics explain individual differences?
1. Basic genetics	
2. Genes and behavior	
II. Biology and Behavior	

Section	What you need to know
A. Eavesdropping on the Brain	What techniques do researchers use to understand the relationship between the brain and behavior?

1. Brain damage
    2. Lesions
    3. Electrical stimulation
    4. Recording brain activity
    5. Brain scans	

B. The Nervous System	What are the major divisions of the nervous system?
C. Brain Structures and their Functions	What functions do major structures of the brain perform?

1. The brain stem and cerebellum
    2. The limbic system
    3. The cerebrum	

D. The Endocrine System	How do hormones influence behavior?
III. The Nervous System in Action	
A. The Neuron	What are the properties of cells in your nervous system?
B. Graded and Action Potentials	How are signals passed by neurons?
1. The biochemical basis of action potentials 2. Properties of the action potential	
C. Synaptic Transmission	How does the signal cross the synapse?
D. Neurotransmitters and their Functions	What substances serve as neurotransmitters?

Section	What you need to know
E. Neural Networks	How do groups of neurons function together to produce complex behaviors?
IV. Hemispheric Specialization and Individual Differences	
A. Cerebral Dominance: Two Brains or One?	What are the characteristic styles of the two hemispheres of the brain?
B. Individual Differences in the Lateralization of Function	In what ways do individual brains differ?
1. Sex differences 2. Individual styles in lateralization	
Close-up: The Biological Roots of Sexuality	Is sexual orientation affected by biological forces?
V. Your Responsive Brain	What perspective should you have on the brain?

Guided Study   ☞ ☞ ☞ ☞

I. Heredity and Behavior (p. 57)

➤ What is meant by the contrast between nature and nurture?

I. A. Evolution (p. 57)

1. What observations led Darwin to propose the mechanism of natural selection? What has Peter Grant's research added to Darwin's observations?

2. What is meant by the phrase "survival of the fittest"?

Define genotype and phenotype.

51

I. B. Human Evolution (p. 60)

➤ Why are bipedalism and encephalization landmarks in human evolution?

➤ How is language important for cultural evolution?

I. C. Variation in the Human Genotype (p. 62)

➤ What is the study of genetics?

1. How many chromosomes did you inherit from each parent? Try to invent a strategy to remember that women have XX pairings and men XY.

2.   What comparisons are necessary to draw conclusions about genetic influences on behavior? What is the role of each of the following groups:

Biological parents

Adoptive parents

Biological siblings

Adoptive siblings

Why should the television viewing result make you cautious about linking genes and behavior?

II. Biology and Behavior (p. 64)

➤ Review the contributions each of these scholars made to contemporary neuroscience:

René Descartes

Sir Charles Sherrington

Santiago Ramón y Cajal

Donald Hebb

II. A. Eavesdropping on the Brain (p. 65)

➤ This section outlines a number of techniques to acquire information from the brain. For each technique, summarize how it is used. Place Paul Broca, Wilder Penfield, and Walter Hess with the appropriate methodology.

1. Brain damage

2. Lesions

3. Electrical stimulation

4. Recording brain activity

5. Brain scans

You might check with your professor to see if you will be held responsible for the explanations of how each type of brain scan works.

II. B. The Nervous System (p. 68)

➤ Make sure you can recall the major divisions of the nervous system. What functions does each division carry out?

Central nervous system (CNS)

Peripheral nervous system (PNS)

Somatic nervous system

Autonomic nervous system

Sympathetic division

Parasympathetic division

➤ How does the sympathetic and parasympathetic divisions work in opposition?

II. C. Brain Structures and their Functions (p. 70)

➤ For each structure, you should study the figures to see where it is located. Then briefly summarize its function.

1. The Brain Stem

Medulla

Pons

Reticular Formation

Thalamus

Cerebellum

2. The Limbic System

Hippocampus

Amygdala

Hypothalamus

3. The Cerebrum

Make sure you are able to locate the four lobes. List them here:

_____   _____

_____   _____

Cerebral Cortex

Cerebral Hemispheres

Corpus Callosum

Motor Cortex

Somatosensory Cortex

Auditory Cortex

Visual Cortex

Association Cortex

II. D. The Endocrine System (p. 77)

➤ What are hormones and what do they do?

➤ Study the figure and table in your book to see the locations of endocrine glands.

➤ What role does the hypothalamus serve in the endocrine system? What functions does the pituitary gland serve?

➤ What are the functions of testosterone and estrogen?

III. A. The Neuron (p. 79)

➤ Draw your own picture of a neuron and label each of its parts.

➤ What are three types of neurons?

➤ What functions do glia serve?

III. B. Graded and Action Potentials (p. 82)

➤ What is the contrast between excitatory and inhibitory inputs?

➤ Define temporal and spatial summation.

1. The biochemical basis of action potentials

This is a section of the textbook with several figures that should help you understand the text. Try to work back and forth between the text and the figures. After you have studied, try to recreate rough versions of the figures on a blank piece of paper.

Define:

Action potential

Resting potential

Ion channels

Depolarization

How is the action potential passed down the axon?

2. Properties of the action potential

Define:

All-or-none law

Myelinated neurons

Nodes of Ranvier

Refractory period (what is its function?)

III. C. *Synaptic Transmission (p. 86)*

➤ Draw a diagram of a synapse and label the parts of the presynaptic and postsynaptic neurons.

III. D. *Neurotransmitters and their Functions (p. 88)*

➤ Summarize the properties of each neurotransmitter:

Acetylcholine

GABA

Catecholamines

   Dopamine

   Norepinephrine

Serotonin

Endorphins (what is a neuromodulator?)

Carbon monoxide and nitric oxide

III. E. Neural Networks (p. 89)

➤ The theme of this section is that combinations of simple neurons produce complex behavior. Make sure you understand the examples given in Figures 3.15 and 3.21.

IV. A. Cerebral Dominance: Two Brains or One? (p. 91)

➤ What is meant by cerebral dominance and lateralization? Give some examples of lateralization.

➤ Make sure you understand the logic of the experiments with split-brain patients. Use the research of Roger Sperry and Michael Gazzaniga as an example.

➤ Make sure you understand the distinction between analytic and holistic processing. Why are both valuable?

IV. B. Individual Differences in the Lateralization of Function (p. 95)

1. What evidence suggests that there are characteristic differences between the brains of males and females? How does Doreen Kimura explain sex differences in aphasias?

2. What have experiments on face recognition demonstrated about individual differences in lateralization? What is meant by "characteristic perceptual asymmetry"?

V. Your Responsive Brain (p. 97)

➤ Summarize the idea of the "responsive brain."

Close-up: The Biological Roots of Sexuality (p. 98)

➤ What have genetic analyses shown about sexual orientation?

➤ What have comparisons of brain structures shown about sexual orientation?

For Group Study   🖐 🖐 🖐 🖐 🖐

I. Heredity and Behavior

You can use a group of friends to make sure you understand the distinctions made in this section. Can you identify different genotypes and phenotypes in the room? Also, you can start to think about the effects of nature and nurture. How would each of you explain differences between you and your brothers and sisters?

II. A., B., and C.

Each of these sections introduces a large number of specialized terms. The best way to learn them is by creating a set of flash cards with your study group. Help each other by going through the cards and making sure each person can reproduce the correct information. You can also devise strategies together for remembering the different terms. (Perhaps, for example, you can remember the function of the "reticular formation" because it reminds you of "tickle" which is something someone could do to keep you alert. We suspect your group can do better than that!) This same advice applies to later sections of the chapter. It will help you to join forces to develop strategies for mastering the material.

IV. A. and IV. B.

Try to think about "analytic" and "holistic" approaches to everyday tasks. Can you detect different approaches that seem characteristic of each member of the group? Do some people seem more analytic or more holistic?

Close-up: The Biological Roots of Sexuality ⌇ ⌇ ⌇

The content of this close-up will strike some readers as controversial. You should discuss how scientific research interacts with people's opinions. If one or more members of your group are themselves gay men or lesbians, you can discuss how this close-up affects them personally. (Note that other material on homosexuality is given in Chapter 12.)

1. A movie director needs to cast someone who looks like a villain. He is most interested in the actor's

a. cultural evolution.
b. chromosomes.
c. phenotype.
d. genotype.

2. What sets gaseous neurotransmitters apart from other neurotransmitters is that they

a. bind with more than one type of receptor molecule.
b. fit the receptor molecule like a key in a keyhole.
c. pass directly through a receptor cell's outer membrane.
d. do not travel across the synaptic cleft.

3. Lara was in an accident that left her with some brain damage. She now has quite a bit of difficulty speaking. If Lara is right-handed, the area of damage is likely to be in the

a. corpus callosum.
b. brain stem.
c. left hemisphere.
d. right hemisphere.

4.   Which pattern of data would suggest that there might be a genetic contribution to sexual orientation?

a. When one dizygotic twin is a gay man there is a high probability that the other one will be as well.
b. When one dizygotic twin is heterosexual there is a high probability that the other one will be as well.
c. One member of a pair of monozygotic twins is more likely to be a lesbian than one of a pair of dizygotic twins.
d. When one monozygotic twin is a lesbian there is a high probability that the other one will be as well.

5. If you suffered damage to your _____ you might experience difficulty learning the names of new acquaintances.

a. hypothalamus
b. hippocampus
c. reticular formation
d. pons

6. Which of the following might be the title of a book about endocrine activity?

a. <u>Be Happy about Hormones</u>
b. <u>My Favorite Synapse</u>
c. <u>Are You Sympathetic to Your Nervous System?</u>
d. <u>Those Nutty Neurons!</u>

7. Which of the following is similar to temporal summation?

a. Several neighbors ask you to turn down your stereo and you comply.
b. A friend gives you tickets to three different movies.
c. You ask each of your professors for an extension but only one agrees to give you one.
d. A leaky faucet drips into a glass until the glass overflows.

8. How do Darwin's finches illustrate the principle of natural selection?

a. They are more likely than other species to live in family clusters.
b. They sought out environments in which it was easy for them to obtain food.
c. Their phenotypes are unrelated to their genotypes.
d. The shapes of their beaks suggests adaptation to different environments.

9. Suppose you were having a conversation with a neuron. Which statement would it be likely to make?

a. "There are a whole lot of us, but I've never touched another neuron."
b. "I wish I had more terminal buttons on my dendrites."
c. "My myelin sheath slows down the rate at which I can transmit an action potential."
d. "Sometimes I generate a large action potential; sometimes I generate a small one."

10. You have decided to attend a costume party dressed as a neuron. Which of the following should NOT be a feature of your costume?

a. Each of your legs could be an axon.
b. You could wear a "soma" tee shirt with a cell nucleus drawn on it.
c. You could use your arms as dendrites.
d. You could paint receptor molecules on each of your fingers.

11. Doreen Kimura has reported that men suffer from more speech disorders following injury to their left hemispheres than do women. What explanation does she give for that finding?

a. Women are more likely to have speech represented in both hemispheres.
b. Men are more likely to have speech represented in both hemispheres.
c. Speech is organized differently within the left hemispheres of men and women.
d. Men are more likely to have surgery to sever their corpus callosum.

12. You and a friend look at a pair of chimeric faces. You think the first one looks happier. Your friend thinks the second one does. What might your preferences suggest?

a. One of you is a man and the other one is a woman.
b. You and your friend do not have the same relationship between visual fields and your brain hemispheres.
c. You have different characteristic ways of lateralizing functions to the two hemispheres of your brain.
d. One of you has suffered from some minor type of brain injury.

13. Which statement is most accurate about the role of your two cerebral hemispheres in carrying out day-to-day life functions?

a. Most functions are performed only in one hemisphere or the other.
b. Their different processing styles contribute to most of the functions you carry out.
c. The left hemisphere is responsible for the "duality of consciousness."
d. The two hemispheres play identical roles except that they control opposite sides of the body.

14. Which of the following statements could NOT be spoken as true by a researcher studying the functions of different brain sites in cats?

a. "Electrical stimulation of different brain sites produces different responses."
b. "I have recorded brain activity from 1000 locations in the brain."
c. "When I stimulate certain brain regions, my cats become aggressive."
d. "The brains of my lesioned cats are identical to the brains of my unlesioned cats."

15. If you DON'T inherit a Y chromosome from your father, you are born with

a. female characteristics.
b. only 45 chromosomes.
c. 200 genes.
d. male characteristics.

16. Researchers in human behavior genetics often study children who live with adoptive parents because

a. adoptive parents treat adopted children identically to their biological children.
b. adopted children share an environment, but not heredity, with the adoptive parents.
c. adopted children follow the same developmental course as do biological children.
d. adoptive parents may provide better hereditary background, in some cases, than biological parents.

17. You are looking at a large painting with a wildly flowing river at the center of the canvas. On the left side of the river, there is a city with an impressive skyline. On the right side, there are acres of open wilderness. Connecting the two banks of the river is a wide bridge. The feature of this painting that should most remind you of your corpus callosum is the

a. wide bridge.
b. city with the impressive skyline.
c. acres of open wilderness.
d. wildly flowing river.

18. While you are under anesthesia, the _____ nervous system still takes care of basic life processes like breathing.

a. somatic
b. autonomic
c. synaptic
d. central

19. What happens when a region of a neuron enters a refractory period?

a. The action potential turns into a graded potential.
b. No amount of stimulation will allow another action potential to be generated.
c. That region of the neuron becomes particularly sensitive to inhibitory inputs.
d. The graded potential can only travel in one direction down the axon.

20. Joe is participating in an experiment that requires him to lift his left hand when he is touched on the right side of his body, and vice versa. Joe feels a gentle tap on his left shoulder, so he lifts his right hand. The "gentle tap" was sensed in the _____ side of Joe's brain and the motor command to lift his hand was issued by the _____ side of his brain.

a. left; left
b. right; right
c. left; right
d. right; left

Practice Test ②

1. When excitatory inputs to a nerve cell are sufficiently strong with respect to inhibitory inputs, the neuron becomes _____ and a(n) _____ occurs.

a. polarized; action potential
b. polarized; refractory period
c. depolarized; refractory period
d. depolarized; action potential

2. There was one house Robbie didn't like delivering the morning paper to. Today, when he saw the big dog coming at him, Robbie's _____ mobilized his body into action and his _____ told the muscles in his legs to run.

a. sympathetic nervous system; spinal cord
b. parasympathetic nervous system; brain
c. sympathetic nervous system; somatic nervous system
d. parasympathetic nervous system; somatic nervous system

3. Marie is walking through an exhibit at the science museum entitled "The Living Brain." She enters through a waiting room called "the spinal cord," and then enters the brain stem. The exhibit takes her from the deepest recesses of the brain to the surface layer. What is the route she will follow?

a. cerebrum, limbic system, cerebral cortex
b. limbic system, cerebrum, cerebral cortex
c. cerebral cortex, limbic system, cerebrum
d. cerebrum, cerebral cortex, limbic system

4. Two-year-old Thelma has just learned how to flush the toilet, and occasionally she will flush for hours. One day she notices that the toilet will not flush properly unless she waits for a while. Thelma doesn't know it, but she is also learning about

a. nodes of Ranvier.
b. ion channels.
c. the synapse.
d. refractory periods.

5. A friend is playing a new game called "Be a Science Detective!" She has just received a clue card which tells her that the suspect has a Y chromosome. From this, it can be deduced that the suspect is

a. male.
b. female.
c. asexual.
d. an albino.

6. Graded potentials are so named because they

a. are all the same size.
b. signal "A," "B," and "C" responses.
c. travel either "uphill" toward the brain, or "downhill" toward the spinal cord.
d. vary in size according to the strength of stimulation.

7. Organisms with a selective advantage are

a. more likely to have a genotype.
b. more likely to have a phenotype.
c. more likely to pass on their genotypes.
d. less likely to pass on their phenotypes.

8. Manny tells you that his aunt recently suffered a stroke that caused damage to the part of her brain which is known as Broca's area. You know that this area is located in the _____ part of the brain, and is associated with processes related to _____.

a. left rear; vision
b. right rear; speech.
c. left front; language.
d. right front; planning.

9. Jack is making flash cards to help him learn the major brain structures and functions. Jill walks by and notices that Jack has incorrectly listed a certain structure as part of the brain stem. She points out to him that the brain stem does NOT include the

a. cerebrum.
b. medulla.
c. thalamus.
d. pons.

10. Studies of split-brain patients have found that the right hemisphere is better than the left at solving

a. problems involving spatial relationships.
b. tasks involving language.
c. mathematics problems.
d. tasks requiring logic and analytical processing of concepts.

11. Behind his back, the people in the town whispered that Bart was "born bad." The viewpoint of the townspeople is most consistent with the idea that human behavior is primarily a result of

a. nurture.
b. heredity.
c. environment.
d. upbringing.

12. Michael has asked Angelo to draw a representation of the relationship between the somatosensory cortex and the body. In his drawing, Angelo should

a. draw a normally proportioned body.
b. include only a head and the reproductive organs.
c. enlarge only the eyes, ears, nose, tongue and hands.
d. enlarge the lips, tongue, thumb, and index fingers.

13. The image of a key fitting into a lock is useful in understanding how

a. synaptic vesicles are opened by an action potential.
b. the end of one neuron fits snugly into another.
c. ion channels open and close.
d. neurotransmitters bind to receptor molecules.

14. Chris and Chrissy are trying to match the lobes of the brain with their various functions. Which pairing do they have wrong?

a. frontal lobe - involved with motor control and cognitive activities
b. parietal lobe - makes plans, decisions, and sets goals
c. occipital lobe - the final destination for visual information
d. temporal lobe - processes auditory information

15. The children in the classroom are acting like neurons. Each is playing the role of a neuron part, and they are arranging themselves in the order that information follows as it passes along the neuron. Beginning with incoming signals, the correct order is

a. dendrites, soma, axon, terminal buttons.
b. axon, dendrites, soma, terminal buttons.
c. terminal buttons, soma, dendrites, axon.
d. soma, terminal buttons, axon, dendrites.

16. The concept of neural networks suggests that the brain operates most like a

a. symphony orchestra.
b. cookbook recipe.
c. simple calculator.
d. typewriter.

17. Although normal as a child, Barney has been showing signs of severe emotional problems. He has become prone to uncontrollable outbursts of temper and often just starts sobbing for no apparent reason. If Barney's problems are the result of a brain injury, it is most likely that damage would be found in the

a. medulla.
b. hippocampus.
c. amygdala.
d. reticular formation.

18. Imagine reading in a popular magazine that scientists have suggested genetics are at least partly responsible for the amount of time that adolescents spend talking on the telephone. Which of the following would be most consistent with the explanation a behavioral geneticist would give to such a finding?

a. The article likely has misinterpreted the actual research findings.
b. Although genetics can explain primitive behavior, genetics cannot explain modern behavior.
c. The behavior of talking on the telephone likely has been encoded into a person's genotype.
d. Some unknown factor must mediate the genetic influence on the behavior of talking on the telephone.

19. Mary is building a computer simulation of a human being, but she is having problems. Her human behaves as though it does not have an endocrine system. When she was designing the brain, Mary probably left out the

a. hippocampus.
b. hypothalamus.
c. thalamus.
d. reticular formation.

20. Donna is an artist who is working on illustrations for an anatomy text. Her current efforts are directed toward cells that are specialized to receive, process, and/or transmit information to other cells within the body. Although these cells vary in size and shape, they all have the same basic structure. Donna is drawing

a. glial cells.
b. neurons.
c. terminal buttons.
d. axons.

Answers, Practice Test ①

1. c (p. 59)

2. c (p. 89)

3. c (p. 91)

4. d (p. 98)

5. b (p. 72)

6. a (p. 77)

7. d (p. 82) In temporal summation, a neuron accumulates inputs spread over time.

8. d (p. 58)

9. a (p. 86)

10. a (p. 80) Neurons only have one axon. You'd have to join your legs together (if you wrap them in myelin, your knees would make a nice node of Ranvier) and then hop all night.

11. c (p. 95)

12. c (p. 96)

13. b (p. 93)

14. d (p. 65) If you lesion part of a brain, you will have made it different from an unlesioned brain.

15. a (p. 62)

16. b (p. 62)

17. a (p. 74)

18. b (p. 69)

19. b (p. 85)

20. d (p. 75) Both sensory signals and motor commands cross over from one side of the body to the other side of the brain (and vice versa).

Answers, Practice Test ②

1. d (p. 84)

2. c (p. 69)

3. b (pp. 70-71)

4. d (p. 85) Just as neurons must "reset" themselves.

5. a (p. 62)

6. d (p. 82)

7. c (p. 59) Organisms with a selective advantage are more likely to reproduce. Only those animals that reproduce can pass on their genotypes

8. c (p. 65)

9. a (p. 71)

10. a (p. 93)

11. b (p. 57) Apparently, the view is that Bart might have inherited a tendency toward bad behavior.

12. d (p. 75)

13. d (p. 86) The shape of the neurotransmitter must match the shape of the receptor molecule as precisely as a key fits into a keyhole.

14. b (p. 74)

15. a (p. 80)

16. a (p. 89) The basic principle by which the brain operates is that a large number of neurons act as a unit to produce complex behavior.

17. c (p. 73)

18. d (p. 63)

19. b (p. 78) Hormones from the hypothalamus are sent to the pituitary, where they stimulate or inhibit the release of other hormones.

20. b (p. 79) Neurons are cells that are specialized to receive, process, and/or transmit information to other cells.

⬛ Chapter 4

Mind, Consciousness, and Alternate States

▤ Chapter Outline

Section	What you need to know
I. The Contents of Consciousness	
A. Awareness and Consciousness	What are the different levels of awareness?
B. Accessibility to Consciousness	To what types of information do you have conscious access?
1. Nonconscious processes	
2. Preconscious memories	
3. Unattended information	
4. The unconscious	
C. Studying the Contents of Consciousness	What techniques allow researchers to examine the contents of consciousness?
II. The Functions of Consciousness	
A. The Mind-Body Problem	Does the mind exist independent of the brain's biological activities?
1. Classical conceptions of body and mind	
2. The emergence of modern theories	

Section	What you need to know
B. The Uses of Consciousness	What functions does consciousness serve?

    1. Aiding survival
    2. Personal and cultural constructions
       of reality

C. Studying the Functions of Consciousness	What techniques allow researchers to study the functions of consciousness?
Close-up: Consciousness and Memory	Can you acquire new information while you are unconscious?

III. Everyday Changes in Consciousness

A. Daydreaming and Fantasy	What are the properties of daydreams?
B. To Sleep, Perchance to Dream	What changes in mental activity accompany sleep?

    1. Circadian rhythms
    2. The technology of sleep and dreams
    3. The sleep cycle
    4. Why sleep?
    5. Individual differences in sleep patterns
    6. Sleep disorders
    7. Dreams: Theater of the mind
    8. The origins of dream content
    9. Nightmares

IV. Extended States of Consciousness

A. Lucid Dreaming	Can you control the content of your dreams?
B. Hypnosis	Is hypnosis real?

    1. Induction of hypnosis
    2. Hypnotizability

Section	What you need to know

3. Pain control
4. The hidden observer

C. Meditation — What benefits can meditation bring to your life?

D. Hallucinations — Are hallucinations just illusions?

E. Religious Ecstasy — How can religious experiences affect consciousness?

F. Mind-Altering Drugs — What are the dangers of abusing drugs to alter consciousness?

1. Dependence and addiction
2. Varieties of psychoactive drugs

Guided Study

☞ ☞ ☞ ☞

I. A. Awareness and Consciousness (p. 102)

➤ Use the three levels of consciousness to summarize the material in this section.

1.

2.

3.

I. B. Accessibility to Consciousness (p. 103)

➤ For each section, summarize an example given in the text.

1. Nonconscious processes

2. Preconscious memories

3. Unattended information

4. The unconscious

➤ How has the idea of the unconscious changed from Freud to contemporary theories? How can information that cannot be conscious have an effect on your behavior?

I. C. Studying the Contents of Consciousness (p. 105)

➤ Describe two techniques:

1.

2.

II. The Functions of Consciousness (p. 106)

➤ If you were an early human, how would you have explained human actions?

II. A. The Mind-Body Problem (p. 106)

1. At what solution to the mind-body problem did these thinkers arrive?

Plato

René Descartes

Ancient Chinese philosophers

Buddhist scholars

2. Why is the position of monism widely accepted by contemporary researchers?

How has the mind evolved? (What was the ultimate evolutionary breakthrough for mind?) What can monkeys do? What can chimpanzees do?

II. B. The Uses of Consciousness (p. 108)

1. What functions does consciousness accomplish to aid survival?

Restrictive

Selective storage

Executive control

2. How does consciousness contribute to your construction of reality?

Personal

Cultural (consensual validation)

II. C. Studying the Functions of Consciousness (p. 110)

➤ Summarize the two research techniques described in this section.

1. SLIP

2. False fame judgments

✍ *Close-up: Consciousness and Memory (p. 112)*

➤ Make sure you understand the distinction between explicit and implicit memory. (You can look to Chapter 10 for some extra help.)

➤ Summarize the circumstances in which researchers have and have not found memories formed when subjects are unconscious.

III. A. Daydreaming and Fantasy (p. 113)

➤ What have researchers discovered about the content of daydreams?

➤ What have researchers discovered about the function of daydreams?

III. B. To Sleep, Perchance to Dream (p. 114)

1. What are circadian rhythms? What variables influence jet lag?

Draw yourself a diagram to help remember how traveling east and west affects your circadian rhythms.

2 & 3. How does the EEG help dream researchers? Make sure you understand the distinction between REM and NREM sleep. Study Figure 4.2 to master the sleep cycle.

4. Suppose someone told you that sleep was unnecessary. How would you respond?

5. How much REM and NREM sleep does someone your age typically get? What factors in your life could make you different from the average? (How is the research of Rosalind Cartwright relevant to this question?)

6. Summarize the major types of sleep disorders.

Insomnia (what is subjective insomnia?)

Narcolepsy

Sleep apnea

Daytime sleepiness

7. Summarize research results about individual differences in dream content.

8. Why did Freud originate the distinction between manifest and latent content? How is the latent content determined?

What is the physiological challenge to Freud? What roles do acetylcholine, serotonin, and norepinephrine play?

9. What are the properties of nightmares?

IV. A. Lucid Dreaming (p. 124)

➤ How are individuals trained to become lucid dreamers?

IV. B. Hypnosis (p. 125)

1. What is hypnosis? How is hypnosis induced?

2. What has been found with respect to individual differences in hypnotizability?

3. How does research on pain control suggest that the effects of hypnosis are not just placebo effects?

4. What is meant by the "hidden observer"? How are automatic writing and automatic talking used to reveal the hidden observer?

IV. C. Meditation (p. 129)

➤ What is the purpose of meditation?

➤ What is controversial about meditation?

IV. D. Hallucinations (p. 129)

➤ Make sure you understand how hallucinations and illusions are different.

➤ Under what circumstances are hallucinations desirable?

IV. E. Religious Ecstasy (p. 130)

➤ What procedures result in religious ecstasy?

IV. F. Mind-Altering Drugs (p. 131)

1. What are physiological and psychological aspects of tolerance, dependence, and addiction?

Give an overview of the consequences of drug use and abuse.

2. Summarize the effects of each type of psychoactive drug. Give examples for each category (consult the text and Table 4.1).

Hallucinogens

Cannabis

Opiates

Depressants

Stimulants

What three psychoactive drugs are common in day-to-day experience? What effects do they have?

1.

2.

3.

For Group Study

II. B. Accessibility to Consciousness

Work through the different categories. Choose everyday experiences and make sure you all agree how to analyze the contributions of consciousness. What types of things do you regularly do outside of conscious awareness?

II. C. Studying the Functions of Consciousness

Try to write down slips of the tongue. Can you analyze how they emerge? Recently, for example, we heard someone say, "He's just like Homer Fudd" (which was a combination of Elmer Fudd and Homer Simpson). There doesn't seem to be much influence from unconsciousness in this example (the textbook returns to these ordinary slips of the tongue in Chapter 11). Can you do better? You should see if you and your friends can find instances in which the slip may indicate some meaning lurking in the unconscious.

III. A. Daydreaming and Fantasy

Have each group member keep track of a few daydreams. Do they fit the generalizations given in the section?

III. B. To Sleep, Perchance to Dream

If you have never seen REM sleep (that is, if you have never seen a sleeper's eyes moving), then you should consider asking a friend or lover for permission to watch him or her sleeping. When during the night would it be best to watch?

Try to have each group member write down whatever dreams he or she can remember for a few mornings. (Trying to remember your dreams is a good way to start remembering more of them.) Do all of the group members' dreams share similar characteristics? Are some of the same concerns expressed in many of your dreams? Can you find sources for individual details? How vivid are your dreams? Do some of you dream in color and others in black and white? Try to understand the theories of dreaming given in this section in terms of your individual experiences.

IV. F. Mind-Altering Drugs

During college, many people experiment with mind-altering drugs. With your group, discuss why this might be so. What are the dangers of this practice? Why do people use drugs even given these risks? Work through the list of psychoactive drugs and try to understand the effects that each of them has on the brain and body.

Practice Test ①

1. A person who practices meditation may minimize external stimulation with the goal of

a. preventing hallucinations.
b. eliminating unconscious processes.
c. improving automatic thinking.
d. enhancing self-knowledge.

2. Which of the following is the best example of an unconscious process?

a. You tell the punch line to a joke.
b. You cover your mouth when you sneeze.
c. You put a key in a lock to open a door.
d. You wave at a friend across the street.

3. Each day that Paul shoots up with heroin, he needs a slightly bigger dose to get the same effect. This is a phenomenon called _____.

a. psychological dependence
b. craving
c. neurotransmitter depletion
d. tolerance

4. Self-hypnosis is particularly valuable for controlling pain because patients can

a. determine whether they are high or low in hypnotizability.
b. avoid the use of placebo medications.
c. use the procedure whenever they need it.
d. avoid the side-effects of other-induced hypnotic trances.

5. Which statement is true about patterns of hypnotizability in adulthood?

a. Women are considerably more hypnotizable than men.
b. People's hypnotizability mostly depends on the skill of the hypnotist.
c. Men are somewhat more hypnotizable than women.
d. People's hypnotizability is relatively stable over time.

6. You find it very difficult to tune out information that is not relevant to the immediate goals you are pursuing. You might be concerned that your consciousness is not serving its proper _____ function.

a. restrictive
b. selective storage
c. executive control
d. monistic

7. Danitra believes that she may suffer from sleep apnea. How could you determine if she is correct?

a. Ask her to report how much sleepiness she experiences during the day.
b. Monitor her eye movement patterns during the night.
c. Monitor her breathing patterns during the night.
d. Follow her for a day and determine how often she spontaneously falls asleep.

8. Which of the following statements is LEAST accurate?

a. Some hallucinations are dismissed when evaluated against reality.
b. Sensory isolation is unlikely to produce hallucinations.
c. Hallucinations are desirable in some cultural settings.
d. Some drug experiences will produce hallucinations.

9. Which of the following is NOT a conclusion from research studying daydreaming?

a. Men and women differ in the content of their daydreams.
b. Young adults daydream more than older adults.
c. Sexual daydreams are most common during sexual activity.
d. Daydreams serve no functions for women.

10. What type of awareness is defined as the top level of consciousness?

a. Awareness of an inner and outer world.
b. Awareness of yourself as a conscious, reflective individual.
c. Awareness that you are perceiving and reacting to perceptual information.
d. Reflection on what you are aware of.

11. Subjects sometimes will incorrectly report that an individual is famous because they fail to remember that they had read the name on an earlier list. What lesson does this result provide about the functions of consciousness?

a. Conscious judgments can affect the construction of unconscious memories.
b. The executive control function of consciousness sometimes fails.
c. Conscious processes contribute to judgment errors.
d. Unconscious memories can influence conscious judgments.

12. You've just had surgery under general anesthesia. While you were under anesthesia, a list of words was played over a tape recorder. If you are tested with an explicit memory test, is it likely that you will show memory for words on the list?

a. No, because explicit memories aren't formed under anesthesia.
b. Maybe, depending on the type of anesthesia that was used.
c. Yes, because explicit memory tests are the most sensitive type of memory test.
d. Maybe, depending on how emotionally charged the words were.

13. The type of mental ability that is most important in the evolution toward human consciousness is the ability to

a. reason about what other animals know and don't know.
b. communicate in some way with other animals.
c. experience dreams and daydreams.
d. have social relationships with other animals.

14. Your friend Nicholas claims that he never dreams. To demonstrate to him that he is wrong, you want to wake him up while he is experiencing REM sleep. If Nicholas typically goes to sleep at 11:30 p.m. and wakes up at 7 a.m., at which time would it probably be best for you to wake him?

a. 12:30 a.m.
b. 2:30 a.m.
c. 4:30 a.m.
d. 6:30 a.m.

15. For a research project, you are asked to wear an electronic pager. At random times during the day, the pager signals you to write down the most recent thoughts you were having. The research project is probably studying the _____ of consciousness.

a. functions
b. levels
c. contents
d. processes

16. You tell your therapist that you had a dream in which "a bear growled at you in the woods, and then chased you." Your therapist tells you that you are concerned about being yelled at by your boss. This interpretation suggests that your therapist believes in the importance of the _____ content of dreams.

a. manifest
b. analytic
c. latent
d. holistic

17. Different drugs can have opposite effects on the body: _____ decrease arousal; _____ increase arousal.

a. opiates; barbiturates
b. cannabinoids; opiates
c. barbiturates; amphetamines
d. cannabinoids; amphetamines

18. Which classical thinker or group of thinkers believed that mental activities could be explained by the actions of the internal organs?

a. Plato
b. Chinese philosophers
c. René Descartes
d. Buddhists

19. Olga claims to be a lucid dreamer which means that she can

a. have vivid dreams during non-REM sleep.
b. have daydreams that are as lucid as night dreams.
c. control the content of her dreams.
d. keep her eyes still during her dreams.

20. Right before you started to read this question, its answer was _____.

a. a preconscious memory
b. a nonconscious process
c. unattended information
d. an unconscious process

Practice Test ②

1. Virginia reads in a pamphlet published by the U. S. Public Health Service that the total negative impact on health of one particular drug is greater than that of all other psychoactive drugs combined. Still, a million people start using this drug each year. The drug is

a. alcohol.
b. nicotine.
c. heroin.
d. cocaine.

2. Imagine that you are an ancient Chinese philosopher.   A friend comes to you complaining of symptoms that in modern times would suggest the individual was suffering from a mental disorder. You would likely look for the causes of these symptoms in

a. your friend's early childhood experiences.
b. social systems that place more value on material goods than on spiritual goals.
c. imbalances in the functioning of your friend's internal organs.
d. your friend's irrational thought patterns.

3. If you are a modern sleep researcher, your work probably has been most influenced by the

a. invention of the EEG and the discovery of rapid eye movements.
b. theories of Sigmund Freud and Carl Jung.
c. discovery of circadian rhythms and the principle of hibernation.
d. phenomenon of jet lag and the invention of the electrocardiogram.

4. One day a friend confides in you that she has narcolepsy. You understand this to mean that she

a. is addicted to narcotics.
b. has a chronic, mildly contagious disease.
c. has a periodic compulsion to sleep during the daytime.
d. experiences total loss of muscle control brought on by emotional excitement.

5. Timothy "sees" nonexistent mice running up and down the building walls, and "hears" voices speaking to him from his unplugged radio. Timothy is apparently experiencing

a. illusions.
b. hallucinations.
c. delusions.
d. a reality check.

6. Which of the following is out of place?

a. NREM sleep
b. REM sleep
c. dreams
d. paradoxical sleep

7. Which of the following procedures would bc most likely to be a part of the SLIP technique?

a. Asking subjects to say a series of words.
b. Distracting subjects while they are memorizing a list of names.
c. Asking blindfolded subjects to run across a wet floor.
d. Rewarding accuracy and punishing errors.

8. Mike thinks participating in research is interesting. He wears an electronic pager which is activated at various random times of the day. Whenever the pager signals, Mike responds to some questions. The research Mike is participating in is using the _____ method.

a. experience-sampling
b. think-aloud
c. "beeper"
d. randomized participation

9. Some developmental researchers believe that changes in the content of children's dreams between the ages of 3 and 9 years is related to

a. maturation of the brain.
b. changes in daytime activities.
c. a decreasing need for sleep.
d. the interaction between the endocrine system and the autonomic nervous system.

10. One day, while looking in some old boxes at your grandfather's house, you come across an old manuscript apparently written by his friend Sigmund Freud. Skimming through it, you realize it is the draft of a sequel to "The Interpretation of Dreams." You can imagine all of the following as titles to this unpublished work EXCEPT

a. "The Royal Road to the Unconscious"
b. "Everynight Madness"
c. "An Uncensored Vision"
d. "Transient Psychoses"

11. Sven wants to be a hypnotist, and is developing an induction procedure. The starting point of his procedure will probably involve

a. the instruction to fall asleep.
b. the use of anesthesia.
c. asking subjects to imagine that they are jogging.
d. minimizing of external distractions.

12. The regulation of blood pressure, the beating of your heart, and the automatic process of breathing, are all examples of

a. preconscious memories.
b. nonconscious processes.
c. self-conscious processes.
d. autobiographical knowledge.

13. Alice tells you that she has learned to become aware of her dreams and to control their direction. It is most likely that Alice is experiencing

a. nightmares.
b. lucid dreams.
c. hallucinations.
d. schizophrenia.

14. If you lived at the time of our early human ancestors, you probably would have favored an "animistic" explanation of behavior. According to this approach,

a. reinforcers and punishers control human behavior.
b. humans are believed to have evolved from lower forms of animal life.
c. the body and spirit are one.
d. spiritual forces that exist in nature exercise control over behavior.

15. Although he is supposed to be studying, Stanley finds his attention shifting to thoughts of what he will be doing on the weekend. Stanley most likely is engaging in

a. narcolepsy.
b. subjective insomnia.
c. rapid eye movements.
d. daydreaming.

16. As used by Ernest Hilgard, the term "hidden observer" refers to

a. a level of consciousness that is aware of the behavior of another level of consciousness.
b. a research design in which the subject of observation is not aware of the observer.
c. a censor that blocks threatening material in the unconscious from entering consciousness.
d. an aspect of consciousness that emerges when psychoactive drugs dominate conscious awareness.

17. Dee Dee is studying botany. She comes across a plant with psychoactive effects, whose active ingredient is THC. It can impair motor coordination, and affects receptors common in the hippocampus. This psychoactive plant is probably a

a. cannabis.
b. cocoa.
c. cactus.
d. mushroom.

18. Hal has written a science fiction novel in which a robot develops a sense of self. It can be inferred that the robot probably

a. has a well-developed personality.
b. experiences consciousness.
c. is highly intelligent.
d. can speak.

19. Nellie sleeps less than average. She is most likely to be

a. energetic and extroverted.
b. nervous and worrisome.
c. artistic and creative.
d. a nonconformist.

20. At a sleep disorder clinic, middle-aged Tyrone learns that he has sleep apnea. When he asks for more information, he learns all of the following EXCEPT that

a. most individuals have a few such apnea episodes a night.
b. the normal treatment is to place the individual in intensive care, attached to a respiratory monitor.
c. when apnea occurs, the body secretes emergency hormones that cause the individual to awaken and resume breathing.
d. it may be possible to control the disorder.

1. d (p. 129)

2. b (p. 105) When you sneeze, you probably bring your hand to cover your mouth without giving it a moment's thought. All the other activities involve at least some involvement of consciousness.

3. d (p. 131)

4. c (p. 127)

5. d (p. 127)

6. a (p. 108)

7. c (p. 120)

8. b (p. 129)

9. d (p. 113)

10. b (p. 103)

11. d (p. 110)

12. a (p. 112)

13. a (p. 108) Can you catch yourself doing this kind of reasoning?

14. d (p. 116) People experience more and more REM sleep as the night goes on. Therefore, the later in the night you try, the more likely you are to catch a REM phase.

15. c (p. 105)

16. c (p. 123)

17. c (pp. 133-134)

18. b (p. 106)

19. c (p. 124)

20. a (p. 104)

Answers, Practice Test ②

1. b (p. 135)

2. c (p. 107)

3. a (p. 115) The development of the EEG and the discovery of rapid eye movements were major breakthroughs in sleep research.

4. c (p. 120)

5. b (p. 129)

6. a (pp. 115-116) REM sleep was initially termed paradoxical sleep. It is during this stage that dreams are most likely to occur.

7. a (p. 110)

8. a (p. 105)

9. a (p. 122)

10. c (p. 122)

11. d (p. 125)

12. b (pp. 103-104)

13. b (p. 124)

14. d (p. 106)

15. d (p. 113)

16. a (p. 128)

17. a (p. 133)

18. b (p. 103) A sense of self emerges from your conscious realization
that others are observing, evaluating, and reacting to what you are doing.

19. a (p. 118)

20. b (p. 120)

📖 Chapter 5

Cognitive Aspects of Life-span Development

🗐 Chapter Outline

Section	What you need to know

I. Studying and Explaining Development

    A. Documenting Development — What methodologies enable researchers to draw conclusions about developmental changes?

    B. Explaining Shared Aspects of Development — Why are some aspects of development nearly constant across all humans?

        1. Nature and nurture
        2. The shared human inheritance
        3. The impact of environments
        4. Errors of the genotype

    C. Individual Genotypes and Environments — How can we begin to understand individual differences?

        1. The role of genes
        2. The impact of environments

II. Physical Development Across the Life Span

    A. Babies Prewired for Survival — With what capabilities do babies enter the world?

Section	What you need to know

1. Sensory abilities and preferences
2. Generating expectations

B. Patterns of Physical Growth and Maturation

What is the pattern of early growth?

C. Physical Development in Adolescence

What physical changes occur in adolescence?

D. Physical Changes in Adulthood

What physical changes accompany aging?

1. Vision
2. Hearing
3. Reproductive and sexual functioning

III. Early Cognitive Development

A. Piaget's Insights into Mental Growth

What processes and stages did Piaget use to explain cognitive development?

1. Schemes
2. Assimilation and accommodation
3. Stages in cognitive development

B. Contemporary Perspectives on Early Cognitive Development

How have contemporary scholars extended and amended Piaget's views?

1. The sensorimotor child revisited
2. The preoperational child revisited
3. Children's theories of mind and world

Close-up: Your Earliest Memories

What happens to the memories from your first few years?

IV. Cognitive Development in Adolescence and Adulthood

A. Postformal Thought

How does thinking improve through adulthood?

Section	What you need to know
B. Cognitive Changes in Late Adulthood	Do older adults always show cognitive impairment?
1. Intelligence	
2. Memory	
V. Acquiring Language	
A. The Context of Acquisition	How do parents talk to babies?
B. Speech Perception Abilities	What sound distinctions are infants prepared to hear?
C. Learning Word Meanings	How are the challenges of acquiring meanings overcome?
D. Acquiring Grammar	What role do innate principles play in the acquisition of grammar?
1. The role of input	
2. The language-making capacity	
3. Critical periods	

Guided Study ☞ ☞ ☞ ☞

I. Studying and Explaining Development (p. 138)

➤ Think about some of the changes you have undergone over your life span, and try to analyze them as combinations of gains and losses.

I. A. Documenting Development (p. 139)

➤ Give an example of how age changes differ from age differences.

➤ What is the purpose of normative investigations?

➤ What is the difference between chronological and developmental age?

Define these research designs and summarize an example for each:

Longitudinal

Cross-sectional

Sequential

I. B. Explaining Shared Aspects of Development (p. 142)

1. The distinction between nature and nurture should be familiar from Chapter 3. (Recall that we warned you that many of the concepts from that chapter would reappear at other places in the book.) You might review that material to help you study Chapter 5. The new material here concerns the application of the distinction to individual lives such as Victor's.

Why was Victor relevant to the debate between John Locke and Jean Jacques Rousseau? What role did Jean Marie Itard play in Victor's life?

2. Contrast qualitative (stage) and quantitative views of development.

3. What are critical periods and the evidence for them?

4. Summarize each of these errors in the genotype.

Down Syndrome

PKU

I. C. Individual Genotypes and Environments (p. 146)

1. Review the material on basic genetics here and in Chapter 3.

What is the difference between dominant and recessive genes? Are all human characteristics controlled by single genes or pairs of genes?

Explain the concept of unused genetic potential.

2. What are some aspects of environments that bring about individual differences?

II. A. Babies Prewired for Survival (p. 148)

➤ What is the difference between an embryo and a fetus?

➤ How has contemporary research responded to William James's and John Watson's ideas about the experiences and capabilities of newborn infants?

1. What capabilities are babies born with in each of these sensory domains?

Taste

Vision

Hearing

2. What is the evidence that infants generate expectations?

II. B. Patterns of Physical Growth and Maturation (p. 152)

➤ Give a description of the typical pattern of early growth.

➤ What is maturation?

➤ How does culture affect walking?

II. C. Physical Development in Adolescence (p. 154)

➤ Give a description of the typical pattern of adolescent growth for girls and for boys. When do concerns about body image emerge?

Boys

Girls

II. D. Physical Changes in Adulthood (p. 154)

➤ Summarize the evidence supporting the motto "use it or lose it."

In each of these domains, what are typical changes across adulthood?

1. Vision

2. Hearing

3. Reproductive and sexual functioning

III. Early Cognitive Development (p. 156)

➤ What does cognitive development involve?

III. A. Piaget's Insights into Mental Growth (p. 157)

1. Define schemes. What role do they play in Piaget's theory?

2. Contrast assimilation and accommodation. Try to understand the distinction in terms of your own experience with acquiring new information.

3. For each stage in Piaget's theory, list the age range and the major acquisitions.

1. Sensorimotor (Ages:)

2. Preoperational (Ages:)

3. Concrete Operations (Ages:)

4. Formal Operations (Ages:)

III. B. Contemporary Perspectives on Early Cognitive Development (p. 160)

➤ Define the distinction between competence and performance.

1. How has the research of Baillergeon and others modified Piaget's views on the sensorimotor child? (Summarize the results.)

2. How has contemporary research modified Piaget's views on the preoperational child? (Summarize the results.)

3. What is meant by children's foundational theories? Summarize research findings for each domain.

Theory of mind

Scientific concepts

In what ways are children like scientists?

Close-up: Your Earliest Memories (p. 164)

➤ What is the typical content of people's earliest memories? Are they accurate?

➤ What theories have been proposed to explain childhood amnesia?

IV. A. Postformal Thought (p. 165)

➤ Describe the life situations that require postformal thought.

IV. B. Cognitive Changes in Late Adulthood (p. 166)

1. What are crystallized and fluid intelligence? How are they affected by aging?

What are the characteristics of wisdom?

Explain each of the components of selective optimization with compensation.

2. What has research revealed about memory changes with aging?

What are the effects (and proposed causes) of Alzheimer's disease?

V. Acquiring Language (p. 169)

➤ Review Table 5.4 to see the types of knowledge children must acquire to be proficient language users.

V. A. The Context of Acquisition (p. 170)

➤ What are the features of motherese? Why is it found cross-culturally?

V. B. Speech Perception Abilities (p. 171)

➤ Outline the logic of speech perception research with infants (habituation studies). What has Janet Werker's research revealed?

V. C. Learning Word Meanings (p. 172)

➤ What is the naming explosion?

➤ Research on meaning acquisition fits the model of the child as junior scientist. How does each of these concepts fit into that perspective?

Overextensions

Underextensions

Mutual Exclusivity (constraints)

Bootstrapping

How does children's vocabulary change over time?

1. What considerations about input led researchers to their conclusions about innate structures? What effects can input have?

2. What are some of the features of the child's language-making capacity (Dan Slobin's operating principles)?

What is telegraphic speech? What does it show?

What are overregularizations? What do they show?

3. What evidence supports the existence of critical periods in the acquisition of grammar?

For Group Study

I. A. Documenting Development

Pose questions to each other about developmental change. For each question, try to invent research projects with different designs. What are the strengths and weaknesses of each design?

I. C. Individual Genotypes and Environments

For Chapter 3, we suggested that you and your friends trade notes about nature and nurture. This would be a good point to renew that discussion. Remind yourselves of the types of conclusions you drew. (Be forewarned, we're going to want you to have this conversation one final time for Chapter 6.) The goal of this discussion is to help you understand the types of causal hypotheses developmental researchers can formulate. What commonalities among people are dictated by the shared genetic inheritance? What differences should be attributed to individual genotypes? What differences point to different environments?

III. Early Cognitive Development

One of the best ways to master the material on cognitive development is to spend time with young children. With the members of your group, see if you can get permission to observe children whose ages range from 0 to 8 years. Before each meeting, review the material in the text. Are there particular tasks you'd like to carry out with each child? Try to develop a model of the types of cognitive activities of which each child is capable. Try to see the way in which even the youngest children are acting like busy little scientists.

IV. B. Cognitive Changes in Late Adulthood

Even by the time you have reached college age, you are probably aware of the decisions you have to make that could be characterized as selective optimization with compensation. Apply this strategy for successful aging to your own life, and to those of your friends. See how you can put good habits in place at as early an age as possible.

V. Acquiring Language

Once again, you should try to make opportunities to spend time with young children. You should note, in particular, the hypotheses the children develop about word meanings (leading, for example, to overextensions and underextensions) and their overregularizations in grammar.

Practice Test ①

1. Your friend is making you guess how old her sister Kara is. Which of these questions will get you off to the best start?

a. Does Kara use assimilation?
b. Does Kara experience accommodation?
c. Does Kara use sensorimotor schemes?
d. Does Kara experience centration?

2. Research on changes in memory performance during adulthood has shown that aging does not diminish people's ability to

a. access their general knowledge stores.
b. control their memory processes.
c. cope with Alzheimer's disease.
d. acquire new information.

3. You overhear part of a lecture in which the professor says that certain behaviors cannot be learned if input from the environment is not available at the appropriate time in development. He is probably lecturing about

a. the nature-nurture controversy.
b. assimilation and accommodation.
c. quantitative changes.
d. critical periods.

4. A child finds it hard to acquire the word "coat" when she already knows the word "jacket." What process may be at work here?

a. mutual exclusivity
b. bootstrapping
c. assimilation
d. overextension

5. Researchers have demonstrated that infants have acquired some knowledge of the world even before they are born. One research result that supports this claim is that children

a. prefer sweet tastes to salty tastes.
b. prefer their mothers' voices to the voices of other women.
c. turn their eyes in the direction of environmental noises.
d. prefer the unmuffled voices of strangers.

6. What conclusion did Janet Werker draw from her studies of the perception of Hindi sound contrasts with adults and infants from English-speaking and Hindi-speaking cultures?

a. Adult speakers of both languages perceive more contrasts in Hindi than in English.
b. English-speaking adults no longer perceive contrasts that would be perceived by their six-month-old children.
c. Infant learners of both languages perceive fewer Hindi contrasts than all adults.
d. Infant learners of both languages perceive as many Hindi contrasts as all adults.

7. Although the average child can transfer objects from hand to hand at age six months, Ismene is unable to do so until about eight months. For this one behavior, Ismene's _____ is less than her _____.

a. ability to assimilate; ability to accommodate
b. chronological age; developmental age
c. developmental age; chronological age
d. ability to accommodate; ability to assimilate

8. An infant's initial collection of schemes is known as

a. sensorimotor intelligence.
b. symbolic representations.
c. preformal intelligence.
d. egocentric representations.

9. Stage approaches to development assume that behavior is _____ different in different age-specific life periods.

a. normatively
b. qualitatively
c. quantitatively
d. sequentially

10. Which of these questions is a three-year-old child most likely to answer correctly?

a. What do dogs have inside of them?
b. Should you look at a toy or sit on it to find out its color?
c. Should you look at a toy or listen to the toy to find out its color?
d. What does this model look like from my side of the table?

11. A visitor from a foreign land laughs when he hears mothers in the United States speaking to their children in motherese. What might you tell this visitor?

a. Parents use motherese because children think it's funny.
b. Parents are not able to communicate an emotional tone when they are using motherese.
c. Parents in many cultures use motherese.
d. Children who hear motherese have trouble learning language.

12. If you are like most people, your earliest memory comes from between ages 3 and 5. Why might that be?

a. Young children may not find their own life experiences to be very interesting.
b. You may need to have a sense of self before you can have autobiographical memories.
c. Young children may not be able to remember what they did from one day to the next.
d. Most people remember early memories in a highly distorted form.

13. Which of these would NOT be an appropriate title for a lecture on physical changes associated with adulthood?

a. "Remedies for Vision and Hearing Losses"
b. "Sexual Experiences are a Healthy Pleasure"
c. "Physical Difficulties are Inevitable"
d. "Aging Doesn't Begin at 65"

14. Children often suffer negative consequences if their mothers used cocaine while they were pregnant. This finding suggests that

a. the environment has an impact even before the child is born.
b. parents can change some aspects of a child's genetic inheritance.
c. heredity is a more powerful force for some children than for others.
d. the environment has its greatest effect late in life.

15. Dan Slobin has suggested that children use an operating principle called *extension* that requires them to try to use the same morpheme, in all cases, to mark the same concept. Which error is explained by the use of this operating principle?

a. A child uses *doggie* to refer to all four-legged creatures.
b. A child would say "Tanya ball" when she means "Tanya wants the ball."
c. A child would say "cow" when he's looking at a horse.
d. A child uses *foots* as the plural of *foot*.

16. Each week, starting at age three months, each child in a group of 30 has been given a test of object permanence. This sounds like _____ research.

a. sequential
b. longitudinal
c. cohort-sequential
d. cross-sectional

17. A friend tells you that his grandfather has decided to give up all games except poker. His goal is to read a series of poker books and to play three times a week in a highly competitive game. Which feature of a strategy for successful aging does this plan omit?

a. selection
b. optimization
c. compensation
d. fluidity

18. Suppose you were asked to defend the point of view that nurture had little impact on Victor, the Wild Boy of Aveyron's inability to become "fully human." Which claim might you make?

a. Victor was abandoned because he was developmentally disabled.
b. Victor could be trained more effectively with modern techniques.
c. Victor's teachers did not provide him with enough social contact.
d. Victor could not have survived in the wild without human assistance.

19. Bernice is bragging that her granddaughter learned to suckle at an earlier age than any of the other children in the neighborhood. Is this likely to be a true claim?

a. No, because most children are born with the ability to suckle.
b. No, because suckling has no survival value.
c. Yes, because suckling is a complex behavior that requires experience in the environment.
d. Yes, because suckling is a behavior that is changed by its consequences.

20. Beyond the stage of formal operations, adults can still learn to

a. use fluid intelligence rather than crystallized intelligence.
b. use centration as a reasoning strategy.
c. think about abstract concepts like truth and justice.
d. reason better about situations involving emotional ambiguities.

Practice Test ②

1. As Clark has gotten older, he has been complaining more about his vision. He is LEAST likely to complain about

a. seeing things at close range.
b. seeing things at a distance.
c. night vision.
d. discriminating certain colors.

2. Nate has been wondering whether he was adopted. His parents are both very short, but Nate is tall. Nate might be relieved to learn that

a. height is determined by the joint effects of heredity and environment.
b. height is a recessive trait.
c. height is a dominant trait.
d. genes have no effect on height.

3. Mary has been reading up on her pregnancy. She has learned that her developing embryo will

a. first respond to stimulation, then develop a heartbeat, and finally engage in spontaneous movements.
b. first engage in spontaneous movements, then develop a heartbeat, and finally respond to stimulation.
c. first engage in spontaneous movements, then respond to stimulation, and finally develop a heartbeat.
d. first develop a heartbeat, then respond to stimulation, and finally engage in spontaneous movements.

4. Aunt Emma hasn't seen little Dorothy for a long time, and is amazed at how much she has grown. Which statement best represents how infants like Dorothy physically grow?

a. Early infant physical growth is fairly smooth and continuous.
b. Early infant physical growth takes place in concentrated bursts.
c. Some infants' physical growth patterns are continuous, but others show concentrated bursts of growth.
d. Physical growth is smooth and continuous in females, but takes place in concentrated bursts in males.

5. Jia-Jen is describing her earliest childhood memory. If Jia-Jen is like most people, it is likely that the memory will be

a. of a very dramatic incident.
b. very inaccurate.
c. of a positive emotion.
d. of an experience when Jia-Jen was three to five years old.

6. Although the learning of language usually comes naturally, Henry has decided to teach his newborn sister Shannon to talk. As a first step in his approach, Henry should consider

a. talking to Shannon, then pausing to let her respond.
b. responding to any gestures that Shannon makes.
c. smiling at Shannon when she uses words that are relevant to the topic at hand.
d. nodding at Shannon when it is clear that she has understood what he has said.

7. Based on the experimental evidence that is relevant to the idea of critical periods, it would be reasonable to conclude that

a. there is no firm support for the idea of critical periods.
b. critical periods may exist in nonhuman animals, but they do not exist in humans.
c. there are critical periods for all human and nonhuman animal functions.
d. critical periods for certain functions occur in human and nonhuman animals.

8. Bonnie and Clyde notice that their eight children have shown a number of similarities in their physical and motor development. For example, they all went through the same stages of creeping and crawling, all took their first steps at about the same age, and all showed marked physical changes in adolescence. According to researchers, the explanation for the equivalence of developmental changes across individuals can be found in

a. a shared human genetic inheritance.
b. the similar environments all humans encounter in childhood.
c. the process of imprinting.
d. chance factors.

9. A two-year-old's speech is characterized as telegraphic because it is

a. short and simple, using mostly nouns and verbs.
b. used to convey emotional content.
c. intense and surprising, as are most telegrams.
d. made up of single words, linked together with no grammatical structure.

10. In a study of three-to five-year-old children, subjects are shown two pictures and told that one is a hungry boy whose mother has given him a cookie, and the other is a hungry boy who is thinking about a cookie. When asked which of the boys could actually eat the cookie

a. only the five-year-olds were able to answer accurately.
b. only the three-year-olds could not answer accurately.
c. children of all ages were able to answer accurately.
d. none of the children was able to answer accurately.

11. Baby Huey is less than a week old. A careful observer will notice that Huey

a. can easily distinguish fine visual details.
b. shows preferences for certain tastes.
c. prefers male voices.
d. behaves as if all sounds are coming from directly in front of him.

12. Little Mario has gotten hold of the car keys again. His older brother cleverly distracts him, and gets the keys back. Little Mario instantly beings to search for the disappearing keys. The youngest age Mario is likely to be is _____ old.

a. 3 weeks
b. 2 months
c. 8 months
d. 3 years

13. Your elderly grandfather tells you that he is a subject in a longitudinal study
that was begun by Lewis Terman shortly after World War I and is still
continuing. You can assume that your grandfather was chosen to participate on the basis of his

a. high intelligence scores.
b. status as a twin.
c. record of juvenile arrests.
d. poor performance in school.

14. A trait is said to be polygenic if it is

a. passed to all the offspring of a parent.
b. determined by genes on the 23 chromosome.
c. expressed in the phenotype of an individual.
d. influenced by two or more pairs of genes.

15. You would probably find the greatest decline with age if you did a _____ study
and tested _____ intelligence.

a. longitudinal; crystallized
b. longitudinal; fluid
c. cross-sectional; crystallized
d. cross-sectional; fluid

16. Ann and Andy are having a discussion. Ann believes that the development of
their newborn child will be more affected by heredity, whereas Andy thinks that
their baby's development will be more a product of learned experiences. Ann
and Andy are continuing the _____ debate.

a. learning-reflexes
b. nature-heredity
c. nature-nurture
d. nurture-environment

17. Contrary to Piaget, contemporary researchers who are studying children's
cognitive abilities

a. study only accommodation.
b. downplay the importance of immediate memory.
c. distinguish between performance and competence.
d. place more emphasis on the stages of development.

18. The authors of your textbook take the perspective that development involves all of the following EXCEPT

a. change.
b. passive processes.
c. active engagement with the environment.
d. gains and losses.

19. Harry has the verbal skills one would expect to see in the typical 5-year-old, but Harry was born 10 years ago. A developmental psychologist would say that Harry has a _____ age of _____ for verbal skills.

a. chronological; 0.5
b. chronological; 5
c. developmental; 5
d. developmental; 10

20. Three-year-old Susan loves sports. Her dad recently taught her how to catch a big beach ball, and now her mom is teaching her how to catch a small tennis ball. At first, Susan tries to "surround" the tennis ball with her arms, the way she did the beach ball. Slowly, she learns to use just her hands. Susan's restructuring of her scheme illustrates Piaget's concept of

a. egocentrism.
b. object permanence.
c. assimilation.
d. accommodation.

Answers, Practice Test ①

1. d (pp. 157-159) For each of the other questions, the answer should be "yes" no matter how old Kara is.

2. a (p. 168)

3. d (p. 178)

4. a (p. 174)

5. b (p. 150) The preference suggests that they have some prior knowledge of their mothers' voices.

6. b (p. 172)

7. c (p. 139)

8. a (p. 157)

9. b (p. 144)

10. b (p. 163)

11. c (p. 171)

12. b (p. 164)

13. c (p. 155) Use it or lose it!

14. a (p. 147)

15. d (p. 177) Saying *foots*, rather than *feet*, suggests that the child is trying to add the same morpheme (sometimes it's an "s" sound, as in docks; sometimes it's a "z", as in dogs) to mark every case of plural.

16. b (p. 140)

17. c (p. 168)

18. a (p. 143) This explanation suggests that Victor suffered from a biological defect that could not be overcome by a change in environment.

19. a (p. 150)

20. d (p. 165)

Answers, Practice Test ②

1. b (pp. 155-156)

2. a (p. 147)

3. d (p. 148)

4. b (p. 152)

5. d (p. 164)

6. a (p. 170)

7. d (p. 145)

8. a (p. 144)

9. a (pp. 176-177)

10. c (pp. 162-163)

11. b (p. 150)

12. c (p. 159)

13. a (p. 141)

14. d (p. 146)

15. d (pp. 166-167)

16. c (p. 143) The extent to which development is determined by heredity (nature) and learned experiences (nurture) is a long-standing debate.

17. c (p. 160)

18. b (p. 139)

19. c (p. 139)

20. d (p. 158) Accommodation restructures or modifies existing schemas.

📖 Chapter 6

Social Aspects of Life-span Development

🗒 Chapter Outline

Section	What you need to know
I. Life-span Theories	
A. Erikson's Psychosocial Stages	What crisis do you face in each phase of your life?
B. Jung's Outward and Inward Directedness	Where are values focused in different periods of life?
C. Neugarten's Changes in Adulthood	How do men and women differ in life-span patterns?
II. The Cultural Context of Development	
A. Changing Conceptions of Childhood	How have children been treated over the centuries?
B. Families and Youth at Risk	What difficulties do many families face?
III. Social Development in Childhood	
A. Social Capabilities of Newborns	With what social skills do babies enter the world?
B. Attachment and Social Support	What are the consequences of children's relationships with their parents?

Section	What you need to know

   1. Assessing the quality and
      consequences of attachment

   2. Parenting styles and parenting
      practices

Close-up: Children in Day Care   What advantages do children receive
                                 from quality day care?

  C. The Costs of Deprivation   What happens when children have no
                                 possibility for attachment?

   1. Contact comfort and social
      experience

   2. Human deprivation

  D. Gender Roles   How do children form
                          their identities as
                          boys and girls?

IV. Adolescence

  A. The Experience of Adolescence   Does "adolescence" exist across cultures?

   1. Transition markers and initiation
      rites
   2. The myth of adolescent "storm and
      stress"

  B. Identity Formation in   What forces shape adolescent identities?
     Adolescence

   1. Social relationships
   2. Future goals

V. Adulthood

Section	What you need to know
A. Intimacy	How do social relationships change during adulthood?
B. Generativity	How do adults contribute to future generations?
C. The Cultural Construction of Late Adulthood	How do cultures contribute to the consequences of aging?
D. At Life's End	How do people deal with death?

    1. Anticipating death
    2. Bereavement

VI. Moral Development

A. Kohlberg's Stages of Moral Reasoning	How does moral reasoning change over time?
B. Moral Reasoning in Adolescents and Adults	How have Kohlberg's views been corrected?
C. Moral Action	What is the basis for moral action?
VII. Learning to Age Successfully	What advice can be given toward unproblematic aging?

Guided Study ☞ ☞ ☞ ☞

I. A. Erikson's Psychosocial Stages (p. 182)

➤ To master the material on Erikson's stages you should use Table 6.1 in conjunction with the text. Try to relate Erikson's insights to children and adults of your acquaintance. For each stage, try to understand why the crisis applies to that period of life. Recreate your own table here:

Crisis	Age	Why then?

➤ How well do Erikson's stages apply cross-culturally?

I. B. Jung's Outward and Inward Directedness (p. 185)

➤ How do values in youth differ from adult values?

I. C. Neugarten's Changes in Adulthood (p. 185)

➤ Contrast chronological age and social age.

➤ With what aspect of Jung's theory does Neugarten agree?

➤ What sex differences did Neugarten identify? How are they affected by age?

II. The Cultural Context of Development (p. 186)

➤ Why is the cultural context particularly relevant to social development?

II. A. Changing Conceptions of Childhood (p. 187)

➤ Summarize the conception of childhood in each of these periods.

Prior to the 16th century:

16th through 18th century:

19th century:

20th century:

II. B. Families and Youth at Risk (p. 187)

➤ Try to relate the material in this section to your own day-to-day experiences and reports in the news. What are the major indicators that children and families are at risk?

III. Social Development in Childhood (p. 188)

➤ Define socialization. How does it come about?

III. A. Social Capabilities of Newborns (p. 189)

➤ With what social capabilities do newborns enter the world? (You might review the "babies prewired for survival" section in Chapter 5 to give yourself a more general picture of infant capabilities.) To what does synchronicity refer?

➤ Summarize the research by Jerome Kagan and by Steven Suomi.

III. B. Attachment and Social Support (p. 190)

➤ What is imprinting?

➤ What has research shown with respect to proximity-promoting signals?

1. How is the Strange Situation Test used to assess attachment? (Summarize the procedure.)

What are the four categories of attachment? Focus, in particular, on the distinction between secure and insecure attachment. It should help you to generate a mental picture of how each type of child behaves when his or her mother leaves and returns.

What are the consequences of secure and insecure attachment?

2. To master the material on parenting styles, make sure you understand the two dimensions given in Figure 6.1. How does each parenting style emerge?

How do parenting styles interact with parents' goals? What long-term effects do parenting styles have?

✍ Close-up: Children in Day Care (p. 194)

➤ What is the best answer to questions about the "dangers" of day care. Why?

➤ Summarize the features of quality day care.

Physical

Education and psychology

Teacher interaction style

III. C. The Costs of Deprivation (p. 195)

1. How did Harry Harlow's research rule out the cupboard theory?

What happened when monkeys from his studies were placed with normally reared peers?

What happened when the monkeys became mothers?

How does cross-fostering work?

2. What is known about the costs of human deprivation?

What is psychosocial dwarfism?

III. D. Gender Roles (p. 197)

➤ What is the difference between sex differences and gender differences?

➤ How are gender differences promoted by culture?

➤ How do children participate in their own construction of gender?

IV. A. The Experience of Adolescence (p. 199)

1. What is the purpose of transition markers and initiation rites? How do cultures define the age limits on adolescence?

2. Why do researchers believe that adolescent "storm and stress" is a myth?

What consequences may adolescent problems bring in later life?

IV. B. Identity Formation in Adolescence (p. 201)

1. What roles do parents and peers play in adolescent lives?

Parents

Peers (note differences for boys and girls)

2. What concerns do adolescents have about their futures?

V. A. Adulthood: Intimacy (p. 203)

➣ What was Erikson's position on intimacy?

➣ Summarize major aspects of adulthood's social relationships. In each case, note any differences that exist for men and women.

Marriage (or other long-term relationships)

Parenthood

What is selective social interaction?

V. B. Generativity (p. 205)

➤ What is generativity? What did George Vaillant find about the importance of generativity for adjustment?

➤ How do most people feel, looking back on their lives?

V. C. The Cultural Construction of Late Adulthood (p. 206)

➤ What are some stereotypes of older adults?

➤ How do expectations affect performance? What is the dependency-support script?

➤ What is ageism? What effects does it have? What did Pat Moore do?

V. D. At Life's End (p. 207)

1. Which age groups express the most death anxiety?

Are there standard stages that everyone passes through to cope with death (as was suggested by Elisabeth Kübler-Ross)?

What is the philosophy of the hospice approach to dying?

2. What are some possible consequences of bereavement?

VI. Moral Development (p. 209)

➤ What is morality and why is it important to society?

VI. A. Kohlberg's Stages of Moral Reasoning (p. 209)

➤ Use Table 6.4 and the text to solidify your knowledge of Kohlberg's proposals about moral development. Try to understand why Kohlberg believed that each level was an advance over the previous one. This should help you to memorize the order of the stages.

Stage	Why is this an advance?

VI. B. Moral Reasoning in Adolescents and Adults (p. 211)

➤ What was Gilligan's concern about Kohlberg's theory? What did she propose?

➤ Has contemporary research revealed consistent differences between men and women?

➤ How does moral action differ from moral reasoning? What did research on children's honesty show to be important?

➤ How might empathy give rise to moral action?

➤ Review the principle of "use it or lose it."

➤ Review selective optimization with compensation.

For Group Study

II. The Cultural Context of Development

In the Guided Study section, we ask you to reflect on the question "Why is the cultural context particularly relevant to social development?" You could also turn this into a useful group discussion. The chapter, in general, has a strong cultural theme. You should also consider the costs of deprivation, and the cultural construction of late adulthood. Keep in mind, in each case, that psychology's goal is not just to describe the problems. Researchers would also like to participate in the solutions.

III. Social Development in Childhood

This is the final time we're going to ask you to reflect on nature and nurture. This section on social development in childhood discusses individual differences in attachment and some of the parenting styles that might bring them about. This is a good opportunity to consider again why you are a different social creature from your friends and your siblings. Do you believe that some aspects of your social style were in-born? What life experiences have made you the way you are? Do your friends have similar ideas?

III. D. Gender Roles

You can have the same discussion as before but now focus it more narrowly on issues of sex differences and gender differences. This will work best if you have both men and women in your group. Each time you come to a disagreement about the origins of a difference--is it biology or culture--think how you might collect data to decide the question.

IV. Adolescence

Many of the students who take Introductory Psychology are not at too great a distance from their own period of adolescence. As a group, try to relate the material in this section to your own life experiences. Pay particular attention to the changing roles of family and peers.

V. Adulthood

At several places in this section, the text warns you not to be too dispirited by research results that raise the possibility of negative consequences from marriage and parenthood. Discuss what expectations might be reasonable, given these results. How can this knowledge help you to avoid typical problems?

Practice Test ①

1. What idea is consistent between Carl Jung's and Bernice Neugarten's theories of adulthood?

a. Adults develop a greater sense of spirituality as they age.
b. Men and women follow different developmental paths in adulthood.
c. Social age matters more than chronological age.
d. Adults shift their focus from the outer to the inner world.

2. What is the relationship between culture and the experience of adolescence?

a. In most cultures adolescence is a period of storm and stress.
b. In most cultures initiation rites prolong the period of adolescence.
c. In some cultures the period of adolescence is very brief.
d. Most cultures have a legal definition of adolescence.

3. Which of the following is an example of empathy?

a. Jill complains to her mother that Jack got a bigger piece of cake.
b. Jack returns a stolen bucket to his neighbor.
c. Jack feels upset when Jill is crying.
d. Jill starts laughing after Jack falls down.

4. Both middle-aged and older adults agree that to be well-adjusted requires an individual to be "others oriented." This is an important part of

a. generativity.
b. autonomy.
c. ego-integrity.
d. competence.

5. In the sixteenth through eighteenth centuries, children were

a. expected to assume adult responsibilities as soon as they were physically able.
b. subject to child labor laws and the juvenile court system.
c. kept out of the labor force to leave jobs for adults.
d. legally protected from abuse and neglect.

6. Researchers use the Strange Situation Test to judge whether a child is securely or insecurely attached. The basis of the judgment is the child's behavior when the mother

a. offers the child an unusual toy to play with.
b. leaves the room and then reappears.
c. has a conversation with a stranger.
d. scolds the child for playing too noisily.

7. If you have an adolescent daughter, it's likely to be the case that she will

a. follow her friends' suggestions in all cases.
b. talk to you about her views on dating and sex.
c. prefer talking to you rather than talking to her friends.
d. be concerned with acceptance and popularity.

8. Which of Erikson's psychosocial stages begins when the child starts to use language and explore the environment?

a. Trust vs. mistrust
b. Autonomy vs. self-doubt
c. Initiative vs. guilt
d. Competence vs. inferiority

9. What are the consequences of marriage and parenthood for adults?

a. Both men and women typically become depressed when they are left with an "empty nest."
b. Women suffer more than men when they are in bad marriages.
c. After the birth of a child, men find themselves less burdened by traditional sex roles.
d. Marital satisfaction is highest when a couple has adolescent children.

10. You are watching a videotape of a mother and her infant. When the mother smiles, the child smiles. When the mother frowns, the child frowns. This phenomenon is known as

a. socialization.
b. imprinting.
c. synchronicity.
d. proximity promotion.

11. Laurie and Stan both need to work to support their family. They are somewhat concerned about placing their children in day care. What can you tell them?

a. Children in day care can benefit from a wider variety of social interactions.
b. Children in day care are always at an advantage over children who stay at home.
c. All children respond to day care positively.
d. There is no stigma associated with putting children in day care.

12. When men and women are asked to reason about the same moral dilemmas,

a. women's responses are most similar to Kohlberg's predictions.
b. men put more emphasis on caring than on justice.
c. they give similar patterns of caring responses.
d. they give responses that are consistent with Gilligan's predictions.

13. According to Erikson, when earlier crises are left unresolved, people are likely to end life with feelings of

a. stagnation.
b. isolation.
c. self-doubt.
d. despair.

14. In Kohlberg's theory, which of these reasons for moral behavior is at a highest level?

a. to follow rules
b. to promote society's welfare
c. to gain acceptance
d. to avoid disapproval

15. Your friend Zelda is concerned about her 80-year-old father. She thinks that he tries to do too many tasks himself, so she tries to finish things for him before he even starts. You might want to explain _____ to Zelda.

a. the dependency-support script
b. generativity
c. the empty nest syndrome
d. stagnation

16. Which of the following was a result from Harry Harlow's experiments with monkeys who were raised with terry cloth and wire mothers?

a. The monkeys did not know how to be mothers themselves.
b. The monkeys were more likely to become attached to the artificial "mother" who provided food.
c. Once the monkeys were allowed to interact with other monkeys, they showed no adjustment problems.
d. The monkeys were able to have normal sexual relationships.

17. You are discussing sex and gender differences with the parents of two young children. Which of the following observations is most likely NOT to be true for typical children?

a. Their nine-year-old daughter prefers to play with other girls.
b. Their four-year-old son plays more roughly than his sister did at the same age.
c. Their four-year-old son prefers to play with other boys.
d. Their nine-year old is less flexible about gender roles than her four-year-old brother.

18. Research with ten-month-old infants showed that they were more likely to smile when their mothers were watching them. This suggests that the infants are already

a. aware that they shouldn't smile all the time.
b. imprinted on their mother's appearance.
c. insecurely attached to their mothers.
d. using smiles to produce an effect on their mothers.

19. When a parent is centered on the child but makes too few demands to socialize the child, the parenting style is called

a. authoritative.
b. indulgent.
c. authoritarian.
d. uninvolved.

20. Typically _____ have more anxiety about death than do _____.

a. older adults; younger adults
b. older adults; adolescents
c. adolescents; older adults
d. adolescents; younger adults

Practice Test ②

1. Hubert has skipped class again. He gets the lecture notes from Margie, but can't quite read her handwriting, so he makes an error in copying information about Kohlberg's stage model of moral reasoning. Which of the following statements did Hubert copy incorrectly?

a. An individual can be at more than one stage at a given time.
b. Everyone goes through the stages in a fixed order.
c. Each stage is more comprehensive and complex than the preceding.
d. The same stages occur in every culture.

2. Patrick and Patricia are twins, but they are not likely to be treated identically. Patrick is likely to

a. receive more negative responses when he engages in cross-gender behavior.
b. be held less often.
c. receive less physical stimulation.
d. be paid less attention for his vocalizations and signals for food.

3. The teacher of your developmental psychology class has decided to show the class the procedure developed by Mary Ainsworth to study the attachment of infants. Due to the fact that no infants are available, you have been asked to play the part of a child, and your friend will be your "mother." You are led into a room filled with toys. After you are playing with the toys, what will happen next?

a. A stranger will tell you to leave the room, so that she can talk to your mother.
b. Your mother will go off with a stranger, leaving you alone in the room.
c. A stranger will enter, and your mother will temporarily leave the room.
d. The toys will break, and your reaction will be judged.

4. Robin is 15-years-old. According to Erikson's life-span model, the question she is probably asking herself is

a. "Can I trust others to meet my needs?"
b. "In what ways can I contribute to others?"
c. "Who am I?"
d. "Am I a capable person?"

5. The idea of adolescence emerged in the nineteenth century as a result of

a. a decrease in the size of families.
b. a decrease in the need for cheap labor.
c. laws concerning compulsory education.
d. the establishment of juvenile court systems.

6. Tamara is several weeks old, and is unknowingly helping researchers investigate the social capabilities of newborns. Tamara's mother is looking at her and speaking to her, but her voice is dubbed with the voice of a stranger. How is Tamara likely to react?

a. She will become upset.
b. She will smile or laugh.
c. She probably will not notice any inconsistency.
d. She will indicate that she understands what is happening.

7. Research on shy monkeys by Steven Suomi demonstrated that

a. shyness was more in the mind of the beholder than in the behavior of the monkey.
b. physiologically, the monkeys did not show any reaction to challenging environments.
c. there was no genetic basis to the trait of shyness.
d. placing the monkeys with calm and supportive foster parents helped the monkeys to adjust.

8. The "proximity-promoting signals" of children may have evolved in humans for the purpose of

a. instigating relationships with peers.
b. eliciting adult responses.
c. controlling their own behavior.
d. stimulating development of neural branching.

9. Based on what is presented in your textbook, which of the following seems to be of LEAST importance among those who want day care to be truly effective?

a. People need to accept the reality that increasing numbers of children will be experiencing day care.
b. The cost of day care must be reduced or even made free to parents who need it.
c. Resources must be directed toward the goal of making all day care, quality day care.
d. People must work to eliminate the stigma associated with "working motherhood" and day care itself.

10. When the "motherless" monkeys from the Harlow studies of attachment had their own children, how did they respond to their offspring?

a. Most of the new mothers were nurturant and responsive to their babies.
b. Most of the new mothers were either indifferent or abusive to their babies.
c. Only the new mothers who had been raised with wire artificial mothers acted normally.
d. Only the new mothers who had been raised with cloth artificial mothers acted normally.

11. In many ways, Phil and his father seem to be opposites. Phil is working hard to establish relationships and make a place for himself in the world, whereas his father is more concerned with a smaller circle of loved ones and a sense of spirituality. In Jung's theory, these contrasting values represent the difference between

a. simplicity and complexity.
b. testing others and testing oneself.
c. outward and inward direction.
d. failure and success.

12. Dawn's parents are thinking about getting divorced, and she is quite upset. She is especially concerned about how a divorce might affect the mental and physical health of her parents. In this context, researchers have shown that

a. neither of her parents likely benefit by being married.
b. men suffer more negative consequences when they stay in an unsatisfying marriage.
c. women suffer more negative consequences when they stay in an unsatisfying marriage.
d. both of her parents are likely to be equally affected if they stay in an unsatisfying marriage.

13. Major theorists seem to share the belief that adulthood is a time when special priority is given to

a. the development of autonomy and initiative.
b. forming an identity and establishing trust.
c. relationships and accomplishments.
d. competence and control.

14. Louis and Bonita are a happily married modern couple, and expect to be parents soon. They might be interested to learn that researchers have found that the birth of children

a. is likely to make their marriage even happier.
b. may be a threat to the overall happiness of a marriage.
c. should minimize the number of conflicts that their marriage will face.
d. is likely to move them in the direction of less traditional sex-roles.

15. The stereotype that college-age adults have of older adults is

a. generally quite positive, especially with respect to the wisdom possessed by the elderly.
b. positive for older adults with whom they are familiar, but negative for most others.
c. in direct opposition to the belief that older adults suffer declines in mental functioning.
d. particularly negative with respect to physical attractiveness and mental competence.

16. Laura baby-sits for a couple who have a two-year-old. Whenever Laura arrives for work, she notices that the parents and child always seem to be involved in a confrontation, with the child demanding to do something, and the parents typically restrictive or critical of the child's efforts. Based on Erikson's theory, Laura realizes that the child may be developing

a. mistrust.
b. inferiority.
c. despair.
d. self-doubt.

17. Martha's husband died a few weeks ago. Every day she thinks about him and wishes he were there to share meals, watch TV with her, and take her shopping. Martha is in the _____ stage of mourning.

a. shock
b. depression
c. recovery
d. longing

18. A longitudinal study of parenting practices that is described in your textbook investigated the relationship between the child-rearing practices mothers used with their 5-year-old children, and the effect of those practices on the social adjustment of the children as long as 35 years later. A major finding of the study was that

a. there was little relationship between early child-rearing practices and later adult social development.
b. adults with parents whose style emphasized the importance of discipline were the most socially well-adjusted.
c. adults with warm, affectionate parents were socially well-adjusted.
d. the adults' social adjustment was best predicted by the number and quality of toys that they had as children.

19. Since she turned 40, Noreen has noticed that her thinking has changed. Her interests and concerns have broadened, and she is now beginning to ask herself how she can contribute more to others. Noreen is experiencing the opportunity for growth that Erikson has called

a. generosity.
b. ego-integrity.
c. generativity.
d. identity.

20. David and Lisa are typical adolescents. When David wants to talk about how things are going in school, he is likely to talk to his _____. When Lisa wants to talk about her new date, she is likely to talk to her _____.

a. peers; parents
b. parents; peers
c. peers; peers
d. parents; parents

Answers, Practice Test ①

1. d (p. 185)

2. c (p. 199) In cultures with initiation rites, adolescence may hardly exist at all.

3. c (p. 212)

4. a (p. 205)

5. a (p. 187)

6. b (p. 191)

7. d (p. 201)

8. b (p. 183)

9. b (p. 204)

10. c (p. 189)

11. a (p. 194)

12. c (p. 211)

13. d (p. 184)

14. b (p. 210)

15. a (p. 207) By trying to protect her father, Zelda may cause him to be unnecessarily dependent on her.

16. a (p. 195)

17. d (p. 198)

18. d (p. 191)

19. b (p. 192)

20. c (p. 208)

Answers, Practice Test ②

1. a (pp. 210-211)

2. a (p. 198)

3. c (p. 191)

4. c (p. 201) In Erikson's description of the life span, the essential task of adolescence is to discover one's true identity.

5. b (p. 187)

6. a (p. 189)

7. d (p. 190)

8. b (p. 190)

9. b (p. 194)

10. b (p. 195)

11. c (p. 185) According to Jung, in youth values expand in an outward direction, whereas in adulthood, values are focused in a more inward direction.

12. c (p. 204)

13. c (p. 203)

14. b (p. 204)

15. d (p. 206)

16. d (p. 183)

17. d (p. 209)

18. c (p. 193)

19. c (p. 184)

20. b (p. 202)

📖 Chapter 7

Sensation

🗐 Chapter Outline

Section	What you need to know
I. Sensory Knowledge of the World	
A. From Physical Energy to Mental Events	What general pattern guides sensory processing?
B. Psychophysics	What is the relationship between physical stimulation and sensory experience?

1. Absolute thresholds
   2. Response bias
   3. Signal detection theory
   4. Difference thresholds	

C. Constructing Psychophysical Scales	How does psychological intensity correspond to physical intensity?
II. The Visual System	
A. The Human Eye	
B. The Pupil and the Lens	How is light received by the visual system?
C. The Retina	What are the early layers of processing in the visual system?

151

Section	What you need to know
D. Pathways to the Brain	What types of analyses occur as visual information makes its way to the brain?
E. Seeing Color	What sensory mechanisms allow you to experience color?

    1. Wavelengths and hues
    2. Theories of color vision

| F. Seeing Form, Depth, and Movement | What mechanisms allow you to experience other important aspects of the sensory world? |

    1. Receptive fields and contrast effects
    2. Complex visual analysis
    3. What neurons "see," the brain perceives

III. Hearing

| A. The Physics of Sound | What are the physical properties of sounds? |
| B. Psychological Dimensions of Sound | How does the psychological experience of sound emerge from those physical properties? |

    1. Pitch
    2. Loudness
    3. Timbre

| C. The Physiology of Hearing | How does the auditory system recover information about the identities and sources of sounds? |

    1. The auditory system
    2. Theories of pitch perception
    3. Sound localization

Section	What you need to know

IV. Your Other Senses

    A. Smell   How do you detect and respond to odors?

    B. Taste   What are basic taste qualities?

    C. Touch and Skin Senses   What information do you obtain through your skin?

    D. The Vestibular and Kinesthetic Senses   How do you monitor your body's movements?

    E. Pain   How do psychological forces affect the interpretation of painful stimuli?

       1. Pain Mechanisms
       2. The Psychology of Pain

Close-up: Taste and Pain   Why do some taste experiences give both pleasure and pain?

Guided Study   ☞ ☞ ☞ ☞

➤ Define the dual functions of survival and sensuality.

I. A. From Physical Energy to Mental Events (p. 217)

➤ Define and give an example of transduction.

➤ What is Johannes Müller's doctrine of specific nerve energies?

➤ What is the importance of the rate and patterning of neural impulses?

➤ Define and give an example of adaptation.

➤ What is meant by stimulus detector units?

I. B. Psychophysics (p. 219)

➤ What is psychophysics and what role did Gustav Fechner play in its history?

1. How are absolute thresholds defined? What is a psychometric function?

2. What are response biases? How do they originate?

How do yea sayers differ from nay sayers? Of what value are catch trials?

3. How does signal detection theory differentiate between sensory processes and decision processes (use yea sayers and nay sayers as an example)?

4. Define and give an example of difference thresholds. What is a JND?

What law did Ernst Weber originate? (Make sure you follow the math shown in Figure 7.4.)

I. C. *Constructing Psychophysical Scales (p. 224)*

➤ What is magnitude estimation and how has it been used in psychophysics?

➤ What equation did S. S. Stevens use to describe the relationship between physical and sensory experiences?

II. *The Visual System (p. 225)*

➤ This section has several figures to aid your understanding. As you read through the text, use the figures to help solidify your knowledge.

II. A. *The Human Eye (p. 226)*

➤ Make sure you understand the analogy between a camera and an eye. What are the components of the analogy? (Consult Figure 7.6.)

II. B. *The Pupil and the Lens (p. 226)*

➤ Explain the physiology of accommodation.

II. C. *The Retina (p. 227)*

For each of these concepts, make sure you understand where you'd find them and give a brief sketch of their function.

Retina

Photoreceptors

Rods

Cones

Fovea

Bipolar cells

Ganglion cells

Horizontal cells

Amacrine cells

Where are your blind spots? Why are you not aware of them?

II. D. Pathways to the Brain (p. 228)

➤ Trace the path of visual information toward your brain.

Optic nerve

Optic chiasma

Lateral geniculate nucleus

Superior colliculus

Visual cortex

➤ How does research support the difference between pattern recognition and place recognition?

➤ What is blindsight? What does it suggest about visual processing?

II. E. Seeing Color (p. 230)

1. What are the physical properties of light waves?

What are the three psychological dimensions of color?

What is the difference between additive and subtractive color mixture?

How do negative afterimages demonstrate the existence of complementary colors?

What is color blindness? What are its most and least common forms?

2. Fill in this chart for theories of color vision.

Name	Who supported it?	What does it explain?

What reconciliation did Leo Hurvich and Dorothea Jameson suggest between the two theories?

II. F. Seeing Form, Depth, and Movement (p. 235)

➤ Where does evidence for subdivisions in the visual system come from?

1. What is a receptive field?

What is a contrast effect? (Make sure you understand the examples given in the figures.)

What is lateral inhibition?

2. Summarize the findings of David Hubel and Thorsten Wiesel.

Simple cells

Complex cells

Hypercomplex cells

What does the spatial-frequency model suggest?

3. How can the brain be fooled into thinking it is sensing the world?

III. Hearing (p. 239)

➤ Why is hearing so important?

III. A. The Physics of Sound (p. 240)

➤ Review the physical properties of sine waves. Distinguish between frequency and amplitude.

III. B. Psychological Dimensions of Sound (p. 241)

➤ What aspects of the physical signal give rise to each of these dimensions?

1. Pitch

2. Loudness (decibels)

159

3. Timbre

III. C. *The Physiology of Hearing (p. 243)*

➤ Use the figures in this section to help you master the material.

1. What role do each of these structures play in the transduction of the sound wave?

Pinna (external ear)

Tympanic membrane (eardrum)

Hammer, anvil, and stirrup

Cochlea

Basilar membrane

Auditory nerve

Auditory cortex

What are the two general types of hearing impairments? Can they be corrected?

2. Fill in this chart for theories of pitch perception.

Name	Who supported it?	What does it explain?

What is the volley principle? How does it help explain pitch perception?

For what range of stimuli do the two mechanisms overlap?

3. What two mechanisms account for sound localization?

IV. Your Other Senses (p. 247)

➤ Pay close attention to the figures.

IV. A. Smell (p. 247)

Define:

Olfactory cilia

Olfactory bulb (note the growth of new neurons)

Pheromones

B. Taste (p. 248)

➢ What is the relationship between odor and taste?

➢ Where do you find papillae? Where do you find taste buds?

➢ What are the basic taste qualities?

➢ How easy is it to damage the taste system?

C. Touch and Skin Senses (p. 248)

➢ Note that these senses are also called cutaneous senses.

➢ What are each of the cutaneous senses?

➢ What are some of the properties of touch?

D. The Vestibular and Kinesthetic Senses (p. 250)

➤ Define each of these senses and note the source of sensory information.

➤ What may cause motion sickness?

E. Pain (p. 251)

➤ Would you want to live without pain?

➤ What are some of the costs of acute and chronic pain?

1. Contrast nociceptive and neuropathic pain. What types of receptors are there for pain?

2. How is the experience of pain affected by psychological factors? Give two extreme examples.

What is placebo therapy?

What is gate-control theory?

Close-up: Taste and Pain (p. 254)

➤ What aspects of physiology can make the same foods both flavorful and painful?

➤ What are supertasters? How does someone become a supertaster?

➤ How can sensory knowledge be used to combat pain?

For Group Study

I. B. Psychophysics

Do you want to try some psychophysics at home? Here's what we suggest. One member of your group should prepare a series of glasses of sugar water, with different amounts of sugar mixed in to each glass (e.g., 1/4 tsp, 1/2 tsp, 1 tsp, and so on). Keep the physical change steady (that's why we suggested multiples of two). The glasses should be labeled so that only the preparer knows which is which. The other group members should take a small taste of each mixture and perform magnitude estimation. What's the relationship between physical intensity and sensory experience?

You could also use the same approach to try absolute and difference thresholds. How much sugar do you need to put in a glass of water before you can differentiate it from a glass of plain water? (Have a friend prepare the two glasses and not tell you which is which.) How much more sugar do you have to add to make two glasses taste different to you? Measure JND's starting with different concentrations. Can you recreate Weber's law?

II. The Visual System

As in Chapter 3, there are many new terms in this chapter. You should take the same approach as you did there. Make sets of flash cards with your group. Help each other develop strategies for remembering the material.

IV. Your Other Senses

There are a number of exercises you can try to give you some first hand experience with the properties of your sensory systems. Here are two suggestions:

For odor and taste, have a meal together. What are the prominent sensory qualities of the food you are eating? Do you all agree about how strong the flavors are? (If you tried the psychophysics experiment described earlier, you may have already discovered some individual differences in taste.) If you have spicy food, do some of you find it unpleasant? Do all flavors taste stronger to those people? What happens to taste when you hold your nose?

To discover properties of your skin senses, you should find two pointed objects (but not too sharp!). The idea is to see how far apart you can touch a partner's skin with the two points simultaneously without the partner being able to tell whether it's one or two. Sometimes you should touch with just one and sometimes with both. Your partner must respond, "One or two?" You may be surprised how far apart you can touch with two stimuli on some parts of the body before your partner will say "two." (You'll have to practice touching them both at once. Time differences will give it away.)

Practice Test ①

1. Thor has been given a new box of crayons. He draws a thick plus-sign with red going one way and blue going the other. Thor notices that the patch in the middle looks purple. He has just discovered the effects of

a. additive color mixing.
b. negative afterimages.
c. subtractive color mixing.
d. complementary colors.

2. Colin's grandmother used to give him a dollar every time she noticed that he had grown. Although he's an inch taller than the last time she saw him, Colin's grandmother didn't give him a dollar. What psychophysical concept might explain why Colin was left empty handed?

a. absolute thresholds
b. response bias
c. difference thresholds
d. adaptation

3. Zvi reminds his son Daniel to stay away from the hot stove. Zvi is afraid that Daniel will experience _____ pain.

a. myelinated
b. nociceptive
c. neuropathic
d. phantom

4. For a classroom presentation, you have built a device that has five lightbulbs (numbered 1 to 5) attached in a row on a board. To demonstrate lateral inhibition, you begin by turning on light 3. Now you should turn _____ light 2 and turn _____ light 4.

a. on; off
b. off; on
c. on; on
d. off; off

5. What do your face, tongue, and fingertips have in common?

a. They all have Meissner corpuscles but no Merkel disks.
b. Sensory information from these areas project to the same location of sensory cortex.
c. They have a great number of nerve endings to sense pressure.
d. They do not have receptor cells for warmth and cold.

6. By restricting the spread of signals within the retina, _____ cells and _____ cells improve the precision of the visual system.

a. ganglion, horizontal
b. amacrine; bipolar
c. horizontal; amacrine
d. bipolar; ganglion

7. You are being paid to babysit a young child. To be a good baby sitter, you must be able to detect potentially dangerous situations. If you care more about the child's safety than embarrassing yourself, you are likely to have many _____ and _____ with respect to detecting these situations.

a. hits; correct rejections
b. hits; false alarms
c. misses; false alarms
d. correct rejections; misses

8. You hear someone call out "Help!" The shout arrives at your right ear shortly after your left ear. The source is likely to be

a. off to your left.
b. directly in front of you.
c. off to your right.
d. directly behind you.

9. David Hubel and Thornton Wiesel studied _____ in the visual system.

a. receptive fields
b. spatial-frequency analysis
c. stimulus contrast effects
d. opponent processes

10. The volley principle suggests that

a. several neurons firing in sequence could signal high frequency sounds.
b. complex sound waves stimulate successive locations on the basilar membrane.
c. combinations of pure tones combine to produce complex waves.
d. low frequency sounds are detected more easily than high frequency sounds.

11. You wash your new pair of blue jeans in bleach so that they have that cool faded look. The dimension of their color you have changed the most is _____.

a. intensity
b. hue
c. brightness
d. saturation

12. If all the cones in your eyes stopped functioning, then you would

a. no longer have color vision.
b. be totally blind.
c. only have sight at the center of the visual field.
d. have poorest vision when illumination was near darkness.

13. Suppose one friend has a flute and the other a guitar. It's possible for them to play a note of the same _____ but not of the same _____.

a. pitch; timbre
b. pitch; loudness
c. loudness; timbre
d. timbre; pitch

14. One thing that the taste and smell systems have in common is that

a. both sensations are processed in the olfactory bulb.
b. they are able to detect pheromones.
c. it is easy to damage them severely.
d. their receptor cells are frequently replenished.

15. Suppose a researcher has determined that your absolute threshold for hearing is x units of sound. Assuming you have no response bias, if the researcher plays you a sound that loud, then you are likely to report hearing something _____ percent of the time.

a. 0
b. 25
c. 50
d. 100

16. Four of your friends claim that they are color blind. Only one of them is telling the truth. For which of the following could there be a physiological basis for his claims?

a. Patrick says that he confuses reds and yellows.
b. Lars says that he confuses reds and greens.
c. Sherwood says that he confuses greens and blues.
d. Arthur says that he confuses yellows and greens.

17. You've been watching television for a while. It seems, over time, that the volume on the TV has been getting softer and softer. This impression may be a consequence of

a. absolute thresholds.
b. response bias.
c. just noticeable differences.
d. adaptation.

18. With your eyes closed, touch your finger to your nose. Your _____ sense allows you to succeed at this task.

a. olfactory
b. kinesthetic
c. auditory
d. vestibular

19. Your friend Barbara finds it very painful to eat food containing hot pepper though it doesn't bother you at all. Compared to Barbara, you are likely to have _____ taste buds and _____ pain receptors.

a. more; fewer
b. fewer; more
c. more; more
d. fewer; fewer

20. The _____ provides part of the link between the eardrum and the cochlea.

a. basilar membrane
b. anvil
c. pinna
d. tympanic membrane

Practice Test ②

1. Joey read a book on the sensory abilities of animals for his science class. One fact that might have surprised him is that

a. human sense of smell is superior to that of rodents.
b. only mammals have information-gathering apparatuses that are specialized.
c. humans process a wider variety of complex sensory input than any other animal.
d. the human species specializes in the visual sensory domain.

2. The children are at a walk-through science museum exhibit entitled "The Ear." They are to act as vibrating air molecules entering the ear. What is the order in which they will encounter the structures listed below, as they move through the ear?

a. tympanic membrane, middle ear, pinna, cochlea
b. cochlea, middle ear, pinna, tympanic membrane
c. tympanic membrane, pinna, cochlea, middle ear
d. pinna, tympanic membrane, middle ear, cochlea

3. The formula for Weber's law is

a. $S=hIb$
b. $S=hb/I$
c. $ÆI/I=k$
d. $ÆI=k-I$

4. If there were a single, true absolute threshold, psychometric functions would resemble

a. an S-shaped curve.
b. an upside-down U.
c. the blade of a saw.
d. a stair step.

5. By using light of various wavelengths, vision researchers have discovered that different cone cells are maximally responsive to

a. dark, light, and shades of gray.
b. blue, green, and red.
c. seven wavelengths of light, representing the seven primary colors.
d. hundreds of different wavelengths, representing all colors.

6. Young Pablo can distinguish between red, yellow, and turquoise because objects of different colors reflect electromagnetic energies of different

a. intensities.
b. frequencies.
c. wavelengths.
d. durations.

7. Bobby has been drawing bizarre cartoon characters again. His latest has a gigantic head and two huge ears that he calls "Cranium-Boy." Bobby's creation should be very good at

a. recognizing musical instruments by their sound.
b. echolocation.
c. localizing the source of high frequency sounds.
d. following a melody played on a cello.

8. Mark's white dress shirt got a bit gray when he washed it with his black t-shirt. If he doesn't want people to notice that his shirt isn't very white, he should wear it with a _____ jacket.

a. black
b. white
c. light gray
d. dark gray

9. While at the art museum, Juán learns a neat trick. If he stares at a painting for a few minutes, then looks away at a blank wall, he "sees" colors that are opposite to those in the original painting. Juán has discovered the

a. opponent-process theory.
b. subtractive color mixture.
c. color blindness.
d. negative afterimage.

172

10. Rudy's mother says that the new "painkillers" she takes for her arthritis work exceptionally well, and don't upset her stomach the way the old medication did. In fact, Rudy's mother is being given an inert substance that has no medicinal value. It sounds as though she is receiving _____ therapy.

a. gate-control
b. endorphin
c. placebo
d. nociceptive

11. The value of the difference threshold is known as a

a. just noticeable difference.
b. barely perceptible minimum.
c. sensory difference threshold.
d. psychological separation unit.

12. Optic nerve is to optic chiasma as auditory nerve is to

a. auditory chiasma.
b. basilar membrane.
c. auditory cortex.
d. cochlear nucleus.

13. When the third-grade class arrived at the pig farm for their field trip, many of the youngsters commented on how bad it smelled. The people who worked there, however, didn't seem to notice. The most likely explanation for this discrepancy is

a. sensory adaptation.
b. temporal coding.
c. psychophysics.
d. the absolute threshold.

14. Jeremy's father is celebrating his 50th birthday. When he tries to read the card his son has given him, he jokes that his arms have gotten too short to be able to read without his glasses. In reality, his vision problem is most likely due to

a. accommodation.
b. flattening of the cornea.
c. the loss of elasticity of the lens.
d. contraction of the ciliary muscles.

15. Valerie is playing a game called "Guess That Brain Part!" She has received hints that the structure in question receives input from the optic tracts and the primary visual cortex, integrates information from the reticular activating system, and performs detailed visual analysis. Valerie should guess that the brain part is the

a. optic chiasma.
b. optic nerve.
c. superior colliculus.
d. lateral geniculate nucleus.

16. The sense that tell us whether the elevator we are riding is going up or down is called the _____ sense.

a. proprioceptive
b. vestibular
c. cutaneous
d. kinesthetic

17. When you walk into your psychology classroom, you notice the words "payoff matrix," "hits" and "false alarms" written on the blackboard. You can conclude that the topic discussed in the previous class was

a. magnitude estimation.
b. signal detection theory.
c. Weber's law.
d. psychophysical scales.

18. Kim has a theory about the senses. Since the eyes are located in the front of the head, and the ears are located on the side of the head, she reasons that the front of the brain must be involved in vision and that the sides of the brain must be involved in hearing. Although Kim doesn't quite have things right, her idea that different sensations are associated with activity in different parts of the brain is consistent with

a. difference thresholds.
b. signal detection theory.
c. psychophysical scales.
d. the doctrine of specific nerve energies.

19. Herbie is a "yea sayer." On a signal detection task, he is likely to be _____ on hits and _____ on false alarms.

a. low; high
b. high; low
c. high; high
d. low; low

20. Rodney reads a science fiction story in which people have personal machines that stimulate distinct circuits of receptive fields of neurons in their visual cortex. In reality, exciting brain cells directly, in the absence of environmental input, would

a. have absolutely no effect.
b. cause confusion in those being stimulated.
c. bring about immediate blindness.
d. cause specific perceptions to occur.

1. c (p. 233)

2. c (p. 222)

3. b (p. 252) Zvi is probably most concerned that Daniel will experience nociceptive pain if he touches the hot stove.

4. d (p. 238)

5. c (p. 249)

6. c (p. 228)

7. b (p. 222) You are a "yea sayer" so you'll have both more hits and more false alarms.

8. a (p. 246)

9. a (p. 238)

10. a (p. 245)

11. d (p. 232) You have added white to the original blue of the jeans, which should make the color look less saturated.

12. a (p. 227)

13. a (pp. 241-242)

14. d (pp. 247-248)

15. c (p. 220)

16. b (p. 233)

17. d (p. 218)

18. b (p. 251)

19. d (p. 254)

20. b (p. 243) The anvil functions along with the hammer and stirrup.

Answers, Practice Test ②

1. c (p. 217)

2. d (p. 243)

3. c (p. 223)

4. d (p. 220) If there were a single, true absolute threshold, you would expect the transition from 0 to 100 percent detection to be very sharp, occurring right at the point where the intensity reached the threshold.

5. b (p. 235)

6. c (p. 231) Colors exist only in your sensory system's interpretation of wavelengths.

7. c (p. 246)

8. d (p. 236)

9. d (p. 232)

10. c (p. 253)

11. a (p. 222)

12. d (p. 243) Fibers from the auditory nerve meet in the cochlear nucleus of the brain stem.

13. a (p. 218) The responsiveness of sensory systems diminishes (adapts) as a function of prolonged stimulus input.

14. c (p. 226) As people age, the lens of the eye becomes more flattened and loses its elasticity.

15. d (p. 229)

16. b (p. 250) The vestibular sense tells you how your body is oriented with respect to gravity.

17. b (p. 222)

18. d (p. 217) The doctrine of specific nerve energies says that the coding for sensory qualities of your different sense modalities takes place according to brain codes in the specific neural pathways activated by each sense.

19. c (p. 222)

20. d (p. 239)

📖 Chapter 8

Perception

🗐 Chapter Outline

Section	What you need to know

II. Attentional Processes

  A. Selective Attention

How do you select among all the information available in the world?

    1. Determining the focus of attention

    2. The fate of unattended information

  B. Attention and Objects in the Environment

What aspects of visual analysis require attention?

    1. Preattentive processing and guided search

    2. Putting features together

III. Organizational Processes in Perception

  A. Region Segregation

How do you find coherent regions in the visual world?

  B. Figure, Ground, and Closure

What becomes prominent in a visual display?

  C. Shape: Figural Goodness and Reference Frames

How do you perceive shapes?

  D. Principles of Perceptual Grouping

What laws govern your organization of the visual world?

  E. Spatial and Temporal Integration

How do you monitor the world across space and time?

  F. Motion Perception

How do you perceive the world in motion?

  G. Depth Perception

How do you experience objects in depth?

Guided Study

➤ How do the caricatures illustrate that sensation is only one component of the overall process of perception?

I. Sensing, Organizing, Identifying, and Recognizing (p. 259)

➤ Make sure you understand each of the stages in the perceptual process. How does each stage differ from the next? (Use Dr. Richard as an example.)

I. A. The Proximal and Distal Stimulus (p. 260)

➤ What are proximal and distal stimuli? Look at objects around the room and try to think about the two-dimensional image they cast on your retina. How can you tell what you're looking at based on that 2D image?

I. B. Reality, Ambiguity, and Illusions (p. 262)

1. Ambiguity is mentioned at the beginning of the chapter to help you understand why perception is a challenge. It is often the case that information arriving from the environment allows several interpretations. Your perceptual system must determine which one is correct (or, at least, must settle on a best guess). Make sure you understand each of the examples.

2. How do illusions differ from ambiguities? From hallucinations? How can the study of illusions be helpful to researchers? (Use the Hermann grid as an example.)

3. What kinds of illusions do you experience on a day-to-day basis? When are illusions helpful?

Close-up: Ambiguity in Art (p. 267)

➤ Enjoy the paintings. They fit the theme of creatively playful perception to which the chapter returns at the end.

I. C. Approaches to the Study of Perception (p. 266)

➤ How does the distinction between nature and nurture apply to theories of perception?

➤ Summarize the major insights of each theory:

1. Helmholtz's classical theory

2. The gestalt approach

3. Gibson's ecological optics

4. Use "Toward a Unified Theory of Perception" to check your understanding of the past few sections. Do you see how this set of questions draws much of the material together?

II. A. Selective Attention (p. 270)

1. Distinguish between goal-directed selection and stimulus-driven capture.

Make sure you understand how the experiment demonstrates stimulus-driven capture.

2. What are the dichotic listening technique and the shadowing procedure? How did Donald Broadbent use these to test his filter theory and what did he discover?

What research results suggest that attention does not function as an absolute filter?

What are the two functions of selective attention?

II. B. Attention and Objects in the Environment (p. 273)

1. Define preattentive processing and guided search.

When is it possible to search the environment in parallel? When must you do a serial search? Give examples.

2. How do the experiments demonstrate that attention is necessary for combining features? What are illusory conjunctions and how have they been studied?

III. Organizational Processes in Perception (p. 278)

➤ As a preview for this whole section, spend a few more minutes looking around your environment. Find objects that should challenge your perceptual system. You might also want to work backwards from the text to look for the types of situations that are described. How do you know, for example, that you're looking at a poster that's hanging in front of a wall? Are there two different regions? Does texture give it away? Or can you tell that the poster is in front of the wall? What depth cues are you using? Why do you take the wall to be the ground and the poster to be the figure?

III. A. Region Segregation (p. 279)

➤ What visual cues do you use to carry out region segregation?

III. B. Figure, Ground, and Closure (p. 279)

➤ How do you decide what is figure and what is ground? Why does it matter?

➤ What is the origin of subjective contours? What role does closure play?

III. C. Shape: Figural Goodness and Reference Frames (p. 280)

➤ What makes a figure good? Why does it matter?

➤ What effect do reference frames have on shape recognition?

III. D. Principles of Perceptual Grouping (p. 281)

➤ List the four laws this section presents. Try to give a different application from the one given in the book, from your real-world experience.

Law	Application

III. E. Spatial and Temporal Integration (p. 283)

➤ Why doesn't your visual memory preserve precise details of scenes? How does this finding apply to "impossible" objects?

III. F. Motion Perception (p. 284)

➤ How do you detect motion from the size of images on your retina?

➤ What is the role of reference frames in induced motion?

➤ Explain apparent motion and the phi phenomenon. What's special about biological motion?

III. G. Depth Perception (p. 285)

➤ Why does depth perception require interpretation of the sensory input?

➤ List the cues for depth perception, and explain why they work.

1. Binocular and motion cues

Cue	Why it works

2. Pictorial cues

Cue	Why it works

III. H. Perceptual Constancies (p. 290)

➤ Define perceptual constancy.

➤ Explain how each type of constancy is possible and give an example.

1. Size constancy

Shape constancy

2. Orientation constancy

IV. A. Bottom-up and Top-down Processes (p. 294)

➤ Define and give examples of bottom-up and top-down processes. Which type of process is also called data-driven? Which is called conceptually-driven? Why?

➤ How does phonemic restoration illustrate the impact of top-down processes?

IV. B. Object Recognition (p. 295)

➤ Study the set of geons given in Figure 8.36. Look around the room and try to construct each object out of geons.

➤ How have researchers demonstrated the importance of parts in object recognition?

➤ Why must you store viewpoint-specific representations of objects?

IV. C. The Influence of Contexts and Expectations (p. 297)

➤ How do expectations affect perception?

➤ Define and give an example of each type of set.

For Group Study

II. A. Selective Attention

Spend some time talking about how your focus of attention is directed both by what's in the world (stimulus-driven capture) and what's in your head (goal-directed selection). Watch a scene out a window. Does everyone notice the same things? Why or why not? Can you detect elements of the scene that you all *had* to look at? Can you detect the goals that made some aspects of the scene more interesting to some people than to others?

III. Organizational Processes in Perception

As we suggested in Guided Study, spend some time looking around the environment trying to apply the material in this chapter directly to the world around you. Ask yourselves questions such as

➤ What aspects of the scene require me to do region segregation? What cues am I using?

➤ How am I determining what is figure and what is ground?

➤ Where do I perceive depth? What cues am I using? (Does anything change when I shut an eye? Why or why not?)

➤ What constancies are at work?

Work through these topics with the group.

IV. C. The Influence of Contexts and Expectations

Take another look out that window. Try to give a pure description of what you are seeing. Your friends should try to catch you letting your expectations affect how you describe what you are seeing.

IV. D. Creatively Playful Perception

This section of the chapter would make a great break from studying! Why don't you take a few minutes to be creatively playful before you get back to memorizing all the different cues to depth?

Practice Test ①

1. When you are in a situation of divided attention, you are particularly likely to experience

a. subjective contours.
b. lateral inhibition.
c. guided search.
d. illusory conjunctions.

2. You walk by a classroom and see a professor drawing a large rectangle on the blackboard. Next he asks his class to tilt their heads about 45 degrees. It's likely that he is making a point about _____ constancy.

a. size
b. dimensional
c. shape
d. orientation

3. Your own professor has drawn a shape on the blackboard. At first you think it's a square, but then he draws some lines around it and now it looks like a diamond to you. Your professor is demonstrating the importance of

a. reference frames.
b. figural goodness.
c. common fate.
d. closure.

4. You are sitting in a dark room looking at a piece of modern sculpture. It consists of a small red square in front of a large yellow circle. The artist informs you that only one of the two shapes is in motion. You are likely to perceive the _____ in motion because

a. circle; it is larger than the square.
b. circle; it is a "better" figure than the square.
c. square; the circle is interpreted as a reference frame.
d. square; it is a brighter color than the circle.

5. To discuss the difference between objects in the world and images on your retina, you have brought to class a large red ball and a cardboard circle painted the same color. In the demonstration, the ball will serve best as the _____ stimulus and the circle will serve best as the _____ stimulus.

a. distal; proximal
b. proximal; invariant
c. invariant; distal
d. proximal; distal

6. Your professor catches you looking out the window during her lecture. To defend yourself, you tell her you couldn't help looking outside because your attention was guided by

a. stimulus-driven capture.
b. goal-directed selection.
c. lateral inhibition.
d. guided search.

7. You have just heard a perception lecture that focused on invariant properties of the environment. The lecture was likely to have been given by a follower of

a. J. J. Oppel.
b. the Gestalt school.
c. Hermann von Helmholtz.
d. James Gibson.

8. How many geons would you need to construct the typical dinner table?

a. 1
b. 5
c. 7
d. 11

9. Ehren is viewing a display that has a row of three red circles on top of a row of three green circles (all the circles are evenly spaced). Ehren reports that she sees three columns, each with a red circle and a green circle. Call the perception police! Ehren's percept violates the gestalt law of

a. common fate.
b. proximity.
c. similarity.
d. closure.

10. Professor Offel is the world's expert on optical illusions. There is one illusion, called the Poggendorf illusion, that he has studied for twenty years. He shows this illusion to his 30-year-old nephew Herman, who has never seen it before, and he looks at it at the same time. The probability that Professor Offel will experience the illusion is _____ percent and the probability that Herman will experience it is _____ percent.

a. 50; 100
b. 100; 100
c. 100; 50
d. 0; 100

11. Suppose it takes you 3 seconds to find a single white rose within an array of 10 red roses. If the number of red roses were increased to 20, it would take you _____ time to find the white rose.

a. the same
b. more
c. less
d. much more

12. Here's another demonstration. You start with small and large cardboard circles. You position them along a table--one to the near left and one to the far right--so that when you sit at the head of the table, each circle projects the same size image on your retina. If you view the two circles _____ they will look nearly side-by-side.

a. in dim illumination
b. with your head tilted
c. with one eye closed
d. in bright illumination

13. A friend asks you to close your eyes and then places an object in your hand. You can tell that it is in the shape of a cube, but not much else. The process of perception has been halted when you reached the stage of

a. perceptual organization.
b. object recognition.
c. sensation.
d. closure.

14. Try this demonstration. Hold your pen or pencil as far away from your head as you can. Now keep your eyes focused on it as you bring it toward you. Can you feel the strain on your eye muscles? You have just experienced the way that _____ can be used as a cue to depth.

a. relative motion
b. occlusion
c. binocular disparity
d. convergence

15. You are playing softball with some friends. Your friend Tina asks you something but because the ballpark is crowded all you hear is "Can I borrow your (noise)at?" Fortunately, _____ processing lets you know that what Tina wanted was a bat.

a. bottom-up
b. preattentive
c. data-driven
d. top-down

16. Ambiguous figures illustrate one of the challenges of perception by suggesting that a

a. distal stimulus can consist of many different objects.
b. proximal stimulus can change from one object to the next.
c. distal stimulus can be stable or unstable.
d. proximal stimulus can have many different interpretations.

17. You are looking at a painting that's a circular canvas with a black circle painted in the middle. The name of the painting is "White Doughnut on Black Table." Suppose the title were changed to "Black Disk on White Iceberg." The black circle should now look _____ you.

a. closer to
b. further from
c. larger to
d. smaller to

18. Your friend Hiram believes that illusions are only things that psychologists make up to trick people in the classroom. To convince him otherwise, you ask him to think about why

a. some of the planets aren't always visible.
b. it looks like the moon is always chasing you.
c. the sun appears to be overhead at midday.
d. the moon is easier to see at night than at day.

19. Dichotic listening tasks have often been used to study the extent to which

a. capacity limitations affect preattentive processing.
b. internal representations become suppressed in memory.
c. unattended information is processed for meaning.
d. the filter applies to attended information.

20. After seeing a horror movie, you think you see a monster lurking in every shadow. This is an example of a _____ set.

a. motor
b. perceptual
c. conceptual
d. mental

Practice Test ②

1. Joyce stared at the lovely trees. Growing together, as they were, their branches intertwined and overlapped, yet the leaves of each variety could easily be seen as separate, somehow grouping themselves together. What Joyce is witnessing is the Gestalt law of

a. proximity.
b. common fate.
c. similarity.
d. effect.

2. For the last twenty minutes, Marjorie has been trying to figure out an illusion known as an "impossible" object. It is a picture of a "perpetual staircase," and no matter how often she moves her eyes around it, it seems to forever ascend or descend. Marjorie is experiencing

a. a violation of the law of closure.
b. a difficulty in spatial integration.
c. a breakdown in shape constancy.
d. the effect of reference frames.

3. When two stationary spots of light in the different positions in the visual field are turned on and off alternately, it can appear as though a single light is moving back and forth between the two spots. This effect is known as

a. relative motion parallax.
b. depth perception.
c. the phi phenomenon.
d. interposition.

4. Nine-year-old Bart is a skillful bike rider. One of his "tricks" is to ride as fast as he can toward a stone wall, then suddenly stop just short of impact. In order to sense how quickly he is approaching the wall, Bart's primary source of information probably is

a. the rate at which his retinal image of the wall expands.
b. feedback concerning how dilated the pupils of his eyes are.
c. the feeling of air rushing into his face.
d. the buildup of pressure as the air between Bart and the wall becomes compressed.

5. Cheri is a subject in a dichotic listening experiment that requires her to shadow the message in her left ear. Cheri is not told that the experimenter will change characteristics of the unattended message. What kind of change, if any, is Cheri most likely to notice?

a. She is not likely to notice any changes.
b. She will notice if the language in which the message is presented changes.
c. She will notice if the message is played backward.
d. She will notice if the speaker's voice changes from male to female.

6. As you read this question, the words stand out against a backdrop. This illustrates the concept of

a. figure and ground.
b. subjective contour.
c. closure.
d. reference frames.

7. Phinneas is taking his first train ride. As he looks out the window, he is amazed at how quickly the objects along the tracks are whizzing by. On the other hand, objects in the distance hardly appear to be moving at all. This best illustrates

a. relative motion parallax.
b. binocular disparity.
c. convergence.
d. interposition.

8. Rosie can finally see the finish line. As she gets closer and closer, the visual images on her retina are constantly changing. According to Gibson's theory of ecological optics, an explanation of Rosie's perceptual processing should emphasize

a. higher level systems of perceptual inference.
b. the raw sensations that are bombarding her.
c. the whole, rather than the sum of the parts.
d. the detection of invariances in her environment.

9. Which of the following statements best captures the nature of the object identification process?

a. Object identification is primarily a data-driven type of process.
b. Object identification is a constructive, interpretive process.
c. Object identification requires considerable conscious effort to be successful.
d. Object identification requires the temporary "suspension of disbelief."

10. From his vantage point at the regatta, Horatio can clearly see the boats working their way up the river. Since the boats are all the same size, his interpretation that the one that looks smaller is farther away is based on the basic rule of light projection called

a. size constancy.
b. the size/size effect.
c. the size/distance relation.
d. the Ponzo illusion.

11. As you career recklessly down the sidewalk on your new rollerblades, you still see the world as invariant and stable despite the dramatic change in stimulation that is being received by your sensory systems. This is referred to as

a. the size/distance relation.
b. relative motion parallax.
c. the Ponzo illusion.
d. perceptual constancy.

12. If you want to reduce the likelihood of forming illusory conjunctions, you should

a. keep one eye closed.
b. use preattentive processing.
c. engage in focused attention.
d. engage in parallel searches.

13. Norman has a strange picture of a woman on his wall. First, it looks as though it is a picture of a young woman, but as one stares at it, it suddenly looks as though it is a picture of an older woman. This important characteristic of ambiguous figures is known as

a. instability.
b. an illusion.
c. lateral inhibition.
d. a hallucination.

14. Johnnie is hurriedly looking for a yellow legal pad on his cluttered desk. It is the only yellow item on the desk. Can preattentive processing help him?

a. No, because preattentive processing is not goal-directed.
b. No, because preattentive processing occurs without awareness.
c. Yes, because he is engaged in a serial search.
d. Yes, because the object he is looking for has a single salient feature.

15. Scarlet was intently reading a romance novel when the movement of a bright red and black scarlet tanager landing on a nearby tree branch momentarily distracted her. The shift in her attention is an example of which component of attention?

a. shadowing
b. dichotic viewing
c. goal-directed selection
d. stimulus-driven capture

16. Sensory evidence is the starting point for _____ processing.

a. top-down
b. bottom-up
c. conceptually-driven
d. contextual

17. Knowing that illusions exist, you can accurately conclude that

a. perceptual systems are sometimes imperfect in recovering the distal stimulus from the proximal stimulus.
b. people are unable to overcome the influence of illusions.
c. sensory receptors do not operate in a predictable manner.
d. either the proximal stimulus does not exist or the distal stimulus does not exist.

18. Otto loves mottoes. If he were a Gestalt psychologist, Otto's motto would be

a. "ask not what's inside your head, but what your head's inside of."
b. "analysis and synthesis make the world go round."
c. "he who hesitates is lost."
d. "the whole is greater than the sum of its parts."

19. You are viewing Uncle Albert's slides of his family vacation. As each new scene appears, your perceptual system springs into action. Your first task of perceptual organization is to segregate regions in the visual pattern, a process accomplished in large part on the basis of information provided by

a. the presence of unfamiliar objects.
b. an up-and-down movement of the eyes.
c. the narrative which accompanies each slide.
d. abrupt changes in color and texture.

20. Transduction occurs in the _____ stage of perceptual processing; synthesis occurs in the _____ stage.

a. sensation; perceptual organization
b. sensation; identification and recognition
c. perceptual organization; sensation
d. perceptual organization; recognition

1. d (p. 276)

2. d (p. 293) If he were demonstrating shape constancy, it's more likely he would manipulate a shape rather than your orientation.

3. a (p. 280)

4. c (p. 284)

5. a (p. 261) The two-dimensional image of the three-dimensional ball should be a circle.

6. a (p. 270)

7. d (p. 268)

8. b (p. 296) One for each leg and one for the flat surface.

9. c (p. 282)

10. b (p. 264) If it is truly an illusion then Professor Offel and his nephew should both see it. There are some illusions that are experienced less strongly by children and people from non-Western cultures (that is, they require sufficient experience in a particular kind of visual environment), but Herman is 30 and he and Professor Offel are very likely to be members of the same culture.

11. a (p. 275)

12. c (pp. 285-286) If both circles cast the same size image on your retina, you will have much less of a sense of depth if you eliminate binocular cues.

13. b (p. 260) You have organized the percept (it's a cube), but without further information you can't recognize what cube-like object it is.

14. d (p. 287)

15. d (p. 294)

16. d (p. 263)

17. a (p. 279) The title change should reverse your interpretation of figure and ground.

18. b (p. 266)

19. c (p. 272)

20. b (p. 299)

Answers, Practice Test ②

1. c (p. 282)

2. b (p. 283)

3. c (p. 285)

4. a (p. 284)

5. d (p. 272)

6. a (p. 279)

7. a (p. 287)

8. d (p. 269)

9. b (p. 298) Identification depends on your expectations as well as on the physical properties of the objects you see.

10. c (p. 288)

11. d (p. 290)

12. c (p. 277)

13. a (p. 263)

14. d (p. 275)

15. d (p. 270)

16. b (p. 294)

17. a (p. 266)

18. d (p. 268)

19. d (p. 279)

20. a (p. 259)

Chapter 9

Learning and Behavior Analysis

▤ Chapter Outline

Section	What you need to know
I. The Study of Learning	
A. What is Learning?	How is learning defined?

1. A change in behavior or behavior potential
    2. A relatively consistent change
    3. A process based on experience	

B. Behaviorism and Behavior Analysis	What are the goals of behavior analysis?
II. Classical Conditioning: Learning Predictable Signals	
A. Pavlov's Surprising Observation	Why did Pavlov undertake the first experiments on classical conditioning?
B. The Acquisition of Classically Conditioned Responses	Under what circumstances will classical conditioning take place?
1. Contingency 2. Informativeness	

Section	What you need to know
E. Schedules of Reinforcement	What happens when behaviors aren't reinforced on every occasion?

1. Fixed-ratio (FR) schedules
   2. Variable-ratio (VR) schedules
   3. Fixed-interval (FI) schedules
   4. Variable-interval (VI) schedules	

F. Shaping and Chaining	What operant techniques allow you to teach behaviors that would rarely appear spontaneously?
IV. Biology and Learning	
A. Instinctual Drift	How do species-specific tendencies affect learning?
B. Taste-Aversion Learning	How do animals avoid eating dangerous substances?
V. Cognitive Influences on Learning	
A. Animal Cognition	What cognitive abilities do nonhuman animals possess?
1. Cognitive maps 2. Conceptual behavior	
B. Observational Learning	How can you learn by watching others?
VI. Formal Models of Learning	How do researchers try to formalize the mental computations underlying learning?

Guided Study

☞ ☞ ☞ ☞

➣ What is the evolutionary perspective on learning?

I. A. What is Learning? (p. 305)

➣ Give an example for each of these components of the definition of learning. What changes in behavior don't fit the definition?

1. A change in behavior or behavior potential (learning-performance distinction)

2. A relatively consistent change

3. A process based on experience

I. B. Behaviorism and Behavior Analysis (p. 306)

➣ What is radical behaviorism?

➣ Summarize the influential ideas of John Watson and B. F. Skinner. What did they have to say about mental states?

What is behavior analysis? Why does it assume that learning is conserved across species?

206

II. A. *Pavlov's Surprising Observation (p. 307)*

➤ What observation prompted Pavlov to study classical conditioning?

➤ Describe the main features of Pavlov's procedure. What did his dogs do?

➤ Define:

Reflex

Unconditional stimulus

Unconditional response

Conditional stimulus

Conditional response

II. B. *The Acquisition of Classically Conditioned Responses (p. 309)*

1. Contrast contiguity and contingency. Make sure you understand how Rescorla's experiment demonstrated the necessity of contingency.

Study Figure 9.5 to master the different timing patterns possible in classical conditioning. Which patterns are most effective? Which patterns are least effective?

2. Define informativeness. Make sure you understand Kamin's blocking experiment.

What is the key to developing a strong conditional response?

II. C. *Processes of Conditioning (p. 313)*

1. Review acquisition.

What is extinction?

What is spontaneous recovery?

What is savings?

2. What is stimulus generalization and how is a generalization gradient produced?

3. How is training in stimulus discrimination given?

Explain why generalization and discrimination must occur in a balanced fashion.

II. D. *Applications of Classical Conditioning (p. 316)*

1. How does classical conditioning explain why some things disgust you?

How does classical conditioning explain the acquisition of fears? Describe Watson and Rayner's experiment.

2. How has classical conditioning been applied to psychoneuroimmunology? For each experiment, make sure you understand what was the UCS, UCR, and so on.

Close-up: Learning to be a Drug Addict (p. 319)

➤ Summarize Shepard Siegel's research on tolerance with rats (identify the UCS, UCR, and son on).

➤ How have his findings been applied to human situations?

III. A. The Law of Effect (p. 320)

➤ What was the purpose of Thorndike's puzzle boxes? What did he conclude about stimulus-response connections, trial-and-error, and the law of effect?

III. B. Experimental Analysis of Behavior (p. 320)

➤ What is the experimental analysis of behavior and why is it not theoretical?

➤ What are operants? What is an operant chamber?

III. C. Reinforcement Contingencies (p. 322)

➤ Make sure you understand how each of these types of reinforcers and punishments are different.

Give examples of each:

1. Positive reinforcers

Negative reinforcers

Operant extinction

2. Positive punishment

Negative punishment

What is a good way to differentiate punishment and reinforcement?

3. What are discriminative stimuli?

Give an example of a three-term contingency.

Distinguish between positive and negative discriminate stimuli and be able to recognize their notation.

How does generalization function in operant conditioning?

4. You should work your way through the questions and answers in the text by calling to mind real-life situations. We repeat each question here. Try to give an answer without looking back at the text.

➤ How can you define the behavior that you would like to reinforce or eliminate?

➤ How can you define the contexts in which a behavior is appropriate or inappropriate?

➤ Have you unknowingly been reinforcing some behaviors?

➤ When is punishment appropriate?

III. D. *Properties of Reinforcers (p. 326)*

1. What is a primary reinforcer? What is a conditioned reinforcer? Give examples.

How do token economies work?

2. What is the Premack principle? Give examples of the Premack principle at work.

III. E. Schedules of Reinforcement (p. 327)

➤ Describe the effect of partial reinforcement.

➤ Make sure you understand the notation (F vs. V; R vs. I). For each of the schedules of reinforcement, bolster your memory by trying to think of a real-life example.

1. Fixed-ratio (FR) schedules

2. Variable-ratio (VR) schedules

3. Fixed-interval (FI) schedules

4. Variable-interval (VI) schedules

III. F. Shaping and Chaining (p. 329)

➤ How does shaping work? (Give an example.)

➤ How does chaining work? (Give an example.)

IV. Biology and Learning (p. 331)

➤ What is meant by biological constraints on learning?

IV. A. Instinctual Drift (p. 331)

➤ Give examples of instinctual drift.

IV. B. Taste-Aversion Learning (p. 332)

➤ Summarize John Garcia's research on taste-aversion learning.

➤ Describe two applications of taste-aversion learning.

V. Cognitive Influences on Learning (p. 334)

➤ What is meant by cognition?

V. A. Animal Cognition (p. 334)

1. What did Edward Tolman's research demonstrate?

To what three uses do animals put spatial cognitive maps?

What are the capabilities of Clark's nutcrackers?

2. Summarize the results of Edward Wasserman's research.

V. B. *Observational Learning (p. 337)*

➤ What is meant by vicarious reinforcement and vicarious punishment?

➤ What is meant by observational learning?

➤ What conclusions have been drawn from studies of observational learning?

➤ How does research on observational learning apply to television and movie viewing (refer to psychic numbing)?

VI. *Formal Models of Learning (p. 338)*

If you understood the blocking experiment presented in an earlier section, it will be easier for you to follow this discussion of formal models.

➤ Review the odd/even example so that you understand the goals of formal models.

➤ What are connectionist models? Describe their two common features.

➤ What is Hebbian learning? Why does it fail on blocking experiments?

➤ What is the delta rule and why is it important?

For Group Study

II. D. Applications of Classical Conditioning

The text challenges you to examine your life for instances of classical conditioning. Take up that challenge with your group. Start with the situations given in the book. Do the examples alarm or disgust you? Why? Are there fears or preferences that any of you can't attribute to conscious processes? For each example remember that classical conditioning must start with a UCS --> UCR pairing. If you can't figure out what that pairing would be, you're not dealing with classical conditioning.

III. C. Reinforcement Contingencies

You should have lots of ideas about how this material applies to day-to-day life. As a group, choose some behaviors you'd like to make more or less frequent (your own behaviors, or others'). Discuss how you might use each of the different types of reinforcement contingencies to bring the change about.

III. F. Shaping and Chaining

Do any of you have pets? Think of something you'd like to train the pet to do and discuss how you might accomplish the goal using shaping or chaining.

You can also practice shaping as a group. Choose one member to leave the room. While he or she is gone, select some behavior that is complex and interesting. You might, for example, want your friend to do a jumping jack, spin, and then touch the ground. You will use applause for reinforcement. After you have chosen the behavior, talk about how you will differentially reinforce each step on the way to performing the full behavior. Bring your friend back in and go to it.

215

Practice Test ①

1. Katie's parents want her to stop screaming. She is warned that if she doesn't stop screaming, she will not be allowed to have a slice of the chocolate cake she loves so well. What type of reinforcement contingency have Katie's parents established?

a. negative punishment
b. positive punishment
c. negative reinforcement
d. operant extinction

2. Which statement might a behaviorist be most likely to make?

a. People cat when they are hungry.
b. Forms of learning are not conserved across species.
c. My goal is the prediction and control of behavior.
d. We can make an objective study of mental states.

3. You are interested in giving a formal model of operant conditioning. You know what stimuli you give an animal as inputs. You know what responses the animal gives as outputs. The formal model provides a hypothesis about the

a. informativeness of the input stimuli.
b. probability that a particular stimulus leads to a particular response.
c. range of responses the animal will produce over time.
d. computations that link the inputs and outputs.

4. Gloria has just come from her doctor. The doctor has prescribed a drug that must be taken on a full stomach, but will inevitably make Gloria feel sick. Gloria, who is an expert on principles of learning, decides to have meatloaf for dinner. You would guess that meatloaf is

a. not one of Gloria's primary reinforcers.
b. one of Gloria's favorite foods.
c. not one of Gloria's favorite foods.
d. one of Gloria's discriminative stimuli.

216

5. You go to the Rialto and watch a horror film that scares you very badly. The next time a friend invites you to the movies you are unwilling to set foot in the Rialto. In this situation, the Rialto is the _____ and your fear response is the _____.

a. CS; UCR
b. CS; CR
c. UCS; UCR
d. UCS; CR

6. You would like to train your new puppy using the Premack principle. To get started, you should determine

a. which behaviors are low- and high-probability.
b. what stimulus you can use as a positive punisher.
c. how often the puppy requires negative reinforcement.
d. what stimuli function as primary reinforcers.

7. You are watching an experiment in which a rabbit's eye blink is being classically conditioned. In the procedure, a tone sounds followed shortly by a puff of air to the eye. However, you notice that the air puff follows a 100 Hz tone but not a 120 Hz tone. It's likely that the rabbit is undergoing _____ training.

a. extinction
b. recovery
c. generalization
d. discrimination

8. You hear on the news that a famous rock star has died of a heroin overdose. Apparently, he shot up twice every day. What other piece of information may have been an important part of the story?

a. He had been using heroin since he was 22.
b. He was shooting up for the first time in his new home.
c. Every time he shot up, he did it in the company of his wife.
d. Other members of his band were heroin users as well.

9. Using classical conditioning, you have trained a rat that a bell predicts an electric shock. You now would like the rat to learn that a light also predicts the shock. In a long series of trials, you provide it with the sequence bell-light-shock. The outcome of this training is likely to be that the rat responds

a. only to the light.
b. only to the bell.
c. to both the light and the bell.
d. to neither the light nor the bell.

10. Shirlee works as a animal trainer for a circus. She is about to try training a ferret for the first time. She has spent the last few days at the library reading up on ferrets' innate behavior patterns. Shirlee is trying to avoid problems with

a. instinctual drift.
b. behavior chaining.
c. discriminative stimuli.
d. operant extinction.

11. You are conducting an experiment in which dogs receive electric shocks and produce fear responses. The whole time the experiment is going on, a loud fan is keeping the room cool. The next time the dogs are brought into the room, will the sound of the fan elicit a fear response?

a. No, because the electric shock is not contiguous with the fan.
b. No, because the electric shock is not contingent on the fan.
c. Yes, because the electric shock is contiguous with the fan.
d. Yes, because the electric shock is contingent on the fan.

12. Which of the following scenarios sounds like an instance in which maladaptive behavior may be reinforced by secondary gains?

a. Each time a young girl throws a tantrum she loses TV privileges.
b. Patients in a psychiatric hospital earn tokens for taking their medication.
c. The grandparents of a shy child bring him extra gifts.
d. A playground bully is rewarded when he helps prevent a fight.

13. Taylor thinks she may have discovered a violation of the law of effect. She has been trying to teach her cat Jeffrey to jump on her lap by scratching him behind the ears each time he does so. Strangely, Jeffrey is spending less and less time in Taylor's lap. You suggest to Taylor that her scratching may not be _____ for Jeffrey.

a. an operant
b. a stimulus
c. contingent
d. rewarding

14. Emily wants her son to learn a new behavior through vicarious reinforcement. She should try to find a situation in which her son can watch someone

a. having a reward taken away for failing to carry out the relevant behavior.
b. having a reward taken away for carrying out the relevant behavior.
c. being given punishment for failing to carry out the relevant behavior.
d. being given a reward for carrying out the relevant behavior.

15. It is not always possible to judge the extent of learning by a person's behavior because some learning

a. lasts for only a very brief time.
b. is not immediately expressed in performance.
c. is the result of physical maturation.
d. does not rely on experience.

16. You are a dog named Mr. Peabody. At first, your owner gave you a dog biscuit every time you sniffed around his slippers. Now you only get the biscuit when you actually pick one of the slippers up. Your owner is probably using _____ to teach you a complex behavior.

a. chaining
b. partial reinforcement
c. conditioned reinforcers
d. shaping

17. For your classical conditioning experiment, you have selected a buzzer as your CS. Which of the following would be the LEAST likely UCR?

a. whistling
b. an eye blink
c. salivation
d. nausea

18. In the first phase of an experiment, pigeons learned to peck an orange key after viewing photographs of people and cars and a red key after viewing a flower or a chair. The second phase only included pictures of cars and chairs. The pigeons learned to peck a green key after seeing cars and a white key after seeing chairs. In the third phase, the pigeons see flowers again. The researcher can conclude that a pigeon has learned a category if it pecks a

a. white key when it sees a chair.
b. white key when it sees a flower.
c. green key when it sees a car.
d. green key when it sees a flower.

19. Edward Tolman's research on cognitive maps demonstrated that rats could

a. press a bar in the right pattern to gain access to a maze.
b. find their way to hidden food after long delays.
c. solve mazes by observing other rats being reinforced.
d. find paths through mazes that had never previously been reinforced.

20. You are watching a rat in an operant chamber. It presses the bar vigorously for a short period of time and then hardly presses at all for about 5 seconds. That pattern is repeated for as long as you watch. You suspect that the rat is on a _____ schedule.

a. FR-5
b. VR-5
c. FI-5
d. VI-5

Practice Test ②

1. You are playing the part of John Watson in a classroom debate on different approaches to the study of learning. Someone raises a question about the use of introspection in psychological research. You should take the position that introspection _____ an acceptable means of studying behavior because it is _____.

a. is; objective
b. is; subjective
c. is not; objective
d. is not; subjective

2. Ms. Crabtree likes to use conditioned reinforcers to help motivate her second graders. If asked why she prefers conditioned reinforcers to primary reinforcers, she is LEAST likely to respond that they

a. satisfy biological needs.
b. are readily available.
c. are portable.
d. can be dispensed rapidly.

3. Using a puff of air as the UCS, Enid classically conditions her dog to blink whenever she says "blink." Her parrot overhears the procedure, and says "blink" all day long when Enid is out. When she returns, Enid says "blink" to her dog, but he does not blink. It appears as though

a. the dog's behavior has generalized.
b. spontaneous recovery has occurred.
c. the dog is now under the parrot's control.
d. extinction has taken place.

4. The research of Robert Rescorla challenged Pavlov's belief that conditioning will occur if the CS and UCS

a. stimulate different sensory modalities.
b. stimulate the same sensory modality.
c. are only spatially contiguous.
d. are only temporally contiguous.

221

5. Every night at supper time, Pauly calls people and tries to get them to buy things that they don't need. On average, he makes a sale after every 72 calls. Every Friday night he treats himself by buying a lottery ticket with part of his earnings. Pauly's telemarketing success is on a _____ schedule, and his gambling behavior is on a _____ schedule.

a. fixed-interval; variable-ratio
b. fixed-ratio; variable-interval
c. variable-ratio; fixed-interval
d. variable-interval; fixed-ratio

6. Clem notices that a classmate is scolded by the teacher for drawing with crayons on the classroom walls. Although Clem would also like to draw on the walls, he decides not to. Clem is exhibiting learning through

a. shaping by successive approximations.
b. vicarious punishment.
c. the application of cognitive maps.
d. the Premack principle.

7. When the young B. F. Skinner economized on his supply of rat pellets, he found that, compared to rats who were reinforced after every response, the animals who were put on a partial reinforcement schedule

a. learned less quickly.
b. responded less frequently during extinction.
c. stopped responding immediately.
d. responded more vigorously during extinction.

8. Reinforcers always are defined in terms of

a. the probability of a response.
b. cultural values.
c. indications of pleasure.
d. the temporary state of the organism.

9. Cory has been having some problems in his social interactions. He has become very possessive, and will not always share his toys when other children come to his house to play. Cory's parents are concerned, and are thinking about punishing Cory's inappropriate behavior. In the long run, it would be most preferable for Cory's parents to

a. spank him when he does not share.
b. try to ignore his inappropriate behavior.
c. keep other children away from him.
d. reinforce his behavior when he does share.

10. Nellie's mom thinks that Nellie could be neater. She is constantly nagging Nellie to keep her room tidy. When Nellie increases her room cleaning, her mom stops nagging her. The nagging is a

a. positive punisher.
b. negative punisher.
c. positive reinforcer.
d. negative reinforcer.

11. The students in the psychology class have decided to get the teacher to lecture from a corner of the classroom. They smile and make eye contact with him only when he moves closer and closer to the corner. If he moves in the wrong direction, they avert their eyes and look bored. The students are using

a. observational learning techniques.
b. primary reinforcement.
c. shaping by successive approximations.
d. chaining.

12. Professor Boone has a pet raccoon named "Danny" that he is trying to teach a trick. He wants Danny to put some coins into a toy bank, and is using food as a reinforcer. Danny, however, simply rubs the coins together in his paws, and won't let go. This sounds like what Keller and Marion Breland referred to as

a. taste-aversion learning.
b. a token economy.
c. instinctual drift.
d. an internal cognitive map.

13. Little Lulu has learned to answer the telephone with a big "hello." Now, wherever she is, if the telephone rings she runs to it and says "hello." This illustrates

a. the learning-performance distinction.
b. the relative consistency of learned changes.
c. that learning always involves permanent changes.
d. that learning can be directly observed.

14. Bud does not like the feeling of being drunk, so when he drinks alcohol he always tries to drink in moderation. Based on the research of Shepard Siegel, Bud should also

a. drink with his eyes closed.
b. drink with good friends.
c. sip, rather than gulp, his drinks.
d. avoid drinking in unfamiliar places.

15. Millicent drank so much champagne at her sister's wedding that she felt ill and had to lie down to get her head to stop spinning. In Millicent's case, feeling sick _____ the behavior of excessive drinking, and the termination of her dizziness _____ the behavior of lying down.

a. positively punished; positively reinforced
b. negatively punished; negatively reinforced
c. positively punished; negatively reinforced
d. negatively punished; positively reinforced

16. Chaining would be most likely to be used to

a. teach children to dress themselves.
b. prepare patients for major surgery.
c. write a research paper.
d. train seals to perform tricks.

17. Dennis has a summer job delivering telephone books. He is bitten by a dog and develops a fear of dogs. During the winter, his fear of dogs disappears, but when delivering telephone books the next summer, his fear returns. The return of his fear is an example of

a. savings.
b. extinction.
c. the informativeness of conditional stimuli.
d. spontaneous recovery.

18. Dr. Thunder is a psychoneuroimmunologist who is preparing to give an invited address based on his research. The title of the talk is most likely to be

a. "The use of placebos as a medical treatment."
b. "The conditioning of fear in Little Albert."
c. "How pigeons can be trained to play table tennis."
d. "Cognitive maps in nonhuman species."

19. As part of a lab exercise on classical conditioning, the students are experimenting with different temporal patterns. In one study, they present the CS, but then turn it off before the UCS is presented. This is known as _____ conditioning.

a. simultaneous
b. delayed
c. backward
d. trace

20. Imagine, for a moment, that you are a pigeon in B. F. Skinner's lab. You have been deprived of food, and placed in an apparatus where you can obtain food by pecking a small disk, which you soon learn to do. According to Skinner, what has caused your behavior?

a. your desire to get the food
b. your feelings of extreme hunger
c. a combination of your innate intelligence and problem solving ability
d. deprivation and the use of food as reinforcement

Answers, Practice Test ①

1. a (p. 323) This is negative punishment. Katie's parents are trying to reduce the probability of a behavior by taking something away.

2. c (p. 306)

3. d (p. 339)

4. c (p. 333) If Gloria anticipates taste-aversion learning, she is likely to eat a food that is not her favorite.

5. b (p. 308)

6. a (p. 327)

7. d (p. 315)

8. b (p. 319) He may have overdosed because of the change in context.

9. b (p. 312) This is a blocking situation.

10. a (p. 331)

11. b (p. 310)

12. c (p. 325)

13. d (p. 322)

14. d (p. 337)

15. b (p. 305)

16. d (p. 329)

17. a (p. 308) Whistling is not a reflex response.

18. b (p. 336)

19. d (p. 334)

20. c (p. 329)

Answers, Practice Test ②

1. d (p. 306)

2. a (p. 326)

3. d (p. 314)

4. d (pp. 309-311) Pavlov believed that classical conditioning was due to the mere pairing of the Cs and the UCS.

5. c (p. 328)

6. b (p. 327)

7. d (pp. 327-328)

8. a (p. 322)

9. d (p. 325)

10. d (p. 322) A negative reinforcer is any stimulus that, when removed, reduced, or prevented, increases the probability of a given response over time.

11. c (p. 329)

12. c (pp. 331-332) The Brelands used the term "instinctual drift" to refer to the tendency of learned behavior to drift toward instinctual behavior.

13. b (p. 305)

14. d (p. 319)

15. c (p. 323)

16. d (p. 330)

17. d (p. 314)

18. a (p. 318) One goal of the field of psychoneuroimmunology is to discover techniques that allow conditioning to replace high doses of drugs.

19. d (p. 311)

20. d (p. 306) Skinner would argue that behavior can be fully explained by environmental events.

📖 Chapter 10

Memory

🗒 Chapter Outline

Section	What you need to know

I. What is Memory?

    A. Ebbinghaus Quantifies Memory   What are the origins of contemporary memory research?

    B. Types of Memory   What varieties of experience are preserved by memory?

    C. Implicit and Explicit Memory   Are you aware of all the memories you possess?

    D. Declarative and Procedural Memory   How do you remember how to do things?

    E. An Overview of Memory Processes   What is the basic flow of information in and out of memory?

II. Sensory Memory

    A. Iconic Memory   What information is preserved from each glimpse of the world?

    B. Echoic Memory   What auditory features of the world are briefly stored?

229

Section	What you need to know

III. Short-Term Memory (STM)

    A. The Capacity Limitations of STM — How much information can you keep in mind all at once?

    B. Accommodating to STM Capacity — How can you make the most of limited capacity?

       1. Rehearsal
       2. Chunking
       3. Retrieval from STM

    C. STM as Working Memory — To what uses is STM put?

IV. Long-Term Memory (LTM): Encoding and Retrieval

    A. Retrieval Cues — How do cues function to guide your search for information in memory?

       1. Episodic and semantic memories
       2. Interference

    B. Context and Encoding — How does context affect your ability to retrieve memories?

       1. Encoding specificity
       2. The serial position effect

    C. The Processes of Encoding and Retrieval — What is the best relationship between encoding and retrieval processes?

       1. Levels of processing
       2. Processes and implicit memory

    D. Improving Memory for Unstructured Information — How can you improve your ability to remember?

Guided Study

➤ What is knowledge compilation? When will it lead to errors?

I. E. An Overview of Memory Processes (p. 348)

➤ Define:

Encoding (and mental representations)

Storage

Retrieval

➤ What is the flow of information through these processes?

II. A. Iconic Memory (p. 350)

➤ How did Sperling's experiments demonstrate the existence of iconic memory?
What properties did he discover?

II. B. Echoic Memory (p. 352)

➤ What is the suffix effect?

➤ How does your interpretation of incoming information affect the suffix effect?

➤ Why do the basic properties of sensory memories make sense?

III. A. The Capacity Limitations of STM (p. 353)

➤ What is memory span? Why does it differ from the capacity of STM?

III. B. Accommodating to STM Capacity (p. 354)

➤ If the capacity of STM is so small, why do you rarely notice?

1. What is maintenance rehearsal? How does a distractor task prevent subjects from rehearsing?

2. What is chunking? How can it be used to expand the capacity of STM? Summarize the research with S. F.

3. What did Saul Sternberg demonstrate about retrieval from STM?

How do capacity and speed of retrieval trade off for STM?

III. C. STM as Working Memory (p. 356)

➤ Why is STM often called working memory? How does STM allow you to carry out mental tasks?

IV. Long-Term Memory (LTM): Encoding and Retrieval (p. 357)

➤ What is long-term memory? How long can long-term memories last?

➤ What general conclusion about memory performance will this chapter support?

IV. A. Retrieval Cues (p. 357)

➤ What is the difference between recall and recognition? How can each be tested?

➤ How do retrieval cues explain why recall is generally more difficult than recognition?

1. Define episodic and semantic memories. Give examples from your own LTM.

2. What is meant by interference? What are proactive and retroactive interference? Try to find examples from your own life. (Why might it help you to sleep after learning new material?)

IV. B. Context and Encoding (p. 361)

1. What is encoding specificity? Describe two research studies of encoding specificity and one real-world example.

2. What is the serial position effect (consult Figure 10.7)? Which is the primacy effect and which the recency effect?

What is contextual distinctiveness? How does it explain the serial position effect? Summarize the logic of the experimental test.

How do findings on the serial position effect apply to the real world?

IV. C. The Processes of Encoding and Retrieval (p. 364)

1. What is meant by levels of processing? What happens when you process information at a deeper level? What makes processing shallow or deep?

2. List and illustrate five techniques that are used to evaluate implicit memory. (Don't forget category association.)

What is priming? How is it shown on implicit memory tests?

Describe the logic of the experiment that demonstrated the importance of a match between processes at encoding and retrieval.

IV. D. Improving Memory for Unstructured Information (p. 366)

➤ Describe and give an example of elaborative rehearsal.

➤ List and describe three types of mnemonics.

IV. E. Metamemory (p. 368)

➤ What is meant by metamemory? What are feelings-of-knowing?

➤ Are feelings-of-knowing generally accurate?

➤ What two theories explain the accuracy of feelings-of-knowing?

V. A. Memory Structures (p. 369)

1. What are concepts? Give your own examples.

2. What are prototypes? What evidence suggests that you form them?

How do prototypes change over time?

Why does typicality matter?

In what domain might it be good to be prototypical?

3. Study Figure 10.12 to see how information can be arranged hierarchically. Could you produce a similar hierarchy for other domains?

What is the basic level? Why is it important?

4. What are schemas? How are they formed?

V. B. Using Memory Structures (p. 373)

➤ What are five uses to which memory structures are put? List and explain each use.

➤What effects do stereotypes have? How have social psychologists studied these effects?

1. In what sense are mental "structures" real?

V. C. Remembering as a Reconstructive Process (p. 375)

➤ Were you able to answer the questions in the text?

1. What processes did Sir Frederic Bartlett find that led to distortions in reconstructive memory?

How can schemas lead to distortions in reconstructive memory (refer to research on the soap-opera effect)?

In what circumstances is it appropriate not to remember exactly what happened? Explain how quotation is relevant.

2. Describe two experiments that demonstrate some of the difficulties of eyewitness memory.

Close-up: Repressed Memories (p. 378)

➤ Who originated the idea of repressed memories? How are they defined?

➤ Why does memory research suggest that it may be quite difficult to identify which reports of repressed memories are accurate?

VI. A. Searching for the Engram (p. 379)

➤ What did Karl Lashley mean by the "engram"? List the conclusions from his research.

➤ What brain structures have been implicated in memory processes?

➤ Summarize research on the role of the cerebellum in classical conditioning.

➤ From what memory problems did Nick A. suffer after his injury?

➤ Summarize the two experiments that suggest that implicit memory may be spared when brain damage impairs explicit memory.

➤ What have PET scans shown about the distribution of encoding and retrieval to parts of the brain?

For Group Study

I. What is Memory?

This section of the chapter makes distinctions between different types of memory. A later section also introduces "semantic" vs. "episodic" memory. Make sure you understand each of these distinctions by talking about examples provided by the group. You should also be able to share problems you've had with different types of memory. If you've learned to drive, for example, talk about what that experience was like. Was it easy or hard for your teacher to try to turn procedural knowledge back into declarative instructions?

You are also probably more likely to benefit from the different memory exercises suggested in the text if you try each of them in the group. Don't focus on who does better and who does worse. Instead, talk about what is important about each exercise.

IV. B. Context and Encoding
IV. E. Metamemory

This chapter should give your group another excuse to have some fun together. One of the best ways to reflect on your memory processes is to play a board game such as Trivial Pursuit (or make up your own trivia questions). As you play, sometimes you'll know the answer right away. Sometimes you'll know right away that you *don't* know the answer (which is a type of metamemory). Often, however, you'll be caught in the middle--you'll have a feeling-of-knowing but not be able to remember. So how can you get the memory out? Try to reconstruct the context in which you first learned the information, right? Even if you only play over the course of a brief study break, playing a trivia game can help make you more comfortable with many of the ideas in the chapter.

IV. D. Improving Memory for Unstructured Information

Try some of these mnemonics as a group. You could, for example, try to make up a mnemonic for the names of each of the type of memory (implicit, explicit, and so on). Choose information in the text you all wish to memorize, and practice with these mnemonics. This is a good habit to get into!

V. C. Remembering as a Reconstructive Process

If members of your group know each other pretty well, it's likely that they will have experienced some events together. Choose two people who have some story in common (as a last resort, they could both talk about one of the lectures in your class). Have one of them leave the room while the first one tells the story. Make sure he or she tells the story in reasonable detail (that is, more than just a plot outline). Take informal notes. Have the second one return and tell his or her version of the story. How different are the versions? Can you trace the differences to the work of schemas? Have they reconstructed parts of the story differently? Do they have any deep disagreements about what happened?

Practice Test ①

1. You see a man walking toward you who is repeating the digits 5-5-5 (pause) 4-6-4-4 over and over, loud enough for you to hear. When you stop him to ask him what he's up to, he looks panicked and says, "I've got to run back to the phone book!" When you interrupted him, he was probably using

a. elaborative rehearsal.
b. maintenance rehearsal.
c. the method of loci.
d. iconic memory.

2. Renaldo is part of a family of acrobats that performs at the circus. When he performs his maneuvers, Renaldo is likely to find _____ memory to be most useful to him.

a. declarative
b. procedural
c. semantic
d. episodic

3. You are at a crowded party. A woman waves to you from across the room. You know she looks familiar, but you can't quite figure out who it is. Finally it dawns on you: it's your dentist's assistant. Your memory difficulty can probably be explained by

a. encoding specificity.
b. proactive interference.
c. retroactive interference.
d. levels of processing.

4. You are dining at a restaurant with a visitor from another planet. When the bill comes at the end of the meal, the visitor is quite bewildered. Apparently he or she (you can't tell) doesn't have the appropriate schema. Because of that, the function of _____ has broken down.

a. communication
b. reasoning
c. prediction
d. explanation

5.   Carol is a researcher working with a patient who has suffered damage to his hippocampus. Carol would like to see if the patient can remember her name. Carol wants to use a technique with the best possibility of showing positive evidence of memory. She should ask her patient

a. which name is right out of the group "Carolyn, Carmen, Carol, Catherine."
b. to try as hard as possible to recall her name.
c. to say what name first comes to mind to complete "Ca_____."
d. to list all the names she can think of beginning with "C" and then choose the one that sounds correct.

6. In research on eyewitness memory, does warning people that postevent information was misleading eliminate its effect?

a. Yes--when they have been warned, people try harder to remember the real events.
b. Yes--the warning allows people to ignore postevent information.
c. No--in eyewitness situations, people can't use reconstructive memory.
d. No--even with the warning, postevent information has an effect.

7. Charlie was attending his 10th high school reunion. He was very disappointed when he entered the room because no one seemed to _____ his face. Of course, he had grown a mustache and beard since high school. Perhaps the _____ weren't good enough. Charlie decided to go back to his hotel room and shave.

a. recognize; retrieval cues
b. recall; retrieval cues
c. recognize; encoding cues
d. recall; encoding cues

8. Josef and Kirsten are in a class in which eight students must make a presentation each day. Kirsten hopes the professor will remember her presentation well. Josef prefers that his be forgotten. Kirsten is thinking, "Please let me go _____." Josef is thinking, "Please let me go _____."

a. in the middle; last
b. in the middle; first
c. last; first
d. last; in the middle

9. You walk into a classroom at the end of a lecture. On the blackboard you see:

_el_p__ne   pleetheon   tel_____

You suspect that the lecture was on tests for _____ priming in _____ memory.

a. physical; implicit
b. meaning; implicit
c. physical; explicit
d. meaning; explicit

10. Your friend Doug doesn't believe that the mental processes used to encode information have much of an effect on retrieval. You should give him a brief summary of research on

a. encoding specificity.
b. feelings-of-knowing.
c. reconstructive memory.
d. levels of processing.

11. People may falsely believe they have recovered a repressed memory because they recall the _____ of a memory but not the _____.

a. context; content
b. content; source
c. source; content
d. content; context

12. You are trying to find out from a friend whether a particular piece of information he can recall is an episodic memory or a semantic memory. A good question to ask would be,

a. "How easy is it for you to remember the information?"
b. "Do you remember the context in which you acquired the information?"
c. "Do you need short-term memory to recall the information?"
d. "Can you remember the information without retrieval cues?"

13. Timmy is getting ready to leave for school. Of these four questions his mother asks him, which is a metamemory question?

a. Did you remember to bring your lunch?
b. Are you going to learn about dinosaurs today?
c. Will you remember to bring your report card home tonight?
d. Did Helene pay you the fifty cents she owes you?

14. You go to an international cat show that includes a large number of breeds you've never seen before. It's likely that by the end of the day, there would be subtle changes in your _____ for the category of cats.

a. basic level
b. stereotype
c. feelings-of-knowing
d. prototype

15. On Friday afternoon you memorized a poem. On Monday morning, you discover that you've completely forgotten it. You wonder if it will be easier to learn a second time around. The research of _____ is most directly relevant to this question.

a. Elizabeth Loftus
b. Saul Sternberg
c. Hermann Ebbinghaus
d. Endel Tulving

16. George Sperling's comparison between a whole-report and partial-report procedure allowed him to conclude that iconic memory

a. is associated with vision.
b. has a large capacity.
c. lasts for at least twenty seconds.
d. preserves letters but not numbers.

17. Which of the following was a conclusion from Karl Lashley's studies in search of the engram?

a. Memories for maze running are not found in the cortex.
b. Memory was not affected by the location of the tissue that was removed.
c. The amount of tissue removed had no effect on rats' ability to relearn the mazes.
d. The engram was localized in small portions of the brain.

18. For a memory experiment, subjects are asked to read a story called, "A Visit to the Doctor." The story includes the sentence, "Velma had to wait for a while to see the doctor." An hour later, subjects had to try to recall the story word for word. Which of the following sentences shows the LEAST evidence that a subject used his or her schema to reconstruct the sentence?

a. Velma read a magazine while she waited to see the doctor.
b. The nurse told Velma she would have to wait a while before she saw the doctor.
c. Before she could see the doctor, Velma had to wait a while.
d. Velma sat in a room full of patients waiting to see the doctor.

19. You ask your friend Kermit to name the three mental processes required for memory. He tells you that he used to know but now he can't remember. If Kermit's report is accurate, his difficulty is with

a. retrieval.
b. storage.
c. representation.
d. encoding.

20. It is best to think of short-term memory as a(n)

a. place to which information gets sent.
b. extension of iconic memory.
c. process that brings representations into focus.
d. repository for procedural knowledge.

Practice Test ②

1. Virginia is participating in an experiment that replicates Sperling's study of iconic memory. A visual display of three rows of letters is presented to her very briefly, then a tone is presented to her immediately after the letters. The purpose of the tone is to

a. keep her awake.
b. signal which row she should report.
c. interfere with her memory trace.
d. make her memory trace last longer.

2. Faye has sent her daughter to the grocery store. As she leaves, Faye can hear her repeating, "a dozen eggs and a loaf of bread" over and over again. Faye's daughter obviously is engaged in

a. episodic memory.
b. elaborative rehearsal.
c. chunking.
d. maintenance rehearsal.

3. The "suffix effect" illustrates that an echoic sensory memory

a. can be displaced by new sensory information that is similar.
b. is composed of two or more word fragments.
c. is an experience that is "tagged on" to our earlier sensory experiences.
d. is in reality an iconic sensory memory.

4. Clara is taking a history test. One of the questions asks her for the name of the founder of the American Red Cross. Clara is sure that she knows the name, but cannot retrieve it from memory. A useful strategy would be for her to

a. make an exhaustive list of all of the names that she knows.
b. try to remember the context in which she learned the name.
c. move on quickly to the next item on the test.
d. write the first name that she can think of, even if she is not sure it is correct.

5. When Professor Boring looks out over his classroom, he notices that many of his pupils have fallen asleep. This reminds him of a classic study by Jenkins and Dallenbach in which subjects who went to sleep immediately after learning new material

a. recalled the new material better the next morning.
b. remembered little of what they had learned when they awoke.
c. continued to learn while they were asleep.
d. showed no evidence of an episodic memory.

6. The finding that subjects typically leave out the word "Liberty" when drawing a picture of a US coin best illustrates the point that

a. schemas are quite resistant to change.
b. most schemas do not represent a person's average experience in the environment.
c. schemas tend to be inaccurate.
d. schemas are based on what people have noticed about the world.

7. A researcher is studying the serial position effect. She has subjects read a list of unrelated words in order, then tests their memory for the words. If she were to draw a graph illustrating the probability of correct recall as a function of the position of the item on the list, the results would look most like

a. the letter U.
b. a straight horizontal line.
c. a diagonal line from lower left to upper right.
d. the letter S placed on its side.

8. Howard is a hypochondriac. He is always worried about having some terrible health problem. One day he notices that he has trouble remembering facts, dates, names, and also memories of emotional significance. You can expect that Howard will believe that he is experiencing problems with his

a. amygdala and hippocampus.
b. cerebral cortex.
c. cerebellum
d. striatum.

9. After traveling backward in your time machine, you find yourself outside of the office of German psychologist Hermann Ebbinghaus. You would be most likely to overhear him say

a. "A great memory does not make a philosopher, any more than a dictionary can be called a grammar."
b. "The proper memory for a politician is one that knows what to remember and what to forget."
c. "Without sufficient study and review, facts crammed at examination time soon vanish."
d. "O Memory! thou fond deceiver."

10. In an experiment on prototypes that was described in the textbook, male and female subjects judged the attractiveness of individual photos of faces and of composite photos that were computer-generated by combining sets of photos of faces. The results indicated that

a. the subjects judged most of the photos of individual faces as more attractive.
b. the subjects judged the photos of composite faces as more attractive.
c. the males preferred the photos of individual faces whereas the females preferred the photos of composite faces.
d. the females preferred the photos of individual faces whereas the males preferred the photos of composite faces.

11. When Jacob moved, he found it difficult to remember his new telephone number. Two years later, he can't remember the old one when he tries to. The difficulties that Jacob has had remembering his telephone numbers can be attributed to

a. proactive interference.
b. retroactive interference.
c. first retroactive interference and now proactive interference.
d. first proactive interference and now retroactive interference.

12. Archie has a big test coming up, and his teacher has suggested that he consider using mnemonics. His teacher is talking about

a. relaxation techniques.
b. procedures to clear his mind of unwanted distractions.
c. short, verbal devices to assist memory.
d. implicit memories.

13. Suppose you wanted to carry out a memory experiment on priming. You would be most likely to assess the effect that

a. a prior experience with a word has on a later experience.
b. a monetary reward has on a subject's future performance.
c. hints have on the ability to remember.
d. a new experience has on the recollection of an earlier experience.

14. Episodic memory

a. is the same as procedural memory.
b. is a type of procedural memory.
c. consists of semantic memories.
d. is a memory for personally experienced events.

15. Alfred is taking an intelligence test. One of the items requires him to listen to a list of numbers, then repeat as many as he can in the order that they were presented. It sounds like Alfred is being given a test of

a. implicit memory.
b. iconic memory.
c. memory span.
d. knowledge compilation.

16. Imagine that you and a friend have witnessed an accident. Afterwards, while discussing what was seen, your friend introduces some inaccurate information into his description of the events. If you are like many of the subjects in research on eyewitness memory, when questioned at some future date,

a. both you and your friend will have little memory of the accident.
b. your memory is likely to be accurate and your friend's memory will be inaccurate.
c. your friend's memory is likely to be more accurate than your memory.
d. your memory is likely to be affected by your friend's inaccurate observations.

17. Jan and Dean are discussing the test they just completed. They feel confident that they answered some of the questions correctly, but both felt uncertain about other questions. Research on these "feelings-of-knowing" has shown that

a. such feelings are generally accurate.
b. such feelings are generally inaccurate.
c. most individuals do not have strong feelings-of-knowing.
d. females are more likely to have feelings-of-knowing than are males.

18. On the way to their class reunion, Ted and Alice are trying to remember the name of the "class flirt." This best illustrates

a. an explicit use of memory.
b. the savings method.
c. procedural memory.
d. the partial-report procedure.

19. The last time they were in the city, Sandy and Dennis had a great time at a restaurant, but now they can't remember its name. Sandy is looking at the restaurant listings in the telephone book in the hope that seeing the name will jog her memory. The procedure Sandy is using is similar to a _____ test of memory.

a. recall
b. recognition
c. word fragment completion
d. word identification

20. Margot's abilities were definitely affected by the accident. Although she could still manage to dress herself and make her own meals, at the end of the day she could not remember what she had done. She also had trouble remembering where things were kept, and sometimes even forgot the names of her children. Margot seems to be having the least problem with her _____ memory.

a. declarative
b. procedural
c. explicit
d. episodic

1. b (p. 354)

2. b (p. 347) We can assume that most of the tricks Renaldo does have been compiled into procedural memory.

3. a (p. 361)

4. d (p. 373)

5. c (p. 382) The patient is most likely to show evidence that implicit memory is preserved. Option c is the only implicit memory test.

6. d (p. 378)

7. a (p. 358)

8. d (p. 362)

9. a (pp. 365-366)

10. d (p. 364)

11. b (p. 378)

12. b (p. 359) If your friend *can* remember the context, the memory is episodic.

13. c (p. 368) This is the only question that asks Timmy to reflect on his memory processes.

14. d (p. 370)

15. c (p. 345)

16. b (p. 351)

17. b (p. 379)

18. c (p. 376) Each of the other sentences show evidence of intrusions from a schema for what happens in a doctor's office.

19. a (p. 348) Kermit has suggested that he encoded and stored it at some point, but can't retrieve it now.

20. c (p. 353)

Answers, Practice Test ②

1. b (p. 351)

2. d (p. 354)

3. a (p. 352)

4. b (p. 359)

5. a (p. 360)

6. d (p. 373)

7. a (p. 362) The subjects will do very well on the first few words and on the last few words, but rather poorly on the middle part of the list.

8. a (p. 380)

9. c (p. 345) Ebbinghaus believed that facts needed to be sufficiently grounded by other study and later subjected to a sufficient review.

10. b (pp. 371-372)

11. d (p. 360)

12. c (p. 367)

13. a (p. 365)

14. d (p. 359)

15. c (p. 353)

16. d (pp. 377-379)

17. a (p. 368)

18. a (pp. 346-347) Explicit memory involves a conscious effort to recover information.

19. b (p. 358)

20. b (p. 347)

📖 Chapter 11

Cognitive Processes

▤ Chapter Outline

Section	What you need to know
I. Studying Cognition	
A. The Emergence of Cognitive Psychology	What types of observations gave rise to cognitive psychology?
B. Discovering the Processes of Mind	What logic do researchers use to uncover mental processes?
1. Donders's subtraction method	
2. Mental processes and mental resources	
3. Evidence from the brain	
II. Language Use	
A. Language Production	What processes allow you to say the right things at the right times?
1. Audience design	
2. Speech execution and speech errors	
B. Language Understanding	How do you determine what you were meant to understand?
1. Resolving ambiguity	
2. The products of understanding	

Section	What you need to know
III. Visual Cognition	
A. Visual Representations	Do you have pictures in your head?
B. Using Visual Representations	How do you put those pictures to use?
C. Combining Verbal and Visual Representations	How do you unite different types of information?
IV. Problem Solving and Reasoning	
A. Problem Solving	What general strategies can guide problem solving?
1. Problem spaces 2. Improving your problem solving	
B. Deductive Reasoning	What factors affect deductive reasoning?
C. Inductive Reasoning	How can the past help you reason about the present?
Close-up: Human Factors and Flight	What lessons from cognitive psychology can make flight safer?
V. Judging and Deciding	
A. Heuristics and Biases of Judgment	Why do rules of thumb sometimes lead judgments astray?

1. Availability
   2. Representativeness
   3. Anchors aweigh!	

B. The Psychology of Decision Making	How do psychological factors affect everyday decision making?
1. The framing of gains and losses 2. Decision aversion	

Guided Study   ☞ ☞ ☞ ☞

➤ What is cognition? Give some examples of cognitive processes.

I. A. The Emergence of Cognitive Psychology (p. 387)

➤ What is Occam's razor? How does it apply to the emergence of cognitive psychology?

➤ Summarize how each of the following individuals contributed to the history of cognitive psychology:

Noam Chomsky

Jean Piaget

John Von Neumann

Herbert Simon and Alan Newell

I. B. Discovering the Processes of Mind (p. 388)

1. Make sure to do the exercise given in Table 11.1 so you can "feel" the extra mental processes.

What mental steps are necessary for each task in Table 11.1?

What aspects of Donders's subtraction method logic do researchers still use and which have they abandoned?

2. Give examples of serial and parallel processes. Why is it difficult to draw conclusions from reaction time studies?

What claims do serial and parallel processes typically make on mental resources?

How is attention defined with respect to mental processes?

Define controlled and automatic processes. What does the Stroop task show about automatic processes?

When do bottlenecks occur?

3. What are the goals of cognitive neuroscience? Summarize results from research using each of these techniques:

ERPs

Brain imaging

Brain damaged patients

260

➤ Define sentence meaning and speaker's meaning.

1. What is audience design?

Use Table 11.2 to help you understand Grice's cooperative principle and each of the maxims. Try to fill in this chart from memory:

Maxim	What it means

Describe the three types of evidence that allow you to believe that information is in common ground.

Summarize the evidence on the use of community membership in language production.

2. What are spoonerisms? Give an example. Make sure you follow the logic of the examples given in Table 11.3. Can you catch yourself making similar slips? Why is the study of speech errors useful?

What is the SLIP technique and what has it shown?

How does Kathryn Bock's research demonstrate opportunism in language production?

II. B. Language Understanding (p. 399)

1. Give examples of lexical and structural ambiguities.

Contrast the predictions of the constant order model and reordering by context models. What have experiments demonstrated?

For lexical ambiguities:

For message-level ambiguities:

2. What are propositions? How have researchers demonstrated that meanings are represented with propositions?

What are inferences? Do understanders draw all possible inferences? Why or why not?

III. A. Visual Representations (p. 404)

➤ What is the dual-coding theory intended to explain? What evidence supports it?

III. B. Using Visual Representations (p. 405)

➤ What anecdotes suggest that great thinkers have used visual images?

➤ How have researchers studied mental rotation and what have they found?

➤ How much are visual images like real perceptual images? What kinds of research show this?

III. C. Combining Verbal and Visual Representations (p. 406)

➤ What are spatial mental models? What evidence suggests that you form them?

➤ How do verbal representations affect visual representations?

IV. A. Problem Solving (p. 408)

1. What three elements define a problem space?

Give examples of well-defined and ill-defined problems.

What are think-aloud protocols and what can researchers learn from them?

2. Why can practice improve your problem solving?

What role do representations play in problem solving (use the monk puzzle as an example)?

What is functional fixedness? Give an example.

IV. B. Deductive Reasoning (p. 412)

➤ Give an example of deductive reasoning (be able to give an example of a syllogism).

➤ What is the belief-bias effect?

➤ What is the Wason selection task and why do pragmatic reasoning schemas improve performance on it?

➤What role do mental models play in deductive reasoning? When do you reason best?

IV. C. Inductive Reasoning (p. 414)

➤ Give an example of inductive reasoning.

➤ What is the role of inductive reasoning in problem solving? How can research on analogical problem solving be applied in educational settings?

➤ What are mental sets and how can they be overcome?

✍ Close-up: Human Factors and Flight (p. 418)

➤ What is human factors psychology?

➤ Summarize applications of cognitive psychology to flight in these three domains:

The aircraft

The flight plan

The pilot

V. Judging and Deciding (p. 416)

➤ What is meant by bounded rationality?

➤ Differentiate judgment from decision making.

V. A. Heuristics and Biases of Judgment (p. 417)

➤ What are heuristics? Why do researchers often focus on the errors that heuristics lead to?

➤ For each heuristic, summarize how it operates and give examples.

1. Availability

2. Representativeness

3. Anchoring

V. B. The Psychology of Decision Making (p. 422)

1. Frames focus attention on the positive and negative (or gain and loss) features of a situation. What are the consequences?

What are reference points and why are they important?

2. What is decision aversion? What factors contribute to its existence?

Under what circumstances are people decision seeking?

For Group Study 🖐 🖐 🖐 🖐 🖐

I. B. Discovering the Processes of Mind

You have almost certainly noticed situations in which your attentional resources were suddenly strained. That's why, for example, you can't carry on much of a conversation if you're trying to drive in difficult traffic. Try to think about other situations in which you have to apportion your resources to different mental processes.

II. A. 2. Speech execution and speech errors

We're back to speech errors. For Chapter 4, we asked you to discuss whether speech errors revealed anything hidden in your unconscious. Here, you should look to speech errors to understand how planning takes place in language production. Have a casual conversation in your group about some lively topic. Every time someone makes an error try to detect its origins. (Did you recognize the "Homer Fudd" example as a type of blend, illustrated in Table 11.3?) This will make people somewhat self-conscious, but it's also a fun game to try to find the roots of your slip-ups.

You can also look for examples of opportunism. If there are a lot of you in the conversation, you'll all have to compete to gain the floor. See what kinds of things people start with, so that they can be the first to get in. Are their utterances always fully prepared when they get started? (Almost certainly not.) So how do they get started?

IV. A. Problem Solving

Encourage some of your group members to reveal problems they have been trying to solve. It should help to think about the problems in the terms described in the chapter. What can you do as a group to assist problem solving?

V. Judging and Deciding

For this section of the chapter, see if you can find real-world examples of your own. Any time you are asked to make a judgment or a decision, you should think about what heuristics are at work and how the issues are being framed. Can you show how people are making errors? Can you see how people on two sides of a debate have different framings of a problem? Practice giving gain and loss frames on issues that matter to you.

Practice Test ①

1. Research has suggested that you have cognitive processes that try to detect potential speech errors. That's why you are LEAST likely to produce a spoonerism based on the words

a. dart board.
b. darn bore.
c. dell bark.
d. duck bean.

2. You present subjects in an experiment with this syllogism:
Premise 1: All mammals walk.
Premise 2: Whales are mammals.
Conclusion: Whales walk.

You find that your subjects are reluctant to accept "Whales walk" as a valid conclusion. This is a case of _____ at work.

a. the belief-bias effect
b. the availability heuristic
c. decision aversion
d. functional fixedness

3. You are visiting New York City for the first time. You stop a man on the sidewalk and ask for directions to the Empire State Building. The man responds, "How well do you know Manhattan?" He is probably trying to figure out whether you share

a. linguistic copresence.
b. community membership.
c. maxims of cooperation.
d. physical copresence.

4. If you must solve problems regularly, it is a good strategy to practice the components of a complex solution because then

a. you won't suffer from functional fixedness.
b. all problems will be well-defined.
c. you can use a visual representation for problem solving.
d. those components will take up fewer resources.

5. If you have reached your attentional limits, it could be because you are trying to carry out too many _____ processes.

a. automatic
b. parallel
c. bottleneck
d. controlled

6. You are waiting to board an airplane with your friend Sandro. He is wondering if you know anything about the cognitive processes of pilots. You tell Sandro that, while you're no expert, you know it to be true that pilots are more efficient at _____ than are nonpilots.

a. mental rotation
b. using judgmental heuristics
c. language comprehension
d. deductive reasoning

7. Which of the following would be an appropriate propositional representation for *The dog pushed the cat off the mat*?

a. OFF (dog, PUSH (cat, mat))
b. OFF (cat, PUSH (dog, mat))
c. PUSH (dog, OFF (cat, mat))
d. PUSH (cat, OFF (dog, mat))

8. For the word *racket*, its sports meaning is more frequent than its noise meaning. Which of the following sentences would allow you to test the reordering by context model?

a. The noisy children created an incredible racket as they raced around the yard.
b. Carlos grabbed his racket and headed out to the tennis court.
c. The tennis ball hit the center of the racket.
d. After all the racket, we were grateful for the silence.

9. The development of the computer contributed to the emergence of cognitive psychology because researchers

a. could perform calculations with greater speed.
b. began to conceive of the mind as an information-processing system.
c. began to conduct more complicated experiments with computer-based methodologies.
d. could disprove behaviorist models with data from computer science.

10. Martha tells you that she is trying to study stimulus categorization using Donders's logic. You would expect her to try to create two experimental tasks

a. that both require stimulus generalization.
b. in which stimulus generalization precedes response selection.
c. that differ by only one mental process.
d. that involve only parallel processes.

11. You are trying to buy a new car. You think the car dealer may try to cheat you. Which of the following questions suggests that he is trying to use the anchoring bias against you?

a. "Doesn't this car have all the features of a luxury car?"
b. "Isn't this a better car than the last three cars you've looked at?"
c. "Don't you want to spend your money on the most popular car in the country?"
d. "What's the most you think someone would pay for a car this beautiful?"

12. Which of these is essential for successful inductive reasoning?

a. valid premises
b. past experience
c. valid conclusions
d. rules of logic

13. Andy wants Eleni to bet on the contents of a paper bag. Andy tells Eleni that he's just been at the grocery store and has picked up some supplies to make juice. Andy gives Eleni the four options listed below. Eleni can bet five dollars. If she guesses what's in the bag, Andy will give her ten. If Eleni is able to overcome the effects of representativeness, she will bet on

a. fruit.
b. oranges.
c. carrots.
d. eggs.

14. Which of the following is NOT an accurate conclusion from research on visual imagery?

a. Mental rotation has very different properties than does physical rotation.
b. Similar brain structures are used to carry out visual perception and to generate visual images.
c. People scan visual images as if they were scanning real objects.
d. People often use mental rotation as part of the process of object recognition.

15. Researchers who use event-related potentials (ERPs) try to discover the _____ that accompany isolated sets of mental activities.

a. patterns of reaction times
b. serial and parallel processes
c. drains on attentional resources
d. characteristic brain responses

16. Which of the following is NOT an explanation for decision aversion?

a. People don't like to be held accountable for decisions that lead to bad outcomes.
b. People like having other people make decisions for them.
c. People don't like to make decisions that will cause some people to have more and some people less of some desired good.
d. People are able to anticipate the regret they will feel if the option they choose turns out worse than the option they didn't choose.

17. You are hearing a debate between a businessman and an environmentalist about whether a new factory should be built. The businessman emphasizes how many new jobs will be created. The environmentalist emphasizes how much plant and animal life will be lost from the pollution. The issue is going to be decided in an election. Each debater is trying to influence your vote by

a. allowing you to carry out deductive reasoning.
b. having you adopt a particular decision frame.
c. encouraging you to use the representativeness heuristic.
d. making sure you can't overcome a mental set.

18. While you are watching a movie on television, you see an advertisement for the soft drink Poopsie during every commercial break. The next day a friend asks you what you need at the store. You ask her to buy you some Poopsie. You might be able to explain this request, in part, by virtue of the _____ heuristic.

a. representativeness
b. anchoring
c. availability
d. rationality

19. Dual-coding theory explains why

a. parallel processes require less attention than serial processes.
b. propositions are easier to remember than inferences.
c. concrete words are easier to remember than abstract words.
d. some heuristics lead to more errors than others do.

20. Researchers on problem solving are most likely to use think-aloud protocols to learn about

a. initial states.
b. well-defined problems.
c. mental operations.
d. goal states.

Practice Test ②

1. Imagine that you are a teacher. You would like to help your students improve their problem solving skills, and you know that analogical problem solving is a useful technique. One difficulty you are likely to face is that your students

a. do not always see the relevance of past problems.
b. try to use analogical problem solving techniques for all problems.
c. do not do well with concrete analogies.
d. prefer to use deductive reasoning techniques.

2. If you were a research assistant to a cognitive psychologist, you would be LEAST likely to be helping to collect data on the

a. acquisition of language skills.
b. development of conditioned fear.
c. role of long term memory in problem solving.
d. perception of visual patterns.

3. Researchers in the area of human factors who work with pilots and commercial airliners would probably be most involved in

a. negotiating the kind of pay incentives that owners should offer airline employees.
b. obtaining high quality control efforts from the maintenance staff.
c. screening flight crew members for personality disorders.
d. determining the shape and positioning of the flight controls in the aircraft.

4. At a party, the hostess suggests that the guests play charades. Although he has never played the game, Norman feels that he will not enjoy it because he does not like to play party games. Norman is using the _____ heuristic.

a. availability
b. anchoring
c. representativeness
d. framing

5. The "Monk" problem, which is presented in the textbook, becomes relatively easy to solve if one uses a _____ representation.

a. verbal
b. mathematical
c. visual
d. hierarchical

6. Her chair has begun to wobble because a screw has gotten loose, but Heather can't find a screwdriver. Her inability to realize that a dime from her purse could also be used as a screwdriver is an example of

a. the representativeness heuristic.
b. functional fixedness.
c. inductive reasoning.
d. belief-bias.

7. While flipping through some old journals, you come across a review of Skinner's book on verbal behavior that was written by linguist Noam Chomsky. You don't have to read it to know that Chomsky's view is that

a. language can be understood in terms of reinforcement contingencies.
b. children have innate mental structures that guide language acquisition.
c. languages are children's own inventions.
d. nonhuman animals can also acquire language, under the right conditions.

8. Bernard Baars and his colleagues have developed the SLIP technique in order to study

a. speech errors.
b. problem solving.
c. memory.
d. reasoning.

9. Stan and Ollie belong to the same communities and share many similar life experiences. If each is asked to guess what the other is likely to know, they will probably

a. err in the direction of believing that they share little common knowledge.
b. be pretty accurate in their guesses.
c. express the opinion that they have little idea what the other knows.
d. be no more accurate than two complete strangers.

10. Imagine that you are participating in an experiment in which you are asked to remember different words. According to dual-coding theory, when you see the word "chair" you will encode it _____ and when you see the word "honesty" you will encode it _____.

a. verbally; imaginally
b. imaginally; verbally
c. verbally; verbally and imaginally
d. verbally and imaginally; verbally

11. Arthur is practicing scales on his piano. His mother can't wait until he learns some chords so that she can hear several notes together, rather than one note at a time. In psychological terms, the scales are equivalent to _____ processes, and the chords are equivalent to _____ processes.

a. serial; parallel
b. parallel; serial
c. stimulus categorization; response selection
d. response selection; stimulus categorization

12. Which of the following is a spoonerism?

a. Life is like a box of chocolates.
b. Come to us for unwanted pregnancies.
c. Let me sew you to your sheet.
d. A rolling stone gathers no moss.

13. Sondra became so involved with the vivid descriptions in the novel that she found herself thinking about the characters and setting throughout the day. She could picture their houses, where they worked, what they wore, and even what they looked like. Sondra's behavior best illustrates

a. the limitations of Paivio's dual-coding theory of mental representations.
b. the difference between literal and structural ambiguity.
c. that readers fill gaps with inferences.
d. that verbal descriptions can be used to form visual representations.

14. Collette has many interests. She is majoring in both psychology and computer science, but also loves philosophy and neuroscience. It sounds as though Collette would find that she is also interested in the interdisciplinary field of

a. linguistics.
b. developmental psychology.
c. cognitive science.
d. exercise physiology.

15. An event-related potential is an electrical signal in the brain that

a. is evoked by a specific stimulus.
b. results only from expected events.
c. represents spontaneous electrical activity.
d. causes interference with ongoing activity.

16. Karl had never seen his uncle at the circus, so it took Karl a few seconds to recognize him. Based on findings in the study of mental imagery, since Karl's relative was hanging upside down on the trapeze, Karl had to

a. first translate an imaginal code into a verbal code.
b. first translate a verbal code into an imaginal code.
c. mentally rotate the visual image to match a memory representation.
d. wait until his uncle was right side up before recognizing him.

17. Cindy has checked out a book entitled Make Better Judgments! from the library. It deals with the pitfalls of heuristic use. Realistically, how is knowing about the kinds of errors that may result from the use of heuristics likely to affect Cindy's making of judgments?

a. Like perceptual illusions, heuristics are immune to learning, so the book will have no effect.
b. Since heuristics are seldom used, the book will have only minimal effect.
c. The book may be helpful, though knowing about heuristic errors does not guarantee that they will not occur.
d. Once Cindy has become familiar with heuristic errors, her future judgments should be error-free.

18. When you enter the classroom, you notice the teacher has already written the words "quantity," "quality," "relation," and "manner" on the blackboard. Immediately, this makes you think that today's lecture topic will be

a. spoonerisms.
b. Grice's Maxims.
c. spatial mental models.
d. functional fixedness.

19. Only when you are working on a well-defined problem do you know

a. where you are and where you want to go.
b. that there is a single solution to the problem.
c. that you will eventually solve the problem.
d. the starting conditions, goal, and things you can do.

20. Professor Holmes is writing a textbook to teach students how to apply formal rules of logic, which will help them to determine valid conclusions about important events in their lives. It sounds as though this book will focus on

a. the use of heuristics.
b. uncertainty.
c. inductive reasoning.
d. deductive reasoning.

Answers, Practice Test ①

1. a (p. 398) Unlike the other three pairs, if you formed a spoonerism from *dart board* you would get a pair of nonwords (i.e., *bart doard*).

2. a (p. 413)

3. b (p. 396)

4. d (p. 411)

5. d (p. 392)

6. a (p. 418)

7. c (p. 402)

8. a (p. 401) To test the reordering by context model, a biasing context (in this case "The noisy children...") must precede the ambiguous word.

9. b (p. 388)

10. c (p. 389)

11. d (p. 421) The salesman wants you to give a very big response, "Oh, I don't know, $30,000?" on which you will anchor.

12. b (p. 414)

13. a (p. 420) If Eleni used representativeness she'd probably choose "oranges." If she can overcome it, she should say "fruit." What do you think is in the bag?

14. a (p. 405)

15. d (p. 393)

16. b (p. 425)

17. b (p. 423)

18. c (p. 419)

19. c (p. 404)

20. c (p. 410)

Answers, Practice Test ②

1. a (pp. 415-416)

2. b (p. 387)

3. d (p. 418)

4. c (p. 420) Norman is using past information to make a judgment concerning a similar present circumstance.

5. c (p. 411)

6. b (p. 412)

7. b (p. 388)

8. a (p. 398)

9. b (p. 397)

10. d (p. 404)

11. a (pp. 390-391) In serial processing, each element is examined separately, one after another. In parallel processing, all the elements in an array can be examined at the same time.

12. c (p. 397)

13. d (p. 406)

14. c (p. 388)

15. a (p. 393)

16. c (p. 405)

17. c (p. 417) Even the most gifted judgment-makers err under some circumstances, but training can help.

18. b (p. 395)

19. d (p. 409)

20. d (p. 412)

Chapter 12

Motivation

▤ Chapter Outline

Section	What you need to know

I. Understanding Motivation

   A. Functions of Motivational Concepts — What must theories of motivation explain?

   B. Sources of Motivation — What internal and external forces motivate behavior?

      1. Drive theory and tension reduction
      2. Instinctual behaviors and learning
      3. Expectations and cognitive approaches to learning

II. Eating

   A. The Physiology of Eating — What bodily processes guide eating behavior?

      1. Peripheral responses
      2. Central responses

   B. The Psychology of Eating — How are bodily needs affected by psychological forces?

Section	What you need to know
1. Obesity and dieting 2. Eating disorders	
Close-up: Can Diets Be Successful?	If you wish to diet, what factors should you consider?
III. Sexual Behaviors	
A. Nonhuman Sexual Behaviors	How is sexual behavior regulated in nonhuman animals?
B. Human Sexuality	How is sexual behavior regulated in humans?
1. Did evolution shape patterns of sexual behaviors? 2. Physiology of human sexual behaviors 3. Sexual arousal 4. Sexual norms and sexual scripts 5. Date rape 6. Homosexuality	
IV. Motivation for Personal Achievement	
A. Need for Achievement	Are some people specially motivated to achieve?
B. Attributions for Success and Failure	How do causal attributions affect motivation?
C. Work and Organizational Psychology	How are workers motivated on the job?
D. Individualistic versus Collectivist Cultures	How does motivation differ across cultures?
V. A Hierarchy of Needs	Can motivation be fit into a unifying perspective?

Guided Study ☞ ☞ ☞ ☞

I. Understanding Motivation (p. 428)

➤ How does the origin of the word "motivation" help define the concept?

I. A. Functions of Motivational Concepts (p. 429)

➤ For what five purposes have psychologists used the concept of motivation?

1.

2.

3.

4.

5.

I. B. Sources of Motivation (p. 430)

➤ Explain the importance of the distinction between internal and external sources of motivation.

1. What scholars introduced drive theory? What were their views?

What has research shown about the idea that tension reduction can explain all motivated behavior?

2. Define instincts and fixed-action patterns. Give examples.

How do instincts represent interactions between internal and external sources of motivation?

What did William James and Sigmund Freud suggest about human instincts?

What criticisms have been leveled at instinct theories?

3. After you read this section, go back and review the *Wizard of Oz* introduction.

What is meant by a subjective interpretation of reality?

Summarize these scholars' ideas:

Julian Rotter

Fritz Heider

II. A. The Physiology of Eating (p. 435)

➤ What are the four tasks for food regulation?

1. What theory did Canon and Washburn test about peripheral hunger cues and how did they do so?

What has contemporary research shown?

2. What roles do the VMH and LH play in regulating food intake? Make sure you understand why the palatability of the food--good or bad taste--modified early models of eating regulation.

VMH

LH

II. B. The Psychology of Eating (p. 436)

1. What evidence suggests that some people may be born with a tendency to become obese? What is an individual's resting metabolic rate?

What distinction did Peter Herman and Janet Polivy originate?

What circumstances prompts disinhibition of eating? Summarize the experimental evidence.

2. Describe these eating disorders:

Anorexia nervosa

Bulimia nervosa

What are some of the factors that may cause eating disorders?

∽ *Close-up: Can Diets Be Successful? (p. 440)*

➤ What is known about the general success of dieting?

➤ In what ways should diets be personalized?

III. A. Nonhuman Sexual Behaviors (p. 441)

III. A. Nonhuman Sexual Behaviors (p. 441)

➤ How do hormones control mating in nonhuman animals?

➤ What are stereotyped sexual behaviors?

➤ What external factors affect mating behavior (don't forget pheromones)?

III. B. Human Sexuality (p. 442)

1. What have theorists suggested about men's and women's strategies toward sexual behavior?

Why is parental investment relevant to the evolutionary perspective?

Why does David Buss make a distinction between short-term and long-term mating? How does research support his ideas?

2. What role do hormones play in human sexual response?

What conclusions did Masters and Johnson reach about response to sexual stimulation?

287

Summarize the phases of the human sexual response cycle.

Excitement:

Plateau:

Orgasm:

Resolution:

3. How do erotic stimuli contribute to sexual arousal?

What factors contribute to impotence or frigidity?

How does touch contribute to sexual arousal?

What are fetishes?

4. How did Alfred Kinsey's work begin to define sexual norms? (You should acquaint yourself with the general patterns of data in Table 12.2.)

What are sexual scripts?

5. Why is date rape so common?

What types of relationships between men and women are the most likely to give rise to date rape?

6. Why do theorists look for the same casual factors for homosexuality and heterosexuality?

Review the evidence that sexual orientation has a biological component. (You may want to reread the close-up in Chapter 3.)

What are societal attitudes toward homosexuality? How do these attitudes affect men and women who perceive themselves to be gay or lesbian?

What are the main sources of anxiety for gay and lesbian individuals?

Is it possible to determine how many gay men and lesbians there are?

IV. A. Need for Achievement (p. 449)

➤ How is the TAT used to evaluate need for achievement?

➤ What has research shown about people who are high in need for achievement? How does a high need for achievement arise?

IV. B. Attributions for Success and Failure (p. 451)

➤ What is a locus of control orientation? How does it apply to causal attributions?

➤ What are two other dimensions along which attributions can vary? Give examples of each.

➤ How do attributions affect a person's motivation?

➤ Summarize research on the consequences of explanatory style. What outcomes would you predict for optimists and pessimists?

➤ Describe the research example of the impact of causal attributions in an academic setting.

IV. C. Work and Organizational Psychology (p. 454)

➤ What are the activities of organizational psychologists?

➤ Summarize equity theory.

➤ Summarize expectancy theory.

IV. D. Individualistic versus Collectivist Cultures (p. 456)

➤ Define the individualistic versus collectivist distinction. How does motivation differ in these two types of cultures?

V. A Hierarchy of Needs (p. 456)

➤ Use Maslow's hierarchy to help you draw together the themes of the chapter. Make sure you understand why he ordered the needs in the way he did. List and define each class of needs here.

1.

2.

3.

4.

5.

6.

7.

8.

For Group Study

I. Understanding Motivation

To begin group study, you might discuss the question that opens the chapter: why did you get out of bed this morning? See if you can classify different people's answers in terms of the motivational forces discussed in the chapter.

II. Eating

Are you ready to have another meal together? It might be easiest to discuss the section on eating in the context of lunch or dinner. Why are some people feeling more hungry than others? How much will you eat of different foods? Can you work through some of the physiology while you eat? (What are your LH and VMH up to?)

You can also have a discussion of issues surrounding dieting and obesity. This will depend to a certain extent on how comfortable the group members are talking about personal matters, but it should be possible for people to relate much of the content of this section to their own experiences. Do members of the group perceive themselves to be restrained eaters? Does the text help them think about escaping that trap? Have you or other people in the group suffered from eating disorders?

III. Sexual Behaviors

This, again, is a section that can relate directly to different life experiences of members of your group. Try to learn the material by making it relevant to each of your lives. You should be able to have an informed discussion of evolutionary explanations for sex differences in mating strategies as well as sexual scripts and date rape. It will also deepen your understanding of human sexuality if you can discuss the themes of this section with classmates who are lesbian or gay.

IV. A. Need for Achievement
IV. B. Attributions for Success and Failure

Both of these sections talk about individual differences: people show different levels of need for achievement; people have different patterns for explaining events. You should take advantage of the diversity in your group to see how these concepts apply.

Practice Test ①

1. Which of the following is in the right order for Maslow's hierarchy of needs?

a. safety needs, cognitive needs, self-actualization
b. biological needs, cognitive needs, attachment needs
c. cognitive needs, esthetic needs, safety needs
d. attachment needs, cognitive needs, esteem needs

2. Which of the following was NOT a common reason men give for having unwanted sex?

a. They had fears about their macho image.
b. They were drunk or on drugs.
c. They wanted to make other people jealous.
d. They feared being labeled as inadequate.

3. Which of these results suggests that tension reduction can't explain all motivated behaviors?

a. Apes copulate for only about 15 seconds.
b. Thirsty rats will drink when they have the opportunity.
c. Food-deprived rats explore a new environment before they eat.
d. Rats will not mate unless hormone levels are appropriate.

4. The concept of sexual scripts explains why

a. men and women have different mating strategies.
b. hormones play little role in human sexual response.
c. the plateau phase follows the excitement phase.
d. sexual practices vary between different cultures.

5. You have cooked a big meal for your friend Jacqueline. She is about halfway through a big plate of pasta when she announces that she is full. What peripheral information may have ended Jacqueline's feelings of hunger?

a. Her stomach is distended.
b. Her VMH is being stimulated.
c. Her LH is being stimulated.
d. Her stomach is contracting.

294

6. Your boss has been doing some reading on expectancy theory. Unfortunately, he doesn't seem to have understood it completely because he ended up setting up a plan with high instrumentality but low valence. Which plan fits that description?

a. Every worker is guaranteed a thousand dollar bonus at the end of the year.
b. Every worker is guaranteed a five dollar bonus at the end of the year.
c. Some workers are guaranteed a thousand dollar bonus at the end of the year.
d. Some workers are guaranteed a five dollar bonus at the end of the year.

7. In Master's and Johnson's description of the human sexual response cycle, the phase in which a maximum level of arousal is reached is called the _____ phase.

a. excitement
b. resolution
c. plateau
d. orgasm

8. You are reading a case study about the sexual behavior of a person who is identified only as S035. S035 reports a long history of one-night stands. Based only on that information, you guess that S035 is a _____ with a _____ mating strategy.

a. female; short-term
b. female; long-term
c. male; short-term
d. male; long-term

9. What is NOT a major source of anxiety for most gay men and lesbians?

a. People's responses to their sexual orientations.
b. The difficulty of establishing a loving relationship.
c. The fact that they are gay or lesbian.
d. Having to decide whether to reveal or conceal their homosexuality.

10. The anthropological work of Ruth Benedict and Margaret Mead undermined instinct theories by showing that

a. collectivist cultures valued instincts more than individualistic cultures.
b. there were large behavior differences between cultures.
c. instincts were different from culture to culture.
d. Freud's ideas only applied to collectivist cultures.

11. Which of the following sounds like a situation in which a restrained eater named Dan would be LEAST likely to become disinhibited and go on a binge?

a. Dan's professor announces his failing test score to the class.
b. Dan got lost while driving two friends to a party.
c. Dan's roommate threatens to beat him up.
d. Dan doesn't get into a play for which he auditioned.

12. For both anorexia nervosa and bulimia nervosa, _____ are diagnosed with the disease.

a. more older women than younger women
b. equal numbers of men and women
c. more men than women
d. more women then men

13. Research by David McClelland and Carol Franz found that the parents of people with a high need for achievement had

a. been easy-going about toilet training.
b. optimistic explanatory styles.
c. pessimistic explanatory styles.
d. been strict about toilet training.

14. Members of collectivist cultures

a. look for immediate personal rewards.
b. desire a varied, exciting life.
c. value personal freedom.
d. put high value on self-discipline.

15. For nonhuman animals, _____ provide internal motivation for sexual behavior and _____ provide external motivation.

a. hormones; pheromones
b. hormones; gonads
c. pheromones; gonads
d. pheromones; hormones

16. Joshua was not surprised that he didn't get the job he wanted. The interview was at 9 a.m. and the woman interviewing him seemed to be barely awake. He didn't think she paid attention to him at all. Joshua's attribution for why he didn't get the job was _____ and _____.

a. internal; specific
b. external; specific
c. internal; stable
d. external; stable

17. You have just attended a lecture that discussed the importance of expectations and personal values in explaining motivation. It is likely that the lecture emphasized the theory of

a. Julian Rotter.
b. Clark Hull.
c. Martin Seligman.
d. Fritz Heider.

18. You are watching a demonstration with a rat that has had part of its hypothalamus lesioned. If the rat only refuses to eat food that tastes _____, you will guess that its _____ has been lesioned.

a. bad; VMH
b. good; VMH
c. bad; LH
d. good; LH

19. You notice that your friend Gabrielle watches TV the whole night before a big exam. You decide that she just must not be very motivated to pass the course. In this context, you are using the concept of motivation to

a. infer private states from public acts.
b. account for behavioral variability.
c. assign responsibility for actions.
d. explain perseverance despite adversity.

20. Which of the following is NOT a question that would help you set a reasonable target weight for a diet?

a. At what weight do you believe you can live with the required changes in eating?
b. How often would you be willing to purge to maintain your desired weight?
c. Is there a history of excess weight in your parents or grandparents?
d. What is the lowest weight you have maintained as an adult for at least one year?

Practice Test ②

1. Suppose you were a subject in one of David McClelland's studies of the need for achievement. You would be given the Thematic Apperception Test and be expected to

a. rate yourself on a series of achievement-related questions.
b. check off those goals that most apply to you.
c. compile a list of your most important lifetime achievements.
d. generate stories in response to a series of ambiguous drawings.

2. Suppose a group of rats has been deprived of food or water. According to a tension reduction explanation of motivated behavior, the animals will eat or drink at their first opportunity. When actually placed in a novel environment with food and water, what do such animals do?

a. eat
b. drink
c. explore
d. drink first, then eat

3. Perhaps because he grew up in a troubled family, Michael has always been interested in trying to figure out why people do what they do. To a psychologist, Michael's general interest is most closely related to the study of

a. emotion.
b. cognition.
c. motivation.
d. development.

4. Your teacher asked the class to read an article on motivation that was written by Julian Rotter. A classmate who was absent and didn't get a chance to read the article asks you what it was about. It would be safe to say that Rotter did NOT place much importance in his theory on

a. expectations.
b. instincts.
c. personal value.
d. social learning.

5. The primary reason why instinct theory was rejected was that

a. it was demonstrated that many "instinctive" behaviors are learned.
b. psychologists and others disliked the mechanistic view of humans.
c. instincts cannot be observed, and must be inferred from behavior.
d. most researchers agreed that instincts are maladaptive for humans.

6. Cliff is working as a consultant to a large company. He is explaining that workers feel satisfied when they can make favorable comparisons between their own inputs and outcomes and those of other workers. Cliff is applying principles from _____ theory.

a. expectancy
b. equity
c. attribution
d. Maslow's

7. In Heider's approach to motivation, attributing a poor test grade to lack of effort will make it more likely that you will

a. try harder the next time.
b. believe the teacher to be biased.
c. find a poor grade to be reinforcing.
d. attribute good grades to intelligence.

8. Waldo is a modern-day male. Assuming that he is typical, evolutionary psychologists would predict that he will

a. consider sex to be something that he gives away to women.
b. be more discriminating about his mates than females will be.
c. be inclined to exchange sex for long-term commitment and support.
d. show a greater desire for a variety of sexual partners.

9. When you get to your friend's house, she is watching a television talk show on the subject of "adopted twins who are overweight." You learn that the reason twins who are reared apart are typically quite similar in weight is that

a. they probably are genetically programmed to eat the same foods.
b. twins have been shown to have larger areas of the brain that are associated with eating.
c. the predisposition to exercise is highly heritable.
d. the rate at which calories are burned is highly heritable.

10. When you are leaving the golf tournament, you overhear one of the competitors saying that the reason he lost was because his opponent got a lucky break when his ball bounced out of the woods. This golfer is making a(n) _____ attribution.

a. unstable internal
b. unstable external
c. stable internal
d. stable external

11. Who of the following is most likely to have either anorexia nervosa or bulimia nervosa?

a. a 40-year-old female
b. a 20-year-old male student
c. a 20-year-old female non-student
d. a 20-year-old female student

12. In early laboratory studies of the mechanisms underlying eating behavior, animals would appear to stop eating if

a. the lateral hypothalamus was stimulated.
b. the ventromedial hypothalamus was lesioned.
c. either the lateral hypothalamus was stimulated or the ventromedial hypothalamus was lesioned.
d. either the lateral hypothalamus was lesioned or the ventromedial hypothalamus was stimulated.

13. His friends think of Charley as a happy-go-lucky kind of guy who always seems to see the glass as "half full" rather than "half empty." Charley is likely to attribute his failure to _____ causes.

a. internal, unstable, and global
b. internal, stable, and global
c. external, unstable, and specific
d. external, stable, and specific

14. The research of Masters and Johnson described several phases in the human sexual response cycle. The plateau phase occurs

a. during the resolution phase.
b. during the orgasm phase.
c. after the excitement phase.
d. after the orgasm phase.

15. In a study of restrained and unrestrained eaters that was described in the textbook, high anxiety was provoked in some subjects, then all subjects were given the opportunity to eat good-tasting and bad-tasting cookies. The results of this study showed that among subjects who were made anxious,

a. the unrestrained eaters ate more of both types of cookies.
b. the restrained eaters ate more of both types of cookies.
c. the unrestrained eaters at more of the bad-tasting cookies.
d. anxiety had little effect on the number of cookies that were eaten.

16. What most sets homosexuality apart from heterosexuality may be that

a. homosexuality is caused whereas heterosexuality is natural.
b. only homosexuality has a genetic basis.
c. there is a continuing hostility toward homosexual behaviors.
d. only homosexuals act on nature's urgings.

17. A cousin of yours tells you that she is a "restrained eater," and yet she is still very heavy. You can conclude most reasonably that she

a. may really be an "unrestrained eater."
b. probably never diets or limits the amount of food she eats.
c. may indulge in high calorie binges.
d. eats small portions but has too many meals throughout the day.

18. Mary Ellen works at a job where good performances are not rewarded, she does not perceive her work to be at all attractive, and she feels that, no matter how hard she tries, she will not be successful. According to expectancy theory, you would predict that Mary Ellen will

a. continue to make a consistently high work effort.
b. demonstrate low levels of work motivation.
c. restore equity by changing the relevant inputs and outcomes.
d. begin comparing her compensation with those of other workers.

19. Sharon copies the words, "androgens," "estrogen," and "gonads" from the class outline the teacher has written on the blackboard. Apparently the topic for today's lecture is

a. dieting.
b. sexual behavior.
c. achievement behavior.
d. locus of control.

20. "Slim" is trying to gain weight. Research has shown that he will eat more food if he is served meals in which

a. there are a variety of foods with different tastes.
b. only his favorite food is presented.
c. small portions of foods he normally would not eat are presented.
d. he eats with a spoon rather than a fork.

Answers, Practice Test ①

1. a (p. 456)

2. c (p. 447)

3. c (p. 431)

4. d (p. 446)

5. a (p. 435)

6. b (p. 455)

7. c (p. 444)

8. c (p. 442)

9. c (p. 448)

10. b (p. 432) Instincts are supposed to be biologically determined patterns of behavior. Variation from culture to culture suggests that behaviors are not instinctual.

11. c (p. 438) All the other situations would present threats to Dan's self-esteem.

12. d (p. 439)

13. d (p. 450)

14. d (p. 456)

15. a (pp. 441-442)

16. b (pp. 451-452) The attribution is external because the cause was in the environment (the sleepy interviewer), and specific because the next time Joshua interviews for a job, she probably won't be there.

17. a (p. 434)

18. a (p. 436)

19. a (p. 429)

20. b (p. 440)

Answers, Practice Test ②

1. d (p. 450)

2. c (p. 431)

3. c (p. 428)

4. b (p. 434)

5. a (p. 432) The behaviorist's empirical demonstrations that important behaviors and emotions were learned rather than inborn were especially damaging.

6. b (p. 455) Equity theory proposes that workers are motivated to maintain fair or equitable relationships with other relevant persons.

7. a (p. 434)

8. d (p. 443)

9. d (p. 437)

10. b (p. 452)

11. d (p. 439)

12. d (p. 436)

13. c (p. 453)

14. c (p. 444)

15. b (p. 438)

16. c (p. 448)

17. c (p. 437)

18. b (pp. 455-456)

19. b (p. 441)

20. a (p. 435)

Chapter 13

Emotion, Stress, and Health

▤ Chapter Outline

Section	What you need to know
I. Emotions	
A. Basic Emotions and Culture	Did evolution give rise to universal emotions?
1. Are some emotional responses innate?	
2. Are emotional expressions universal?	
3. How does culture constrain emotional expression?	
4. Basic emotions	
B. Theories of Emotion	What is the relationship between the physiology and psychology of emotions?
1. Physiology of emotion	
2. James-Lange theory of body reaction	
3. Cannon-Bard theory of central neural processes	
4. Lazarus-Schachter theory of appraisal	

Section	What you need to know
C. Functions of Emotion	What roles do emotions play in your day-to-day experience?

   1. Motivation and arousal
   2. Social functions of emotion
   3. Emotional effects on cognitive functioning

II. Stress of Living

A. Physiological Stress Reactions	How does your body respond to stress?

   1. Emergency reactions to acute threats
   2. The general adaptation syndrome (GAS) and chronic stress
   3. Psychoneuroimmunology

B. Psychological Stress Reactions	How do you appraise and respond to different categories of stressors?

   1. Appraisal of stress
   2. Major life stressors
   3. Catastrophic and traumatic events
   4. Chronic stressors
   5. Day-to-day hassles
   6. Individual differences in stress responses

C. Coping with Stress	What can you do to lessen the impact of stress?

   1. Modifying cognitive strategies
   2. Social support as a coping resource

Section	What you need to know

III. Health Psychology

    A. The Biopsychosocial Model of Health   What combinations of factors influence health?

        1. Traditional health practices
        2. Toward a biopsychosocial model

    B. Health Promotion   What lessons from psychology can help promote good health?

        1. Smoking
        2. Nutrition and exercise
        3. Heart disease
        4. AIDS
        5. Health promotion as a national and international concern

    C. Treatment   How can psychological insights help make treatment more efficient?

        1. Patient adherence
        2. Harnessing the mind to heal the body

Close-up: Is Laughter the Best Medicine?   Are there medical benefits to humor?

    D. Personality and Health   Does personality help explain individual differences in health?

        1. Type A and Type B behavior patterns
        2. Type C and optimism

    E. Changing the Health Care System   What advice do psychologists give about the structure of the health care system?

    F. A Toast to Your Health   What can you do to ensure your good health?

Guided Study

I. Emotions (p. 460)

➤ The introductory section defines emotion as a complex pattern of bodily and mental changes. By the end of the emotions section, make sure you understand why that definition is appropriate.

I. A. Basic Emotions and Culture (p. 461)

➤ What was Darwin's perspective on emotions? How are emotions adaptive?

1. Summarize the evidence that some emotional responses might be innate.

2. What has Paul Ekman's research revealed about the universality of emotional expressions?

What is the neurocultural theory of emotional expression?

3. Summarize the two examples given in the text of the constraints cultures put on emotional expression.

310

4. Study Figure 13.2 to master Robert Plutchik's emotion wheel. Do you understand how all the emotions fit together?

I. B. Theories of Emotion (p. 465)

1. What are the roles of the sympathetic and parasympathetic divisions of the autonomic nervous system in producing emotional responses? (You might want to review the appropriate material in Chapter 3.)

What role does the limbic system play in emotional response? Summarize Joseph LeDoux's research on the amygdala.

How are emotional responses distributed to the two hemispheres of your brain?

2. Each of the next three sections describes a theory that specifies the relationship between physiological and psychological experiences of emotions. Use Figure 13.3 to help you learn the differences among the theories.

What position did William James and Carl Lange originate?

3. What criticisms did Walter Cannon level against the peripheralist James-Lange theory?

What position did Walter Cannon and Philip Bard originate?

4. Why is cognitive appraisal central to the emotion theories of Richard Lazarus and Stanley Schachter?

Summarize the research evidence that supports the appraisal theory.

What two types of criticisms have been offered of the appraisal theory?

I. C. Functions of Emotion (p. 469)

1. In what ways do emotions affect motivation?

What relationship does the Yerkes-Dodson law capture?

2. How do emotions affect social interactions and communication?

3. Define and give an example of mood-congruent processing.

Define and give an example of mood-dependent retrieval.

II. Stress of Living (p. 472)

➤ What is stress? What are stressors? (Make sure you understand that both positive and negative events are stressors.)

II. A. Physiological Stress Reactions (p. 473)

➤ How are acute and chronic stress defined? Give an example of each.

1. Define the flight-or-fight syndrome and then summarize its physiology (use Figure 13.6 to help you learn the pattern of response).

Is the flight-or-fight response always adaptive?

2. What reaction pattern did Hans Selye document? Describe the stages (study Figure 13.7).

What are psychosomatic disorders? How does Selye's work explain them?

3. What is psychoneuroimmunology?

How does stress affect the functioning of the immune system? What are the effects of interpersonal relationships?

1. What are stress moderator variables?

What is cognitive appraisal?

Define:

Primary appraisal

Secondary appraisal

2. Summarize the techniques that are used to measure life changes.

Social Readjustment Rating Scale:

Life Experiences Survey:

What is the difference between retrospective and prospective studies?

3. What special conditions hold true for catastrophic events? What responses may people suffer to catastrophic and traumatic events?

What is posttraumatic stress disorder and what can bring it about?

What is the residual stress pattern?

4. What are chronic stressors? Give examples.

What evidence suggests that discrimination produces negative health consequences?

How does chronic stress affect intellectual development?

5. What relationship has been found between day-to-day hassles and health?

What is the effect of positive day-to-day events?

6. Are there individual differences in stress responses?

What is hardiness? What can you predict about hardy individuals?

II. C. Coping with Stress (p. 486)

➤ What is anticipatory coping? Give examples.

Summarize the uses to which these coping strategies can be put.

Problem-solving focus:

Emotion-regulation focus:

1. How can cognitive reappraisal help you cope with stress?

What is Donald Meichenbaum's stress inoculation technique? What are it's three phases?

Phase 1:

Phase 2:

Phase 3:

How did Ellen Langer and Judith Rodin demonstrate the benefit of perceived control?

What are four types of control for effective coping?

2. What are different types of social support?

How does the situation determine which forms of social support are most useful?

When will social support increase anxiety?

III. Health Psychology (p. 491)

➤ How is health defined? What are the goals of health psychology?

III. A. The Biopsychosocial Model of Health (p. 491)

1. Summarize traditional health practices from non-Western cultures.

2. How does the biopsychosocial model of health embrace the insights of these traditional health practices? (Make a contrast to the biomedical model.)

Define wellness and health behaviors.

III. B. Health Promotion (p. 492)

➤ What is the role of psychology in health promotion?

1. What personality and social factors lead people to smoke?

What stages do people pass through on their way to quitting smoking?

2. What factors help foster healthy eating?

How can you make exercise a part of your life?

3. Summarize the study that tried to change life-style risks for heart disease.

4. What is known about the transmission and time-course of AIDS?

Who is at risk for AIDS?

What are the components of a successful AIDS intervention? Why?

5. Why has health promotion become a national and international concern?

III. C. Treatment (p. 498)

1. How can psychological interventions improve patient adherence?

2. What techniques have been developed to help the mind heal the body? Summarize the applications of these techniques.

The relaxation response:

Biofeedback:

Group therapy:

Confiding in others:

319

➤ Can positive emotions affect healing?

➤ What physiological mechanism may be at work?

III. D. Personality and Health (p. 501)

1. Define Type A and Type B behavior patterns.

What is the critical element of Type A behavior that poses a health risk?

Can Type A behavior be changed?

2. What are the consequences of Type C behavior? Why?

What are the health consequences of optimism?

III. E. Changing the Health Care System (p. 503)

➤ What is job burnout?

➤ What recommendations can be made to change the health care system?

III. F. A Toast to Your Health (p. 504)

➤ Try to understand how each of these "year-round resolutions" emerges from the research reported in this chapter.

For Group Study

I. A. Basic Emotions and Culture

Are any members of your group from a different culture? You can discuss the different sorts of emotional responses that are considered appropriate across cultures. Even if you are all from the same culture, you can discuss the reasons why different people feel more or less comfortable with overt emotional expressions.

I. C. Functions of Emotion

This may be a good opportunity to focus on the emotional life of your group. What emotions have dominated your group interactions? Does it seem as if the group has a particular emotional tone? Where does it come from? Have there been moments of extreme emotion? If, for example, people got angry at each other, what function did that anger serve? Were you able to diagnose the roots of the anger? As you try to master the material on emotions, treat the group as a laboratory in which you can study the emotions that arise spontaneously.

II. B. Psychological Stress Reactions

What are the stressors in your life? Are they pretty similar across group members? Can you develop coping strategies as a group? How can the group provide appropriate social support?

III. B. Health Promotion

It is very likely to be the case that every member of your group can acknowledge some types of behaviors he or she performs that are contrary to good health. Do some of you eat poorly or get no exercise? Do some of you smoke? Do some of you not practice safer sex? You should explore these departures from good health practices. Apply the ideas presented in the chapter to discuss why they occur. Can you use the chapter to improve your own attitudes about health promotion?

Practice Test ①

1. Which of these behavior patterns would be predicted by the Yerkes-Dodson law?

a. When Kathryn is angry she finds it hard to drive.
b. When Ray is sad he likes to eat ice cream.
c. When Jamie is happy he sleeps very well.
d. When Celia is surprised she begins to cry.

2. Kingston is in a wonderful mood. As he walks down the street with you, he points to all the other people who seem to be having a good time. He may do this as a consequence of

a. mood-congruent processing.
b. cognitive appraisal.
c. mere exposure.
d. mood-dependent retrieval.

3. The type of social support cancer patients find most helpful from their family or friends is

a. informational support--information about the disease.
b. tangible support--money.
c. emotional support--just having them be there.
d. outcome support--talking about the small impact of the disease.

4. You are participating in an experiment. The researcher has told you to relax, and that she will turn on a light on a display in front of you. As you try to relax, you see the light turning on more and more. It's likely that the experiment is concerned with

a. biofeedback.
b. the general adaptation syndrome.
c. stress inoculation.
d. cognitive appraisal.

5. Which of the following hormones does NOT play a role in the fight-or-flight syndrome?

a. epinephrine
b. cortisol
c. thyrotrophic hormone
d. norepinephrine

323

6. Research on the psychological after-effects of catastrophe and trauma has shown that

a. few people pass through recognizable stages.
b. people readily ignore the emotional impact of the tragedy.
c. a residual stress pattern may persist indefinitely.
d. people rarely seek social contact after a tragedy.

7. If you want to decrease the likelihood of caretaker burnout in the health care system, you could

a. increase the number of patients each practitioner sees.
b. ensure that practitioners are in direct contact with patients for long periods of time.
c. avoid the use of teams in health care settings.
d. arrange practitioners' schedules so they get temporary breaks from patient care.

8. You are talking to your friend Carlton about his new romantic interest. Carlton says, "Feel how hard my heart is beating. I guess I must be in love." Carlton's remark comes closest to the _____ theory of emotion.

a. James-Lange
b. Cannon-Bard
c. Tompkins-Plutchik
d. Lazarus-Schachter

9. The major difference between the biomedical model and the biopsychosocial model is that the

a. biopsychosocial model minimizes the importance of physical illness.
b. biopsychosocial model acknowledges the link between the mind and the body.
c. biomedical model draws on traditional health practices.
d. biomedical model is largely concerned with psychosomatic illnesses.

10. Charles Darwin did NOT believe that emotions

a. are vague, unpredictable personal states.
b. serve adaptive functions.
c. deal with recurring situations in the world.
d. evolved alongside other important human functions.

11. Paul Ekman's research on the universality of facial expressions revealed that

a. members of Western cultures were unable to recognize most facial expressions produced by people from the Fore culture.
b. one or two facial expressions are universal.
c. people from the Fore culture recognized almost all the Western facial expressions.
d. people from different cultures use the same expressions to convey different meanings.

12. You think that your friend Rudy has a Type A personality. You worry that his personality will put him at risk for disease because he is so _____ all the time.

a. competitive
b. aggressive
c. hostile
d. impatient

13. If you were a researcher of psychoneuroimmunology, you might study

a. people's emotional responses to acute stress.
b. the role of the autonomic nervous system in the fight-or-flight syndrome.
c. psychological aspects of the general adaptation syndrome.
d. the effects of chronic stress on the body's ability to fight disease.

14. Beth has been smoking for several years. She hasn't done anything concrete yet, but she has started to think seriously about quitting. She is most likely at the _____ stage.

a. contemplation
b. preparation
c. precontemplation
d. maintenance

15. Neuroscientist Joseph Ledoux has suggested that some people may be overemotional because their _____ is unable to control strong responses from their _____.

a. limbic system; amygdala
b. cortex; amygdala
c. hypothalamus; cortex
d. limbic system; hypothalamus

16. All of the following are consequences of chronic stress EXCEPT the

a. prevalence of high blood pressure in the African American community.
b. greater rate of smoking among sensation-seeking men.
c. low birthweight babies of socially disadvantaged mothers.
d. impaired intellectual development of underprivileged children.

17. AIDS intervention programs should include training on behavioral skills because people must

a. know which behaviors are safer sex behaviors.
b. be taught how to put safer sex knowledge to use.
c. be motivated to practice AIDS prevention behaviors.
d. avoid situations in which AIDS could be transmitted.

18. Which of the following statements would you most likely hear from a Type C person?

a. "I'm just going to have to get used to the fact that I'm dying."
b. "I'm going to fight this disease as hard as I can."
c. "I know I'm going to get better."
d. "I can't believe how many people are out to get me."

19. You want to give a friend advice on coping with stress that shows an emotion-focus. Which of the following might you say to her?

a. "You have to find ways to fight the threat."
b. "Is there some kind of compromise you can find?"
c. "Can you do anything to get out of the situation?"
d. "You have to plan ways to distract yourself from the situation."

20. You walk into a classroom and see this list of questions on the blackboard:
    1. What are your personal resources?
    2. What are your social resources?
    3. What action options are available?

You decide that the lecture was probably about

a. stress inoculation.
b. secondary appraisal.
c. primary appraisal.
d. perceived control.

Practice Test ②

1. Suppose you wanted to test the Lazarus-Schachter theory of emotion. You would be most likely to

a. see whether environmental cues are used to help label a subject's arousal.
b. surgically separate the viscera from the central nervous system.
c. measure how long it takes for autonomic nervous system responses to appear.
d. see whether subjects experience emotions in familiar situations.

2. Louie is in a police lineup. He is breathing quickly, his heart is racing, and his blood pressure is sky-high. In addition, Louie's stomach feels bad. The symptoms of stress that Louie is experiencing are produced by the

a. autonomic nervous system.
b. thalamus.
c. stress moderators.
d. immune system.

3. You are playing "Famous Scientists." To win the game, you must identify the first modern researcher to investigate the effects of continued severe stress on the body, and the originator of the "general adaptation syndrome." You should guess

a. Walter Cannon.
b. Donald Meichenbaum.
c. Suzanne Kobasa.
d. Hans Selye.

4. Clarissa is going on a job interview. Just before she steps into the personnel office, she imagines the members of the committee that will interview her as circus performers, and it makes her laugh. Clarissa is using the coping strategy known as

a. stress inoculation.
b. cognitive reappraisal.
c. socioemotional support.
d. decision control.

5. Jeanne is a very perceptive individual. She can sense people's emotional states even when they have not said a word. She knows when people can be approached and when it is best to leave them alone. Jeanne's use of emotional cues best illustrates

a. the Yerkes-Dodson law.
b. the social communication function of emotion.
c. the James-Lange theory of emotion.
d. that emotional expressions are innate.

6. The "mere exposure effect" refers to the phenomenon in which

a. people prefer stimuli that are presented repeatedly, even when the stimuli are not consciously recognized.
b. people stop responding emotionally to a stimulus, simply because it has become familiar.
c. males will express sexual interest in a female with whom they are not familiar.
d. people become emotionally upset upon the simple presentation of a neutral stimulus.

7. Paul Ekman has identified _____ facial expressions that are recognized and produced worldwide.

a. 7
b. 12
c. about 50
d. more than 100

8. Now that Mandy is on her own, she feels much more in control of her life. Taking care of her newly acquired dog is an example of _____ control, and choosing when to go to bed is an example of _____ control.

a. behavioral; decision
b. information; cognitive
c. behavioral; information
d. decision; cognitive

9. Randy is lowering his blood pressure in an unusual manner. He is trying to turn a green light on in a box in front of him. Wires lead from the box to a cuff placed around Randy's finger. The technique that Randy is using is probably based on

a. classical conditioning.
b. the relaxation response.
c. biofeedback.
d. socioemotional support.

10. Hope sees her new job as a challenge. She is anxious to get involved in it and is confident that her performance will be outstanding. Suzanne Kobasa would say that Hope possesses

a. stress tolerance.
b. hardiness.
c. a delusion.
d. adaptability.

11. Adam was pleased to see that Eve had sent him a birthday card and the _____ division of his autonomic nervous system reacted. When he read on the card that she wasn't coming to his birthday party, the _____ division reacted.

a. sympathetic; sympathetic
b. sympathetic; parasympathetic
c. parasympathetic; sympathetic
d. parasympathetic; parasympathetic

12. In a study described in the textbook, residents of the San Francisco area were interviewed at varying time periods after the 1989 earthquake. The researchers found a pattern of three distinct phases of stress reactions that they characterized as

a. alarm, resistance, and exhaustion.
b. emergency, inhibition, and adaptation.
c. denial, bargaining, and acceptance.
d. anger, frustration, and love.

13. With respect to social support mechanisms, researchers have suggested that

a. additional social support is not always helpful.
b. additional social support is always beneficial.
c. social support from family members is most beneficial.
d. tangible social support is most beneficial.

14. Donna and Debbie are in the same book club. This week, they are reading a romance novel that is filled with happy and sad parts. Donna is in a happy mood when she reads the novel, and Debbie is feeling sad. How will their moods affect their processing of the novel?

a. Donna will pay more attention than Debbie to the happy parts.
b. Donna will pay more attention than Debbie to the sad parts.
c. Both Donna and Debbie will pay more attention to the happy parts.
d. Both Donna and Debbie will pay more attention to the sad parts.

15. Research on the relationship between arousal and performance suggests that the key to determining the optimal arousal level for best performance is to take into consideration

a. the strength of your motivation.
b. task difficulty.
c. how important the task is.
d. whether the task is enjoyable.

16. The clinical symptoms of posttraumatic stress disorder are described as

a. hallucinations.
b. conditioned responses.
c. delusions.
d. psychosomatic disorders.

17. Which of the following is an example of a daily hassle?

a. having an abusive, alcoholic spouse
b. losing all of your possessions in an apartment fire
c. going through a divorce
d. getting annoying telephone calls

18. Titus didn't get frightened when he passed the graveyard at night unless he started running. When he ran, he got very frightened. Titus' experience best supports the theory of emotion suggested by

a. Cannon-Bard
b. James-Lange.
c. Lazarus-Schachter.
d. Darwin.

19. The Social Readjustment Rating Scale was developed in order to assess

a. differences in the psychological characteristics of well-adjusted and poorly-adjusted people.
b. the relationship between moving one's residence and later social adjustment.
c. the effect of negative stressors on the development of psychosomatic disorders.
d. the degree of adjustment required by pleasant and unpleasant life changes.

20. Stimulus is to response as

a. acute stress is to chronic stress.
b. fight is to flight.
c. stress is to stressor.
d. stressor is to stress.

Answers, Practice Test ①

1. a (p. 470) Only the first option specifies a relationship between arousal and performance on a task.

2. a (p. 471) Mood-congruent processing suggests that Kingston would be more likely to attend to other happy people or events when he is in a happy mood.

3. c (p. 490)

4. a (p. 500)

5. b (p. 474)

6. c (p. 482)

7. d (p. 504)

8. d (p. 468) It sounds like Carlton is appraising his physiological response.

9. b (p. 492)

10. a (p. 461)

11. c (p. 462)

12. c (p. 502)

13. d (p. 476)

14. a (p. 494)

15. b (p. 466)

16. b (pp. 482-484 and p. 494)

17. b (p. 498)

18. a (p. 503)

19. d (p. 486)

20. b (p. 478)

Answers, Practice Test ②

1. a (p. 468) According to the Lazarus-Schachter theory, emotional experience grows out of ongoing transactions with the environment that are evaluated.

2. a (p. 473)

3. d (p. 375)

4. b (p. 487)

5. b (p. 471)

6. a (p. 469)

7. a (p. 462)

8. a (p. 489) Behavioral control involves taking actions and decision control involves being able to decide on alternative actions.

9. c (p. 500)

10. b (p. 485)

11. c (p. 465)

12. b (p. 481)

13. a (pp. 490-491)

14. a (p. 472)

15. b (p. 470)

16. b (p. 482)

17. d (p. 484)

18. b (pp. 466-467) The James-Lange theory suggested that emotion stems from bodily feedback.

19. d (p. 478)

20. d (p. 472) A stressor is a stimulus and stress is the pattern of responses an organism makes.

Chapter 14

Understanding Human Personality

Chapter Outline

Section	What you need to know
I. The Psychology of the Person	
A. Strategies for Studying Personality	How do researchers study personality?
B. Theories about Personality	What are the goals of personality theories?
II. Type and Trait Personality Theories	
A. Categorizing by Types	Are there different types of people in the world?
B. Describing with Traits	What dimensions underlie diversity in personalities?
1. Allport's trait approach 2. Identifying universal trait dimensions	
C. Traits and Heritability	Do you inherit personality traits from your parents?
D. Do Traits Predict Behaviors?	What can you predict from a trait description of an individual?

Section	What you need to know
E. Evaluation of Type and Trait Theories	What are the strengths and weaknesses of these theories?
III. Psychodynamic Theories	
A. Freudian Psychoanalysis	What unconscious forces did Freud think guide behavior?
1. Drives and psychosexual development 2. Psychic determinism 3. The structure of personality 4. Repression and ego defense	
B. Evaluation of Freudian Theory	What are the strengths and weaknesses of this theory?
C. Post-Freudian Theories	How did Freud's followers modify his views?
IV. Humanistic Theories	What is the significance of the drive toward self-actualization?
A. Evaluation of Humanistic Theories	What are the strengths and weaknesses of these theories?
V. Social-Learning and Cognitive Theories	
A. Kelly's Personal Construct Theory	How do personal constructs define personality?
B. Mischel's Cognitive Social Personality Theory	How is behavior determined by interactions between people and situations?
C. Bandura's Cognitive Social-Learning Theory	What cognitive processes guide social learning?

Section	What you need to know
D. Cantor's Social Intelligence Theory	What expertise do people bring to life tasks?
E. Evaluation of Social-Learning and Cognitive Theories	What are the strengths and weaknesses of these theories?
VI. Self Theories	
A. Dynamic Aspects of Self-Concepts	How do you define your self?
B. Self-Esteem and Self-Presentation	How do you present your self to the world?
C. Evaluation of Self Theories	What are the strengths and weaknesses of these theories?
Close-up: What If You Could Design Your Own Personality?	Do drugs such as Prozac allow you to tune your personality with chemistry?
VII. Comparing Personality Theories	What features individuate each theory?

Guided Study

I. The Psychology of the Person (p. 508)

➤ What two basic concepts do definitions of personality share?

➤ Why does personality research most often rely on correlational designs?

337

I. A. Strategies for Studying Personality (p. 509)

➤ What are the major sources of evidence researchers use to study personality?

1.

2.

3.

4.

5.

➤ Contrast the idiographic approach and nomothetic approach. Give examples of each.

Idiographic approach:

Nomothetic approach:

I. B. Theories about Personality (p. 510)

➤ What two goals do personality theories serve?

II. A. Categorizing by Types (p. 511)

➤ What four types were proposed by Hippocrates?

1.

2.

3.

4.

➤ What three types were proposed by William Sheldon?

1.

2.

3.

➤ How are these type theories viewed by contemporary researchers?

➤ Give an example of a type theory for which there is research evidence.

II. B. Describing with Traits (p. 512)

➤ How are type theories and trait theories different?

1. Based on Gordon Allport's theory, give examples of these types of traits:

Cardinal traits:

Central traits:

Secondary traits:

What did Allport mean by "The same fire that melts the butter hardens the egg?"

2. What three trait dimensions emerge in Hans Eysenck's analyses of personality?

How does Eysenck believe individual differences arise?

How were the dimensions of the five-factor model derived?

What are the dimensions of the five-factor model? How widely applicable are they?

How may the five factors have developed as a response to evolutionary pressures?

II. C. Traits and Heritability (p. 515)

➤ How have researchers demonstrated that personality traits are inherited?

➤ What aspects of the environment are most important in shaping personality?

II. D. Do Traits Predict Behaviors? (p. 516)

➤ What findings led to what is called the consistency paradox?

➤ How is the paradox resolved, to some extent, by changing levels of analysis?

➤ Summarize Wright and Mischel's research evidence on the predictive value of traits.

➤ How does the situation influence the extent to which traits become relevant?

➤ How do *you* influence the extent to which your friends' traits become relevant?

➤ How do consistency and coherence differ?

II. E. *Evaluation of Type and Trait Theories (p. 517)*

➤ What are criticisms of type and trait theories?

III. *Psychodynamic Theories (p. 518)*

➤ What assumption unifies psychodynamic personality theories?

III. A. *Freudian Psychoanalysis (p. 518)*

➤ Why did Freud believe that all behavior was motivated?

1. Summarize Freud's ideas about basic biological drives.

Self-preservation:

Eros:

Thanatos:

What are erogenous zones? What role do they play in psychosexual development? (Make sure you have studied the material in Table 14.1.)

What is the Oedipus conflict?

What is fixation and what causes it? What are the consequences of fixation at each stage of psychosexual development?

Stage	Consequences of Fixation

2. Define and illustrate psychic determinism.

What role does the unconscious play in guiding behaviors? How do the manifest and latent content of a behavior differ?

What is the origin of Freudian slips? Give examples.

3. Summarize the operation of these components of personality structure.

Id:

Superego:

Ego:

4. What is repression and what function does it serve?

What function do ego defense mechanisms serve? For each of the mechanisms in Table 14.2, try to generate a concrete example of the mechanism at work. Devise a strategy to link the name of each mechanism to your example.

How does anxiety trigger the use of defense mechanisms?

III. B. *Evaluation of Freudian Theory (p. 522)*

➤ Explain five criticisms of Freud's theory:

1.

2.

3.

4.

5.

➤ What are important aspects of Freud's theory that have gained acceptance?

1.

2.

III. C. Post-Freudian Theories (p. 523)

➤ What are four general differences between Freud's theory and those of his followers?

1.

2.

3.

4.

➤ What striving is at the center of Alfred Adler's theory?

➤ What role did the collective unconscious and archetypes play in Carl Jung's theory?

➤ What is analytic psychology?

IV. Humanistic Theories (p. 524)

➤ Why is self-actualization so important in humanistic theories?

➤ What is unconditional positive regard? To whom does it apply?

➤ Summarize each feature of humanistic theories.

Holistic:

Dispositional:

Phenomenological:

Existential:

➤ Why was the humanistic view a welcome treat?

IV. A. Evaluation of Humanistic Theories (p. 526)

➤ What criticisms have been leveled at humanistic theories?

➤ What is the practice of psychobiography?

➤ Why does the analysis of narratives or life stories match particularly well with humanistic concerns?

V. Social-Learning and Cognitive Theories (p. 527)

➤ Summarize the historical roots of contemporary social-learning theories.

V. A. Kelly's Personal Construct Theory (p. 528)

➤ How did Kelly use science as a metaphor?

➤ What are personal constructs and how do they define personality?

V. B. Mischel's Cognitive Social Personality Theory (p. 528)

➤ What variables affect how you respond to particular situations?

1.

2.

3.

4.

5.

➤ Why does Mischel view behavior as the interaction of personality and situation? Give examples.

V. C. Bandura's Cognitive Social-Learning Theory (p. 530)

➤ What is reciprocal determinism and what role does it play in Bandura's theory?

➤ What do people acquire through observational learning?

➤ What is self-efficacy? What are the sources for self-efficacy judgments?

➤ How does self-efficacy affect outcomes?

V. D. Cantor's Social Intelligence Theory (p. 532)

➤ What three types of individual differences does social intelligence theory recognize?

1.

2.

3.

➤ What strategies are used by people who are optimists and defensive pessimists?

➤ What happens when normal strategies are disrupted?

V. E. Evaluation of Social-Learning and Cognitive Theories (p. 533)

➤ What two sets of criticisms have these theories weathered?

1.

2.

➤ What is self-monitoring?

VI. C. Evaluation of Self Theories (p. 537)

➤ What are criticisms of self theories?

✍ Close-up: What If You Could Design Your Own Personality? (p. 538)

➤ Summarize the views of proponents and critics of cosmetic psychopharmacology.

Proponents:

Critics:

VII. Comparing Personality Theories (p. 537)

➤ Summarize the grounds for similarity and difference among the different types of personality theories.

1.

2.

3.

4.

5.

For Group Study

I. The Psychology of the Person

For a group exercise, choose some well-known figure and have each member of the group write a brief (one paragraph) personality sketch. Do you all agree in your characterization of your subject's personality? What dimensions or theoretical ideas do you use to describe him or her? As you work your way through the chapter, discuss how each different approach to personality can add to your description.

II. D. Do Traits Predict Behaviors?

Discuss the way in which people use trait terms loosely in everyday conversation ("She's very friendly"; "He's not very reliable"). What do people intend when they use these terms? Do they seem to allow for accurate predictions of behavior?

III. A. Freudian Psychoanalysis

What did you all know about Freud before you began this psychology class? Did you have an accurate impression of his ideas? How has the description of Freud's theory changed your views?

IV. Humanistic Theories

Discuss the idea of self-actualization. How would you reach it in your own lives?

VI. Self Theories

The topic of the self is pretty personal, but see if you can discuss as a group the material about different aspects of the self. Are there noticeable differences in the way you each talk about or present your selves? What are your ideas about possible selves? Has your sense of self changed from adolescence into adulthood?

Practice Test ①

1. Toby is supposed to build a bird house. You are told that Toby is low in self-efficacy. From this prediction you are most likely to predict that Toby may NOT

a. have the ability to build the bird house.
b. want to build the bird house.
c. believe that he can build the bird house.
d. understand the plans for the bird house.

2. Jesse has spent most of his life plagued by feelings of inadequacy. No matter how hard he tries, he always ends up feeling inferior to other people. Jesse's life is best understood in terms of the personality theory of _____.

a. Carl Jung
b. Hans Eysenck
c. Joseph Breuer
d. Alfred Adler

3. Fred and Ginger have many of the same friends. When Fred puts the friends into categories, he tends to group together those people who are good versus bad dressers. Ginger categorizes people according to their ability to dance well or poorly. It sounds like Fred and Ginger have different _____.

a. archetypes
b. instinctual drives
c. expectancies
d. personal constructs

4. Research on self-verification has demonstrated that people with _____ self-concepts prefer to stay in relationships with people who _____.

a. negative; view them negatively
b. positive; have low self-esteem
c. negative; have low self-esteem
d. negative; view them positively

5. You have built a very life-like robot whose personality is structured along the lines of Freudian theory. Unfortunately, you forgot to build in the capacity for repression. As a consequence the robot's

a. id is guided by the reality principle.
b. superego never comes into conflict with its id.
c. ego is aware of the dangerous impulses coming from its id.
d. ego is not able to strive for its ego ideal.

6. Which of the following statements is NOT consistent with Walter Mischel's theory?

a. People with different personalities may act the same in some situations.
b. You cannot tell that much about people by knowing how they behave on average.
c. Most behavior results from the interaction of personality and situations.
d. Most situations overwhelm individual personality differences.

7. Critics such as Peter Breggin and Ginger Ross Breggin disapprove of the over-prescription of drugs such as Prozac because such drugs

a. are not effective enough at ending psychological distress.
b. are often prescribed by people with inadequate training.
c. rob people of experiences that promote personal growth.
d. disrupt the effects of other forms of therapy.

8. According to Freud, it may be difficult to discover the causes of some behaviors because

a. the roots of the behaviors lie in the unconscious.
b. the manifest content of behavior is difficult to uncover.
c. not all people possess libidos.
d. the Thanatos instinct guides psychosexual development.

9. Professor Samuel studies personality using an idiographic approach. Which of these would most likely be the title of an article he would write?

a. "Happiness and Friendliness: Are They Related?"
b. "The Effects of Instinctual Drives on Conscientiousness"
c. "The Personality of Axl Rose: A Case Study"
d. "How Does Self-Esteem Affect Self-Presentation?"

10. Suppose you want to use Nancy Cantor's social intelligence theory to make comparisons between two of your best friends. You might ask them to describe to you what

a. important behaviors they have acquired by watching other people.
b. situations make them feel most inadequate.
c. life goals or life tasks matter most to them.
d. they consider to be important aspects of their possible selves.

11. You are reading a book that describes a new personality theory that divides people into Type D, Type E, and Type F. If this is truly a type theory, which of these sentences should NOT appear in the book?

a. All people who are Type D enjoy late night snacks.
b. John Wayne was recognizable as a Type E from early childhood onward.
c. A larger number of people are Type F than are Type E.
d. Marilyn Monroe was partially Type D and partially Type F.

12. You are reading a case study that describes a patient in therapy as "orderly and obstinate." If you are a follower of Freud, you would guess that this patient is fixated at the _____ stage.

a. anal
b. phallic
c. oral
d. genital

13. Imagine a play in which each character was based on one aspect of Freud's conception of personality structure. The ego would be most likely to say

a. "You've got to wait."
b. "I want it now!"
c. "I don't care what it costs."
d. "That would be wrong."

14. Your friend Elaine has just ended a bad relationship with Larry. His brother Gary has now asked her out on a date. Elaine wonders how likely it is that Gary will share personality traits with Larry. You tell her that it's most likely if they

a. are identical twins.
b. share the same mother.
c. share the same father.
d. are fraternal twins.

15. You have decided to write a psychobiography of pop star Madonna. Because you take a humanistic perspective on personality, your book is likely to interpret events in her life as

a. the triumph of her id over her superego.
b. the product of archetypes from her collective unconscious.
c. a striving toward self-actualization.
d. the products of reciprocal determinism.

16. Dorothy is playing with a beach ball in the living room of her family's apartment. The ball knocks into her mother's favorite lamp, which falls to the ground and breaks. When Dorothy's mother appears, she punishes Dorothy for playing with the ball inside but she also reminds Dorothy how much she loves her. This parenting style follows the advice of

a. Carl Jung.
b. Carl Rogers.
c. Rollo May.
d. Abraham Maslow.

17. Which of Hans Eysenck's three trait dimensions does not appear in the five-factor model?

a. extraversion
b. psychoticism
c. agreeableness
d. neuroticism

18. You'd like to be able to predict how friendly Paul is likely to be if you invite him to your birthday party next month. The best data you could collect to make this prediction would be to

a. ask a large sample of Paul's acquaintances how friendly they think he is.
b. observe how friendly Paul is in other party settings.
c. follow Paul for a day, and see how friendly he typically is.
d. ask Paul's mother how friendly he usually is.

19. Although you don't believe there's any one trait that organizes your life, you do believe that you possess several major personality characteristics. In Gordon Allport's terms, you believe that you are better described by _____ traits than by a _____ trait.

a. central; cardinal
b. cardinal; secondary
c. secondary; central
d. cardinal; central

20. You're about to take a major exam. Which of these statements might be made by a classmate who is engaging in self-handicapping?

a. "I studied really hard, but I'm still not sure I'm going to do well."
b. "I couldn't study last night because I let my sister come visit."
c. "I think this professor gives really tough tests."
d. "I bet I do better on this test than I did on the last one."

Practice Test ②

1. In terms of the modifiability of personality development, _____ theory has a pessimistic view; the most optimistic view is held by _____ theory.

a. Freudian; humanistic
b. social-learning; trait
c. trait; Freudian
d. humanistic; social-learning

2. Six-year-old Juliette says that she loves watching Barney, can't stand fast food, and thinks that people who are bald are funny. In Allport's theory, Juliette is describing some of her _____ traits.

a. central
b. primary
c. secondary
d. cardinal

3. Imagine walking down the street, doing some shopping. You see a beautiful watch in a store window, but you cannot possibly afford it. If you were pure _____, you would break the window and take the watch, but you are prevented from doing so by the _____.

a. ego, superego
b. libido; id
c. id; ego
d. superego; ego

4. The district attorney never stops his campaign to rid the city of pornography. He gets extremely agitated when speaking against the evils of "adult" magazines, and quotes scripture endlessly to back up his tirades. Freud might suggest that his behavior is possibly a sign of

a. reaction formation.
b. repression.
c. regression.
d. denial of reality.

5. As part of a job application process, Felipe is taking a paper-and-pencil type of personality test. He has been answering hundreds of questions about his own behavior, attitudes, and traits for the past hour. The information that Felipe is providing is an example of _____ data.

a. specific behavioral
b. observer-report
c. life-events
d. self-report

6. Floyd has just finished reading a very interesting article on the famous painter, Vincent Van Gogh. It tells of Van Gogh's troubled childhood, and uses the letters he wrote to his brother in an attempt to produce a coherent explanation of both his artistic creativity and his later mental problems. It sounds as though the author has used the technique of

a. psychobiography.
b. social-learning.
c. self-monitoring.
d. observational learning.

7. 0n the first day of school, Wally's fourth-grade teacher asks the class to write a short paragraph. She wants each student to describe things about themselves that are unique, but also ways that they behave that stay the same from one situation to another. The teacher is really asking each student to describe his or her

a. personality.
b. motivation.
c. achievement needs.
d. superego.

8. On personality tests, Morgan scores high on introversion, and most of his friends think of him as quiet and shy. Everyone is surprised when he tries out for a part in the school play and wins a major role. This illustrates

a. the defense mechanism of denial.
b. the consistency paradox.
c. self-monitoring.
d. observational learning.

9. Zelda has low self-esteem. When compared to her friend, Dobie, who has high self-esteem, Zelda is likely to have

a. stronger levels of motivation.
b. a less precise sense of self.
c. a wider range of life successes.
d. a more positive self-concept.

10. Jules and Jim have different biological parents, but both were adopted in infancy by the Truffaut family. Heredity as a determiner of personality would be supported if the personalities of Jules and Jim

a. are more similar to the personalities of their adoptive parents than to their biological parents.
b. are similar to the personality of Jeanne, the Truffaut's biological daughter.
c. are more similar to each other than they are to their own biological siblings.
d. are less similar to each other than they are to their own biological siblings.

11. After the students have left the classroom following their test, the teacher notices a slip of paper on the floor. He picks it up and reads the words, "neuroticism, psychoticism, extraversion." Apparently, a student needed a "reminder" concerning _____ theory of personality.

a. Sheldon's
b. Allport's
c. Freud's
d. Eysenck's

12. Polly faces situations with high expectations and little prior thought. Anna sets low expectations and expends considerable effort thinking through possible positive and negative outcomes. In the context of Cantor's social intelligence theory, Polly is a(n) _____ and Anna is a(n) _____.

a. rationalist; irrationalist
b. optimist; defensive pessimist
c. positive non-thinker; negative thinker
d. conformist; realist

13. According to Walter Mischel, how we respond to a specific environmental input depends in part on what we know, what we can do, and our ability to generate certain cognitive and behavioral outcomes. These are examples of what he calls

a. expectancies.
b. competencies.
c. encoding strategies.
d. self-regulatory systems and plans.

14. When talking to her roommate about her blind date, Marcie describes him as having a lot of "libido." Her roommate understands that Marcie's date apparently

a. is prone to mental illness.
b. wanted to kill himself.
c. demonstrated a strong sex drive.
d. did not have a superego.

15. Brian reads his brother Jack a children's story about a little locomotive that reaches the top of a hill because it thinks it can. The idea in the story sounds most like Bandura's notion of

a. self-efficacy.
b. reciprocal determinism.
c. observational learning.
d. wishful thinking.

16. According to the five-factor model of personality, personality can be classified along the dimensions of

a. egocentrism, reticence, creativity, faithfulness, and energy.
b. honesty, emotional stability, punctuality, hostility, and persistence.
c. agreeableness, extraversion, openness to experience, neuroticism, and conscientiousness.
d. degree of quiescence, egocentrism, introversion, hostility, and emotional instability.

17. Imagine that Carl Rogers is on a talk show handling questions about child-rearing practices. A parent calls in and asks how he should handle his son, who deliberately pushed another child off of a bicycle. Carl Rogers' advice would most likely be to

a. push the child off of his own bicycle, to show him how it feels.
b. tell the child, "Go to your room without supper."
c. tell the child, "Daddy and I don't like you because you are bad."
d. tell the child, "Trying to hurt another child is a bad thing to do."

18. Modern personality theorists suggest that memories about the self, self-schemas, and self-esteem are all components of

a. the self-concept.
b. one's "spiritual me."
c. the "material me."
d. self-verification.

19. In George Kelly's theory of personality, most emphasis is placed on

a. the undeniable fact of past experiences.
b. the assumption that people are victims of the present environment.
c. each person's cognitive construction of the world.
d. the inner drive toward self-actualization.

20. Laura's theory of personality is based on eye color. For example, she says that people with dark eyes are warm and honest, whereas people with blue eyes can't be trusted. Laura's use of eye color as the basis for determining personality is an example of a _____ theory.

a. trait
b. social-learning
c. type
d. self

Answers, Practice Test ①

1. c (p. 531) People with low self-efficacy may have the ability and the desire. They just don't believe they can succeed.

2. d (p. 523)

3. d (p. 528)

4. a (p. 535)

5. c (p. 521)

6. d (p. 529)

7. c (p. 538)

8. a (p. 520)

9. c (p. 509)

10. c (p. 532)

11. d (p. 511) If it is truly a type theory, then Ms. Monroe should be placed exclusively in one type or the other.

12. a (p. 519)

13. a (p. 521) Options b and c sound like the id; option d sounds like the superego.

14. a (p. 515) If they're identical twins, what advice would you give her?

15. c (p. 524)

16. b (p. 525) Carl Rogers suggested that parents express unconditional positive regard.

17. b (pp. 513-514)

18. b (pp. 516-517)

19. a (p. 512)

20. b (p. 536)

Answers, Practice Test ②

1. a (pp. 537-538)

2. c (p. 512) Secondary traits are specific, personal features such as food or dress preferences.

3. c (pp. 520-521)

4. a (p. 522)

5. d (p. 509)

6. a (p. 526)

7. a (p. 508)

8. b (p. 516)

9. b (p. 536)

10. d (p. 515)

11. d (p. 513)

12. b (p. 533)

13. b (p. 529)

14. c (p. 518)

15. a (p. 531)

16. c (p. 514)

17. d (p. 525)

18. a (p. 534)

19. c (p. 528)

20. c (p. 511)

Chapter 15

Assessing Individual Differences

Chapter Outline

Section	What you need to know
I. What is Assessment?	
A. History of Assessment	What are the roots of contemporary assessment practices?
B. Purposes of Assessment	What are the goals of formal assessment?
II. Methods of Assessment	
A. Basic Features of Formal Assessment	How do researchers safeguard the conclusions of formal assessment?
1. Reliability	
2. Validity	
3. Norms and standardization	
B. Sources of Information	What types of evidence are used for formal assessments?
1. Assessment techniques	
2. Self-report methods	
3. Observer-report methods	

Section	What you need to know

Why and how was intelligence first
measured?

What is measured by IQ tests?

How should intelligence be defined?

Why has intelligence so often become a
matter of public debate?

Why have scientists argued so strongly
against the conclusions of this book?

How is creativity assessed?

366

Section	What you need to know
IV. Assessing Personality	
A. Objective Tests	How are personality inventories constructed?
1. The MMPI 2. The CPI 3. The NEO-PI	
B. Projective Tests	How is personality revealed by ambiguous stimuli?
1. The Rorschach 2. The TAT	
C. Evaluation of Personality Assessment	How can personality tests reveal total personality?
V. Assessment and You	
A. Vocational Interests and Aptitudes	How can you be matched to the right job?
1. Assessing interests 2. Assessing abilities 3. Assessing jobs	
B. Political and Ethical Issues	Why does testing become controversial?

Guided Study   ☞ ☞ ☞ ☞

I. What is Assessment? (p. 542)

➤ Why is most assessment concerned with individual differences?

367

I. A. History of Assessment (p. 542)

➤ What kind of assessment was carried out in ancient China?

➤ What ideas did Sir Francis Galton contribute to the history of assessment?

1.

2.

3.

4.

Why did Galton start the eugenics movement?

I. B. Purposes of Assessment (p. 544)

➤ Summarize the goals of assessment.

II. Methods of Assessment (p. 544)

➤ What is psychometrics?

➤ How do theoretical and empirical approaches to test construction differ?

368

➤ Define each of these features of formal assessment. Give examples of the different ways of assessing reliability and validity.

1. Reliability

   Test-retest reliability

   Parallel forms

   Internal consistency

   Split-half reliability

   Coding schemes

2. Validity

   Face validity

   Criterion validity

   Construct validity

3. Norms and standardization (give examples)

II. B. Sources of Information (p. 549)

1. Summarize four examples of assessment techniques.

2. Describe self-report methods. What is their greatest shortcoming?

3. Describe observer-report methods. How do situational behavior observations differ from ratings?

Define and give examples of halo and stereotype effects.

What is the importance of interjudge reliability?

III. Intelligence and Intelligence Assessment (p. 551)

➤ What three skills contribute to definitions of intelligence?

III. A. The Origins of Intelligence Testing (p. 552)

➤ What role did Alfred Binet play in the history of intelligence testing?

➤ What was Binet's method and how did he define mental age and chronological age?

➤ What are four important features of Binet's approach?

1.

2.

3.

4.

➤ What happened when Binet's ideas were brought to the United States?

III. B. IQ Tests (p. 553)

1. Describe Lewis Terman's role in the development of IQ tests. How was the intelligence quotient measured?

How has the Stanford-Binet test changed over time? Is it accurate?

How is IQ calculated nowadays?

2. Why did David Wechsler develop a new intelligence test?

What attributes does his test measure?

How have the Wechsler tests changed over time? Are the Wechsler tests valuable?

III. C. Theories of Intelligence (p. 555)

1. What theoretical tradition uses factor analyses? What are factor analyses and what insights do they yield?

Summarize the work of these scholars.

Charles Spearman:

Raymond Cattell:

J. P. Guilford:

2. Summarize Earl Hunt's ideas about problem-solving intelligence.

3. Explain and give examples of the three components of Robert Sternberg's triarchic theory of intelligence.

Componential intelligence:

Experiential intelligence:

Contextual intelligence:

How can people be made to look intelligent?

4. What are Howard Gardner's seven intelligences? (Study Table 15.1.) What cross-cultural arguments does Gardner make?

III. D. The Politics of Intelligence (p. 559)

1. What opinions did Henry Goddard hold? What evidence did he use to bolster those opinions?

What did Lewis Terman conclude from mass testing by the U.S. Army?

2. How do comparisons of monozygotic and dizygotic twins contribute to analyses of the genetic bases of IQ?

What is a heritability estimate?

Can heritability estimates be applied to comparisons between groups?

What has Stephen Jay Gould suggested about differences between racial groups?

What has been shown by research on degree of European stock?

3. Summarize evidence on the impact of environments on IQ.

How is IQ affected by a change in environment?

What lessons does the Head Start program teach about environments and IQ?

4. How are minority students affected by testing situations?

Why might IQ tests become self-fulfilling prophecies?

✍ Close-up: _The Bell Curve_ (p. 566)

➤ What are the major conclusions of The Bell Curve?

➤ What three major research themes contradict these conclusions?

➤ How might Harold Stevenson's research explain The Bell Curve's warm welcome?

III. E. Creativity (p. 567)

➤ How is creativity defined?

1. What is divergent thinking and how and why have creativity tests measured it?

What is the relationship between divergent thinking and IQ?

What other measures of creativity have been devised?

2. Are there commonalities among "exemplary creators"?

What has research revealed about the link between madness and creativity?

IV. A. Objective Tests (p. 570)

➤ How are objective tests defined? What is a personality inventory?

Summarize the major features of these tests. To what uses are they typically put?

1. The MMPI

2. The CPI

3. The NEO-PI

4. The BFQ

IV. B. Projective Tests (p. 574)

➤ How are projective tests defined?

➤ How common is the use of projective tests?

Summarize the major features of these tests.

1. The Rorschach

2. The TAT

IV. C. Evaluation of Personality Assessment (p. 576)

➤ How do different tests contribute to an overall personality assessment?

➤ What is personology?

V. A. Vocational Interests and Aptitudes (p. 577)

➤ Summarize how assessment is done for each component of matching people to jobs.

1. Assessing interests

2. Assessing abilities

3. Assessing jobs

V. B. Political and Ethical Issues (p. 578)

➤ Summarize the ethical concerns raised by testing practices.

1.

2.

3.

For Group Study

II. A. Basic Features of Formal Assessment

As a group, choose some attribute you'd like to measure (you can choose any psychological dimension on which you think people differ). Discuss how you'd measure the attribute. How would you assure yourself of reliability? How about validity? What would you like to be able to predict from your measure?

III. Intelligence and Intelligence Assessment

Discuss your experiences with intelligence testing. It's very likely that everyone in the group will have been evaluated at some point in his or her schooling. What impact did the testing have on each of your lives? Did you take standardized exams for college entrance? Do you believe those exams really captured your intelligence or potential?

Do you believe the theories of intelligence presented in the text capture everything that's meant by "intelligence"? Try to develop a definition of intelligence with which everyone in your group is content. Was it easy or hard to do so?

Why do you think <u>The Bell Curve</u> received so much attention when its conclusions have been so overwhelmingly contradicted by scientific evidence? Discuss why intelligence so often becomes a subject of public controversy.

III. E. Creativity

Have a group discussion about what constitutes creativity. How much agreement can you reach?

IV. Assessing Personality

Have any group members undergone personality testing? What was the purpose of the testing? Did the outcomes reveal useful information?

V. A. Vocational Interests and Aptitudes

Have there been jobs for which group members thought they were well suited or poorly suited? How could they have discovered that ahead of time? What attributes do you think should be measured to assist job placement?

Practice Test ①

1. The Occupational Analysis Inventory gives you information about

a. your aptitudes with respect to specific job requirements.
b. the jobs that best fit your interests and abilities.
c. the psychological profiles of workers in different fields.
d. the knowledge and skills required for different jobs.

2. Which of these is an example of a halo effect?

a. People who are rated as friendly are also rated as more gullible.
b. Children who are rated as bullies are also rated as more intelligent.
c. Physically attractive people are rated as more manipulative than those who are unattractive.
d. Physically attractive people are rated as more interesting than those who are unattractive.

3. Research described in the textbook demonstrated that a group of racetrack regulars were able to handicap horse races with astonishing accuracy, despite their average IQs. In Robert Sternberg's triarchic theory, this research is most relevant to _____ intelligence.

a. componential
b. contextual
c. fluid
d. experiential

4. Sir Francis Galton did NOT originate the idea that

a. differences in intelligence could be measured.
b. intelligence is distributed in the form of a bell curve.
c. intelligence could be measured as a ratio of mental to chronological age.
d. the relationship between test scores could be represented as a correlation.

5. Robert Weisberg examined the relationship between Robert Schumann's state of mental health and his musical creativity. Weisberg's analysis revealed that Schumann produced _____ compositions when he was in a manic state than when he was in a depressive state. The manic compositions were of _____ the depressive compositions.

a. more; the same quality as
b. fewer; higher quality than
c. fewer; the same quality as
d. more; lower quality than

6. You have developed a new test that is intended to measure a person's emotional stability. After having a large sample of students take the test, you obtain from them lists of their friends. You plan to approach all these friends and collect their ratings of the original sample students' emotional stability. If you hope that the students' test ratings will be highly correlated with their friends' ratings, you are concerned with

a. test-retest reliability.
b. interjudge reliability.
c. face validity.
d. predictive validity.

7. Research by Harold Stevenson has demonstrated that Japanese children have much _____ mathematics achievement than U.S. children. People in the U.S. believe that "innate intelligence" is _____ important than "studying hard."

a. higher; less
b. higher; more
c. lower; less
d. lower; more

8. A major difference between the NEO-PI and the MMPI-2 is that the

a. NEO-PI was first used as a projective test of intelligence.
b. MMPI-2 has fewer clinical scales than the NEO-PI.
c. NEO-PI has not been found to be reliable.
d. NEO-PI was designed to be used with nonclinical adult samples.

9. Mrs. Mines and Mrs. Best are bragging about their children. Mrs. Mines says, "Carlos has the most linguistic intelligence in his class." Mrs. Best says, "Ruth has the most bodily-kinesthetic intelligence in her class." If the mothers are speaking truthfully, Howard Gardner's theory would suggest that Carlos might become a _____ and Ruth might become a(n) _____.

a. journalist; athlete
b. poet; sculptor
c. mathematician; dancer
d. scientist; therapist

10. When the _____ was constructed, each item had to demonstrate its validity by being answered similarly by members within a group but differently by people between groups.

a. TAT
b. MMPI
c. Rorschach
d. WISC-III

11. You are attending a lecture on the uses of the Rorschach test. The lecturer is LEAST likely to make the claim that

a. most responses to the inkblots are highly individualistic.
b. responses are scored for the location on the card that was used.
c. a comprehensive scoring system exists to compare responses.
d. Rorschach results can be used to make valid assessments.

12. Research on the Head Start program suggests that preschool interventions

a. cannot overcome many of the negative effects of poverty.
b. permanently change the IQs of children who participate.
c. have little effect on IQs, even in the short-run.
d. cannot overcome genetic deficits in intelligence.

13. Professor Kaskel is doing an analysis of your performance on her midterm. Although each question is meant to be equally hard, you got 91% of the even-numbered questions right but only 23% of the odd-numbered questions. This pattern suggests that the test has low

a. test-retest reliability.
b. split-half reliability.
c. face validity.
d. construct validity.

14. Wit respect to heritability estimates for IQ, it is NOT true that

a. they are computed by comparing people with different degrees of genetic overlap.
b. the estimate is an average for a population and cannot be used to make predictions for individuals.
c. they allow researchers to make claims about genetic differences between racial groups.
d. they represents the proportion of variability in test scores that can be attributed to genetic factors.

15. Jorge is a Latino student who is about to take an IQ test. Jorge is likely to obtain a lower IQ score than some of his white classmates because

a. he believes that Latinos generally score poorly on IQ tests.
b. his genetic make-up is inferior to that of his classmates.
c. he has less contextual intelligence than his classmates.
d. he has less fluid intelligence than his classmates.

16. When Alfred Binet developed the first intelligence test, his goal was to

a. demonstrate the genetic inferiority of immigrant populations.
b. show that important aspects of intelligence are inherited.
c. prove that mental age is generally higher than chronological age.
d. identify developmentally disabled children for special instruction.

17. If you took the WAIS-R, all of these scores would be reported to you EXCEPT _____ IQ.

a. Performance
b. Problem-Solving
c. Full Scale
d. Verbal

18. A psychologist gives you a test in which you are asked to think of all the things you can do with a pencil. This is likely to be a test of

a. crystallized intelligence.
b. convergent thinking.
c. divergent thinking.
d. spatial intelligence.

19. You are visiting a museum show on theories of intelligence. In one case there is a large red sphere marked "g" surrounded by many small yellow spheres marked "s". It's likely that this display is on the theory of

a. J. P. Guilford.
b. Earl Hunt.
c. Charles Spearman.
d. Raymond Cattell.

20. Which of the following is NOT among the primary ethical concerns that were discussed for psychological assessment?

a. Tests are used unfairly to reject minority job applicants.
b. Teachers spend too much time preparing students for standardized exams.
c. Test creators make large profits from over-testing.
d. Students cannot overcome the labels that test scores put on them.

Practice Test ②

1. George has an IQ of about 115, and Gracie has an IQ of about 85. Based on research findings, what can you predict about their creativity as assessed by typical measures?

a. George and Gracie will be equally creative.
b. Gracie is likely to be more creative.
c. George is likely to be more creative.
d. It is impossible to predict who will be more creative.

2. At the end of his job interview, Homer is given the Minnesota Multiphasic Personality Inventory. He wants to make a good impression, so when he sees questions such as "I sometimes worry about things in my life," and "I don't always tell the truth," he answers that these statements are not true. How will the tester evaluate Homer's responses?

a. The tester will not notice anything unusual about Homer's responses.
b. The tester will conclude that the test in not valid.
c. The tester will be impressed with Homer's moral character.
d. Homer will be scored as abnormal and possibly psychopathic.

3. After Bridget hired 50 widget wirers for the new plant, she gave all of them Bridget's Widget Wiring Skills Test. If Bridget later correlated scores on the test with the average daily production of widgets by the wirers, she would be assessing the _____ of the test.

a. face validity
b. construct validity
c. criterion validity
d. reliability

4. Which of the following is true of Binet's approach?

a. He interpreted scores on his test as a measure of innate intelligence.
b. He wanted to use test scores to identify children who needed special help.
c. He tied the development of his test to a fairly complex theory of intelligence.
d. He chose problems for the test that could only be scored subjectively.

5. Based on recent assessments of the Head Start program, it can be concluded that

a. good programs can have a positive effect on life outcomes.
b. Head Start can negate the effects of poverty.
c. environmental factors are not important determinants of life success.
d. participation in Head Start is more important than adequate nutrition.

6. Suppose you wanted to use a test of fluid intelligence to test your hypothesis that intelligence changes as people grow older. You should probably choose a test of

a. knowledge of vocabulary.
b. arithmetic skills.
c. general information.
d. abstract problem solving.

7. The California Psychological Inventory is LEAST likely to have been used in a study of

a. the differences in the personalities of civil service employees and self-employed people.
b. how adult personality traits are related to earlier life events.
c. the differences in the assertive behaviors of people with different forms of schizophrenia.
d. which individuals are best suited to a special training program for emergency technicians.

8. Imagine that you were one of the first children to be assigned an IQ. As a 4-year-old, you take a test, and your mental age is determined to be equivalent to that of a 5-year-old. Your IQ score would be

a. 5.
b. 80.
c. 125.
d. impossible to determine from the given information.

9. When evaluating the various personality assessment devices, the authors of the textbook come to the conclusion that

a. whenever possible, computer-based analyses are preferable to clinical interpretations.
b. the projective tests appear to be the most reliable and valid instruments.
c. each device has the potential to provide unique insights into personality.
d. it is best for clinicians to choose and stick with one single form of assessment.

10. Noelle has recently landed a job as a job analyst. In this capacity she probably will be involved in

a. listing and categorizing available jobs for a computerized job bank.
b. determining the skills, effort, responsibilities, and stresses of a job.
c. matching job requirements with the aptitudes and abilities of applicants.
d. assessing job satisfaction among employees in a major corporation.

11. The "halo effect" and the "stereotype effect" are most likely to occur when

a. people are completing inventories.
b. objective tests are being scored.
c. self-report measures are used.
d. observer ratings are used for assessment.

12. Which statement best summarizes the state of scientific evidence on the role of genetics in the determination of individuals' and group IQ scores?

a. Genetics is important in individuals' IQ scores, but does not explain racial and ethnic group differences.
b. Genetics does not explain individual IQ scores, but it is important in racial and ethnic group differences.
c. Genetics does not seem to play a role in either individual IQ scores or in racial and ethnic group differences.
d. No conclusions can yet be drawn on the role of genetics in either individual or groups IQ scores.

13. After his friend recites the names of the 7 dwarfs, Howie tries to recite the names of Gardner's 7 intelligences. Unfortunately, when he gets to the last half of the list, he gets mixed up and winds up with 8 intelligences rather than 7. Which of the following abilities should Howie have omitted?

a. philosophical
b. musical
c. bodily-kinesthetic
d. interpersonal

14. Twenty-year-old Lorraine has just finished taking the Block Design test, the Digit Symbol test, and the Picture Arrangement test. She has been working on the

a. nonverbal subtests of the WISC-III.
b. nonverbal subtests of the WAIS-R.
c. verbal subtests of the WISC-III.
d. Stanford-Binet Intelligence Scale.

15. Guilford's Structure of Intellect model is analogous to

a. an auto mechanic's car repair manual.
b. a telephone answering machine.
c. a recipe in a cookbook.
d. a chemist's periodic table of elements.

16. If you wanted to calculate the test-retest reliability of your bathroom scale, you should

a. weigh several of your friends on it, with and without clothes.
b. weigh yourself on it, then weigh yourself on a scale you know to be accurate.
c. weigh yourself on it several times in succession.
d. ask a friend who is an engineer to look at the schematic drawing of the scale.

17. Barbara is taking a course on interviewing techniques. One of the things she learns is that an interviewer is LEAST likely to always have to

a. establish and maintain feelings of rapport with the respondent.
b. know how to elicit the desired information.
c. maintain control of the direction and pace of the interview.
d. ask very specific questions in a very specific way.

18. Orson is playing a game called "Who Am I?" His clues read "I am a half-cousin to Charles Darwin, in 1869 I wrote the highly influential book "Hereditary Genius," and I attempted to apply evolutionary theory to the study of human abilities. If Orson let you help him, you would say

a. Alfred Binet.
b. Sir Francis Galton.
c. Lewis Terman.
d. David Wechsler.

19. The Cerebral Circumference Index is a measure of intelligence based on the circumference of the head just above the eyebrows. It is most reasonable to assume that the test is

a. reliable but not valid.
b. valid but not reliable.
c. both valid and reliable.
d. neither valid nor reliable.

20. One advantage of using an inventory when conducting an assessment is that inventories

a. force people to report objectively on their own behavior.
b. are not standardized, so they can be tailored to fit the individual.
c. tap into an individual's personal experiences and feelings.
d. rely on the input of individuals other than the one being assessed.

1. d (p. 578)

2. d (p. 551) The halo effect suggests that people will be given consistently positive or negative evaluations from one dimension to the next.

3. b (p. 558)

4. c (p. 543)

5. a (p. 570)

6. d (p. 546)

7. b (p. 567)

8. d (pp. 571 and 574)

9. a (p. 559)

10. b (p. 571)

11. a (p. 575) The comprehensive scoring system is made possible by the commonality of responses.

12. a (p. 565)

13. b (p. 545)

14. c (p. 562)

15. a (p. 565) As the text explains, believing that one will do poorly can easily bring about that outcome.

16. d (p. 552)

17. b (p. 554)

18. c (p. 568)

19. c (p. 555)

20. c (pp. 578-580)

Answers, Practice Test ②

1. c (p. 568)

2. b (p. 572)

3. c (p. 546) To assess criterion validity, you compare a person's score on a test to his or her score on some other criterion which is associated with what the test measures.

4. b (p. 552)

5. a (p. 565)

6. d (p. 555)

7. c (p. 573)

8. c (p. 553)

9. c (p. 576)

10. b (p. 578)

11. d (p. 551)

12. a (p. 562) Genetics has a necessary (but not sufficient) role in the understanding of scores on IQ tests, and does not constitute an adequate explanation for IQ differences between racial and ethnic groups.

13. a (p. 559)

14. b (p. 554)

15. d (p. 556) Like chemical elements, intellectual factors can be postulated before they are discovered, using Guilford's Structure of Intellect model.

16. c (p. 545)

17. d (p. 549)

18. b (p. 543)

19. a (pp. 547-548) Measures of the circumference of the head will be consistent, but unrelated to intelligence.

20. c (p. 550)

📖 Chapter 16

Social Processes and Relationships

🗒 Chapter Outline

Section	What you need to know

I. The Power of the Situation

  A. Roles and Rules in Situations — How do situations define appropriate behaviors?

  B. Conformity: Social Norms — How do groups bring about conformity?

    1. Sherif's autokinetic effect
    2. Bennington's liberal norms
    3. Social norms in contemporary college life

  C. Conformity: Informational Influence — How do groups supply information?

    1. The Asch effect: Yielding to lying lines?

  D. Minority Influence and Nonconformity — When can minorities resist pressures to conform?

  E. Authority Influence — How do people respond to authority figures?

Section	What you need to know

1. Lewin's group dynamics
2. Milgram's obedience to authority

   F. Bystander Intervention — When will people help others in distress?

   G. "Candid Camera" Revelations — When do social norms lead to humorous situations?

Close-up: The Wily Salesperson — How can social forces work against you in a department store?

II. Constructing Social Reality

   A. Social Perception — How do people understand the behaviors of others?

1. The origins of attribution theory
2. The fundamental attribution error
3. Self-serving biases
4. Expectations and self-fulfilling prophecies
5. Behaviors that confirm expectations

   B. Social Reality and Personal Attitudes — How do attitudes interact with social reality?

1. Dissonance theory
2. Self-perception theory
3. Is there a "real" social reality?

III. Social Relationships

   A. Prejudice — What forces push people apart?

1. The origins of prejudice
2. Reversing prejudice

394

Section	What you need to know
B. Interpersonal Attraction	What forces draw people together?
1. Liking 2. Loving	
IV. Solving Social Problems	
A. Environmental Psychology	How can social psychology be applied to improve environmental conditions?
B. Peace Psychology	How can social psychology be applied to foster international harmony?

Guided Study

☞ ☞ ☞ ☞

➤ Define the "social context."

I. A. Roles and Rules in Situations (p. 585)

➤ What is a social role? Give examples. How are you affected by them?

➤ What is a social rule? Give examples. Are they always explicit?

➤ Summarize the methodology of the Stanford Prison Experiment.

➤ Summarize the results of the Stanford Prison Experiment. What does it teach you about roles and rules?

I. B. Conformity: Social Norms (p. 587)

➤ What two processes give rise to conformity? (You should review these ideas as the chapter progresses.)

➤ What are social norms? How do people adjust to them? How are they enforced?

1. How did Muzafer Sherif's research demonstrate norm crystallization?

What happened when "new generations" were formed?

2. What did Theodore Newcomb learn at Bennington College? How did he explain the shift from conservatism to liberalism? What is a reference group?

What happened when the young women of Bennington graduated?

What is a total situation? Give examples.

3. What does the research on alcohol use at Princeton University demonstrate about the perception of norms?

What happens when people become aware that the norm doesn't really exist?

I. C. Conformity: Informational Influence (p. 591)

➤ How do groups satisfy information needs?

1. Summarize the methodology Solomon Asch used to study conformity.

What three factors did Asch vary to examine the effect on conformity? What did he discover?

Describe the individual differences that Asch found.

➤ Is it possible for a minority to withstand group pressure? What did Moscovici find?

➤ What are the consequences for the group?

➤ Why were early social psychologists interested in the authoritarian personality?

1. Why and how did Kurt Lewin study group dynamics?

Summarize the effects of having each type of leader.

Autocratic leaders:

Democratic leaders:

Laissez-faire leaders:

How can you be sure that it was leadership style, and not individual leaders, who brought about these effects?

2. Why does Stanley Milgram's research have so much real-world relevance?

Summarize the basic procedure of Milgram's experiment.

How did the experimental participants (the teachers) respond to the request that they continue to give shocks? Did they continue?

Why were psychiatrists wrong in their predictions about the outcome of the experiment?

Describe the experiment that was cited to rule out the possibility that the Milgram result arose from a flawed cover story.

What are demand characteristics? Describe the experiment that ruled out the possibility that the result arose from them.

Summarize the explanations for people's willingness to obey authority. What factors influence compliance?

What lessons from the Milgram's research can you apply in your own life?

I. F. Bystander Intervention (p. 600)

➤ What real-life event gave rise to research interest in bystander intervention?

➤ Summarize Bibb Latané and John Darley's experiment on bystander intervention. How did it demonstrate the diffusion of responsibility?

➤ Summarize the experimental findings that are described under each heading.

Bystanders must notice the emergency:

Bystanders must label events as an emergency:

The bystander must feel responsibility:

The situational cost of helping must not be too high:

➤ What can you do to ensure you obtain help in an emergency?

I. G. "Candid Camera" Revelations (p. 604)

➤ Think about the "Candid Camera" moments you could invent on your own. How can you influence the people around you?

✍ Close-up: The Wily Salesperson (p. 605)

➤ Summarize the three strategies described for the wily salesperson.

Reciprocity:

Commitment:

Scarcity:

➤ How can you defend yourself against wily salespeople?

II. Constructing Social Reality (p. 604)

➤ How does the Princeton-Dartmouth football game illustrate the construction of social reality?

1. Summarize early contributions to attribution theory.

Fritz Heider (What did he mean by "intuitive psychologist"?   What categories of attributions do people make?):

Harold Kelley (What is the covariation principle?   Define and give examples of distinctiveness, consistency, and consensus.):

2. What is the fundamental attribution error (FAE)? Give examples.

Why do people commit the FAE?

What did Joan Miller's research demonstrate about the influence of culture on the FAE?

3. What are self-serving biases? How do they apply in gambling situations?

4. What is a self-fulfilling prophecy? Summarize the experiment on the Pygmalion effect.

Under what circumstances are self-fulfilling prophecies most likely to occur? Summarize the Keith/Karen experiment.

5. How did Mark Snyder define behavioral confirmation?

When do expectations have their greatest effect?

II. B. *Social Reality and Personal Attitudes (p. 612)*

➤ How is "attitude" defined?

1. How did Leon Festinger define cognitive dissonance?

What motivation is provided by dissonant beliefs?

How can dissonance change attitudes? (Summarize the $1/$20 experiment.)

2. According to Daryl Bem, how are attitudes affected by self-perception?

3. Is there a "real" social reality?

III. A. Prejudice (p. 615)

➤ Why have social psychologists studied prejudice?

1. Define prejudice. Under what circumstances will prejudice arise?

To what does social categorization refer? What are minimal groups? What is an in-group bias?

2. What experimental procedures have been used to diminish prejudice? (Refer to the Robbers Cave experiment and Aronson's use of jigsawing.)

III. B. Interpersonal Attraction (p. 618)

1. Summarize the factors that contribute to liking.

Proximity and mere exposure:

Physical attractiveness:

Similarity versus dissimilarity:

Reciprocity:

2. Summarize the factors that affect loving.

The "other" in the "self":

Dependence:

Adult attachment style:

Passionate versus companionate love:

IV. Solving Social Problems (p. 621)

➤ How did Kurt Lewin get people to eat liver?

➤ What management ideas were adopted by the Japanese?

➤ What are the goals of environmental psychology?

➤ What was the most effective way to get students to conserve water?

➤ What are some of the goals of peace psychology?

1.

2.

3.

For Group Study

I. B. Conformity: Social Norms
I. C. Conformity: Informational Influence

The time has come to think about your study group as a group. What norms do you think govern behavior in your study group? Discuss how the group became what it is today. Does everything you do make sense? How much did individual people contribute to the formulation of the norms? How do you make decisions? When you make decisions, are minority opinions respected?

You can also ask the same types of questions about the norms that govern life on your campus. How much does each member of your group think he or she has changed by virtue of internalizing social norms?

I. C. 1. The Asch effect: Yielding to lying lines?
I. E. 2. Milgram's obedience to authority

How do you all feel about the results of these experiments? How do you think you would have behaved as subjects? These experiments teach important lessons about the power of situations. How do the members of the group feel about those lessons?

II. A. Social Perception

People are constantly making causal attributions in everyday conversation. Listen for occasions in which people are explaining why what happened happened. Have each member of the group collect 5 to 10 everyday causal explanations. Are people making the fundamental attribution error? (Do you know enough about the situation to tell?) Are people using self-serving biases?

IV. Solving Social Problems

As a group, agree on some social problem that you think you'd like to help solve. Use the knowledge of social psychology you have gained in this chapter to start to plan out a solution.

1. You work as a stand-up comedian. On some nights, the audience finds you hilarious. On other nights, you tell the very same jokes in the very same way with the very same intention to be funny, but no one laughs at all. You may be victim of

a. norm crystallization.
b. a self-fulfilling prophecy.
c. authority influence.
d. in-group bias.

2. You overhear a conversation among a group of students. One of them says something that leads you to believe that he is particularly sensitive to the normative influence of his peer group. He is most likely to have said,

a. "I'm not sure what would be the best way to act in this situation."
b. "I didn't help because I wasn't sure it was an emergency."
c. "I'm not going to go the party because I'm sure I won't have a good time."
d. "It's really important to me to be liked and accepted by my friends."

3. Professor Reilly plans to replicate the Stanford Prison Experiment. He wants to reproduce exactly the methodology of the original experiment. It's most important for him to ensure that the students

a. chosen for guard roles be more aggressive.
b. chosen for guard roles be more passive.
c. be assigned to guard and prisoner roles randomly.
d. have the option of choosing to be prisoners or guards.

4. You are working as the campaign manager for Greta Wurz in her congressional race against Polly Badd (who currently holds the position). If you want to get people to shift their support from Badd to Wurz, you might pay Badd supporters _____ to tell you what they _____ about her.

a. $20; like
b. $1; like
c. $20; dislike
d. $1; dislike

5. You are reading descriptions of decisions made by ten small groups of people. Some of the decisions immediately strike you as more thoughtful and creative. You are willing to guess that the more thoughtful groups

a. included someone who defended a minority opinion.
b. were willing to abide consistently by group norms.
c. were more affected by informational influence processes.
d. agreed without any dissent on an obvious solution.

6. In a social psychology lecture, the professor tells you a story about a time when she was invited to a birthday party by a friend. Her car broke down along the way so she never got to the party. Since that time, her ex-friend always tells people that she is "very unreliable." Your professor's story is an example of _____ at work.

a. normative influence processes
b. a total situation
c. a self-fulfilling prophecy
d. the fundamental attribution error

7. You are trying to decide whether to get a $200 VCR or a $300 VCR. While you are trying to make up your mind, the salesperson points to the $300 VCR and says, "If you buy the better model, I'll give you a free three-pack of blank video tapes." This salesperson is acquainted with the use of _____ as a marketing technique.

a. modeling
b. scarcity
c. reciprocity
d. commitment

8. In Stanley Milgram's research, what typically happened when the teacher (the experimental subject) began to dissent verbally with the experimenter's instructions to continue administering shocks?

a. The subjects refused to administer any more shocks.
b. The experimenter allowed the subject to stop.
c. The subjects continued to give higher shocks.
d. The experimenter threatened the subjects so that they would continue.

9. In Solomon Asch's experiments on conformity he found that

a. the presence of an ally greatly reduced conformity.
b. most subjects conformed on a majority of occasions.
c. the discrepancy between the correct and incorrect line did not influence the rate of conformity.
d. all subject conformed on at least one occasion.

10. Research on alcohol use at Princeton University suggests that

a. older students put pressure on younger students to adopt their level of drinking.
b. men believe that women drink more than they should.
c. perceptions of social norms sometimes differ from the actual norms.
d. social norms have less of an effect on older than younger students.

11. Your friend Sadie has invited you to a party. Unknown to you, Sadie has told all the other guests that you are painfully shy and introverted. You stay at the party for about an hour. Is it likely that the other guests will still believe you to be introverted at the end of the hour?

a. Yes--if you have a strong conception of yourself as outgoing.
b. Yes--if you have a weak conception of yourself as outgoing.
c. No--because behavioral confirmation does not affect social judgments.
d. No--because the party setting creates cognitive dissonance.

12. Which of these statements shows the effect of a self-serving bias?

a. "I would've done better on this test if I had studied a couple of more hours."
b. "I would've caught that ball if the field hadn't been so muddy."
c. "I wouldn't have won today if I didn't have such a good coach."
d. "I wouldn't have lost so much money if I'd listened to my brother's advice."

13. It would NOT be likely that a peace psychologist would try to

a. understand how nations negotiate and make judgments about each others' actions.
b. help military leaders improve techniques for dehumanizing enemies.
c. assist people in reshaping their lives to cope with democratic principles.
d. understand the forces that lead to crises between nations.

14. Your friend Matt is asking you how likely you think it is that he would help out if he were in a bystander situation. One thing you tell him that is NOT very important is whether

a. he believes the situation is an emergency.
b. other people are also present at the time of the emergency.
c. he is made to feel directly responsible for providing assistance.
d. he thinks of himself as a nice person.

15. Researchers at the University of Santa Cruz tried to determine how best to promote water conservation. They found that students followed the desired pattern of water use

a. when other students modeled the appropriate behavior.
b. when instructions were given on a prominent sign.
c. after they attended discussions sessions about water conservation.
d. after they heard a lecture about environmental issues.

16. There's a person named Dale who you'd really like to have become your friend. Which of these is NOT a good strategy for making that happen?

a. You could try to spend a lot of time in places where you know Dale hangs out.
b. You could try to disagree with Dale on some issues so that you earn a reputation as a free thinker.
c. You could try to make yourself appear more physically attractive to Dale.
d. You could try to do a series of small favors for Dale so that it's clear you wish to be friends.

17. Harold Kelley's covariation principle

a. predicts that people will be less prejudiced if they interact more.
b. explores the relationship between situational factors and bystander intervention.
c. concerns the way in which people make causal attributions about events.
d. explains the transmission of social norms across generations.

18. Which of the following questions will best allow you to predict whether someone will stay in a loving relationship?

a. Is companionate love more important to you than passionate love?
b. Could your important needs be satisfied by someone else?
c. Do you share similar opinions with your partner?
d. Do you consider yourself to be physically attractive?

19. In Kurt Lewin's research on group dynamics, _____ leadership produced groups that were inefficient and did poor quality work.

a. democratic
b. laissez-faire
c. indulgent
d. autocratic

20. You are asked to help design summer camp activities that will reduce tension between black and white campers. You should recommend activities that

a. allow the groups to express their aggression in safe ways.
b. require the groups to spend time together.
c. require cooperative action by the groups.
d. allow each group to perceive the other as a minimal group.

Practice Test ②

1. Shakespeare wrote that "one man in his time may play many parts." Social psychologists refer to these "parts" as

a. social roles.
b. social goals.
c. social norms.
d. demand characteristics.

2. A _____ group is a formal or informal group from which an individual derives attitudes and standards of acceptable behavior, and to which the individual refers for information and support for a given lifestyle.

a. standardized
b. social
c. crystallized
d. reference

3. According to the study of Kurt Lewin and his colleagues, bullies who identify scapegoats among their classmates to use as targets for their hostility and aggression are most likely to be found in the classes of teachers who use a(n) _____ leadership style.

a. autocratic
b. democratic
c. laissez-faire
d. authoritative

4. When you answer the telephone, you are asked to make a minimal contribution to your school alumni fund. You agree to the requested amount. The next year, the amount that is requested is much larger. This is similar to the sales technique known as

a. commitment.
b. scarcity.
c. reciprocity.
d. entrapment.

5. When Fritz Heider suggested that all people are "intuitive psychologists," he was expressing his belief that people

a. generally do not agree with the Freudian perspective on behavior.
b. try to figure others out and what causes their behavior.
c. prefer inductive reasoning to deductive reasoning.
d. respond on the basis of emotions and "hunches."

6. Isabel expected Hunter to be self-centered, so when she asked him questions about himself, his willingness to talk so much about himself was not surprising. Isabel's conclusions that her expectations were correct is an example of

a. an adult attachment style.
b. reciprocity.
c. behavioral confirmation.
d. mere exposure.

7. When Juanita does well on a test, she immediately takes the credit, saying that she did well because she studied hard or because she is a "brain." When she does poorly, however, she blames the teacher for making up an "impossible" test, or her roommates for interrupting her study. Juanita is demonstrating

a. the fundamental attribution error.
b. the Pygmalion effect.
c. prejudice.
d. the self-serving bias.

8. In the meeting with the other executives, Ms. Kim is focusing attention on the motion that has just been presented. While others simply accept what is said, she consistently brings up important, relevant ideas that contradict the majority view. Based on the research on minority influence, Ms. Kim's behavior is likely to result in

a. a more thoughtful analysis by the other group members.
b. a strengthening of the "status quo."
c. an increased likelihood that those present will forget the information that Ms. Kim presents.
d. resentment and ridicule by the other members of the group.

9. In a series of experiments on prejudice that were described in the textbook, children in Holland might have said, "She is not very nice because

a. her father is a farmer."
b. her socks are not the same color as her dress."
c. her family came from Germany."
d. she writes on blue paper with a blue pen."

10. The most accurate description of the results obtained by Solomon Asch in his studies of conformity is that usually subjects _____ conform, and the number of those who always conform is _____ the number of those who never conform.

a. do; much greater than
b. do; about the same as
c. do not; about the same as
d. do not; much greater than

11. Dick and Dee-Dee have been involved in a loving relationship for a short period of time. Ralph and Alice have been involved for many years. Dick and Dee-Dee's relationship is more likely to be characterized as _____ love; Ralph and Alice's relationship is more likely to be called _____ love.

a. positive; negative
b. attached; sad
c. pragmatic; erotic
d. passionate; companionate

12. In an experiment by Robert Rosenthal that was described in the textbook, elementary school teachers were led to believe that some of their pupils were "academic spurters" who would show unusual gains during the academic year. The outcome of this study demonstrated the importance of

a. cognitive dissonance.
b. the self-fulfilling prophecy.
c. self-perception theory.
d. interpersonal attraction.

13. Based on the findings of an experiment on bystander intervention that is described in the textbook, if you are at the airport and leave your suitcase long enough to make a telephone call, you should

a. tie it to a chair with your belt or shoelaces.
b. ask someone to "keep an eye on it."
c. put a note on it saying that you will return shortly.
d. sit in the smoking section to take advantage of the "outcast effect."

14. The tendency of people to believe that the subjects in Milgram's experiments were sadistic, or that people who do not intervene in emergencies are apathetic, are both examples of

a. the fundamental attribution error.
b. self-serving biases.
c. self-fulfilling prophecies.
d. cognitive dissonance.

15. There are five houses on Mirth Street, with the street addresses of 10, 18, 24, 36, and 44. Based on the research on interpersonal attraction, the members of the family that lives at 18 Mirth Street are most likely to like people who live
a. in another town.
b. on another street in the same town.
c. at 44 Mirth Street.
d. at 10 Mirth Street.

16. Which of the following people will be most motivated to reduce cognitive dissonance?
a. Edie, who decided at the last minute to go to a movie.
b. Henny, who always gets a warm response to the jokes that he tells.
c. Muriel, who completed a "stop-smoking" program but has started smoking again.
d. Justin, who was a volunteer campaign worker for a successful political candidate.

17. The authors of the textbook suggest that one deterrent to behaving in the blindly obedient manner exhibited by many of the subjects in Milgram's research is to

a. be willing to be a "team player" if that behavior is required of you.
b. institute psychological training programs to make people less evil.
c. leave the decision making up to those who are in authority.
d. be aware that situational forces are powerful enough to affect you.

18. The results of Stanley Milgram's obedience experiments revealed all of the following EXCEPT that

a. the majority of subjects obeyed the authority fully.
b. nearly two-thirds of the subjects delivered the maximum 450 volts.
c. the subjects behaved in a way contrary to psychiatrists' predictions.
d. those subjects who dissented verbally refused to administer shocks.

19. When Louie goes on a campus tour with his older brother, he notices that all of the students are wearing turned-around baseball caps. If he asks his brother why they are doing so, his brother should say that this is an example of

a. conformity.
b. obedience.
c. co-variation.
d. a demand characteristic.

20. One day your sister comes home from school happy as a lark. She received an "A" on her geography test. In applying the covariation principle to understand the cause of her good grade, the "consensus" dimension refers to whether

a. she receives "A's" in most of her courses.
b. she has received "A's" consistently from this teacher in the past.
c. most other people taking the test also received "A's."
d. she studied especially hard for this particular test.

Answers, Practice Test ①

1. a (p. 588) The idea here is that each audience develops a norm for whether they're going to think you're funny or not (because, presumably, each audience includes people who could go either way).

2. d (p. 588)

3. c (p. 585)

4. d (p. 613) If they list what they dislike about Badd for only $1, they might think "I really don't like her as much as I thought I did."

5. a (p. 593)

6. d (p. 608)

7. c (p. 605)

8. c (p. 597)

9. a (p. 593)

10. c (p. 590)

11. b (p. 612)

12. b (p. 609)

13. b (p. 624) Peace psychologists are typically interested in working to decrease feelings of animosity.

14. d (pp. 600-603) Research suggests that personality plays a small role in bystander intervention.

15. a (p. 623)

16. b (pp. 618-619)

17. c (p. 607)

18. b (p. 620)

19. b (p. 595)

20. c (p. 617) Just spending time together (option b) will often not be enough.

Answers, Practice Test ②

1. a (p. 585)

2. d (p. 589)

3. a (p. 595)

4. a (p. 605) People who agree to small requests are more likely to subsequently agree to a large request.

5. b (p. 607)

6. c (p. 612) Behavioral confirmation labels the process by which someone's expectations about another person actually influence the second person to behave in ways that confirm the original hypothesis.

7. d (p. 609)

8. a (p. 593)

9. d (p. 616)

10. c (p. 593)

11. d (p. 621)

12. b (pp. 610-611)

13. b (p. 603)

14. a (p. 608) People tend to overestimate dispositional factors and to underestimate situational ones when searching for the cause of behavior.

15. d (p. 618)

16. c (p. 613)

17. d (p. 600)

18. d (p. 597)

19. a (p. 587)

20. c (p. 607)

📖 Chapter 17

Psychological Disorders

📑 Chapter Outline

Section	What you need to know
I. The Nature of Psychological Disorders	
A. Deciding What is Abnormal	What are the many definitions of *abnormal*?
B. Historical Perspectives	How have concepts of abnormality changed over time?
1. Emergence of the medical model	
2. Emergence of psychological models	
C. The Etiology of Psychopathology	How do different theoretical perspectives specify the causes of psychopathology?
1. Biological approaches	
2. Psychological approaches	
II. Classifying Psychological Disorders	
A. Goals of Classification	Why is classification useful?
B. DSM-IV	What are the standards for diagnosis?

Section	What you need to know

    1. Evolution of diagnostic categories
    2. Is DSM-IV effective?

III. Major Types of Psychological Disorders

    A. Personality Disorders   What personality traits are maladaptive?

    B. Dissociative Disorders   What happens when people lose control of their identity?

    C. Anxiety Disorders: Types   In what different ways are people affected by severe anxiety?

        1. Generalized anxiety disorder
        2. Panic disorder
        3. Phobias
        4. Obsessive-compulsive disorders
        5. Posttraumatic stress disorder

    D. Anxiety Disorders: Causes   How do different perspectives explain anxiety disorders?

        1. Biological
        2. Psychodynamic
        3. Behavioral
        4. Cognitive

    E. Mood Disorders: Types   In what different ways do people experience disturbances in mood?

        1. Unipolar depression
        2. Bipolar disorder

    F. Mood Disorders: Causes   How do different perspectives explain mood disorders?

        1. Biological
        2. Psychodynamic
        3. Behavioral
        4. Cognitive

Section	What you need to know
G. Sex Differences in Depression	Why do more women than men suffer from depression?
H. Depression and Suicide	How can depression lead to suicide?

IV. Schizophrenic Disorders

Section	What you need to know
A. Major Types of Schizophrenia	In what different ways do people experience losses of reality?

1. Disorganized type
2. Catatonic type
3. Paranoid type
4. Undifferentiated type
5. Residual type

Section	What you need to know
B. Causes of Schizophrenia	How do different perspectives explain schizophrenic disorders?

1. Genetic approaches
2. Brain function and biological markers
3. Family interaction and communication
4. Cognitive processes

Section	What you need to know
Close-up: The Insanity Defense	When should people not be held responsible for their crimes?

V. Judging People as Abnormal

Section	What you need to know
A. The Problem of Objectivity	Who gets to decide what is abnormal?
B. The Problem of Stigma	Why is mental illness stigmatized?

Guided Study

I. The Nature of Psychological Disorders (p. 628)

➤ Define psychopathological functioning.

➤ What is the subject matter for the field of abnormal psychology?

I. A. Deciding What is Abnormal (p. 629)

➤ Summarize each of the seven criteria for abnormality.

1.

2.

3.

4.

5.

6.

7.

I. B. Historical Perspectives (p. 630)

➤ Summarize the historical interpretation of mental illness as possession.

➤ What was thought to cause hysteria? What may really have affected the "witches" of Salem?

1. Summarize the roles these scholars played in the emergence of the medical model.

Philippe Pinel:

Emil Kraepelin:

2. Summarize the roles these scholars played in the emergence of psychological models.

Franz Mesmer:

Jean Charcot:

I. C. The Etiology of Psychopathology (p. 633)

➤ Define etiology.

➤ What are the main assumptions of each of these approaches?

1. Biological approaches

2. Psychological approaches

Psychodynamic:

Behavioral:

Cognitive:

➤ What is an interactionist perspective?

II. A. Goals of Classification (p. 635)

➤ What are three goals for a classification system?

1.

2.

3.

➤ Describe the emergence of DSM-IV.

➤ What are the five DSM-IV axes? (See Table 17.1.)

1.

2.

3.

4.

5.

1. How have diagnostic categories changed over time?

2. What can be said so far about the effectiveness of DSM-IV?

III. Major Types of Psychological Disorders (p. 638)

➤ Review the categories of disorders that are not treated at length in this chapter.

➤ What is the source for prevalence statistics used in this chapter? What is meant by comorbidity?

III. A. *Personality Disorders (p. 639)*

➤ What is a personality disorder?

➤ What are the main features of each of these disorders?

Paranoid personality disorder:

Antisocial personality disorder:

Histrionic personality disorder:

Narcissistic personality disorder:

➤ Why are personality disorders controversial?

III. B. *Dissociative Disorders (p. 639)*

➤ What are dissociative disorders? What is dissociative amnesia?

➤ What are the major features of dissociative identity disorder (DID)?

➤ What role might self-hypnosis play in the etiology of DID?

➤ What role might childhood physical and sexual abuse play in the etiology of DID?

III. C. Anxiety Disorders: Types (p. 641)

➤ Summarize the major symptoms of each anxiety disorder.

1. Generalized anxiety disorder

2. Panic disorder

Agoraphobia

3. Phobias

Social phobias

Specific phobias

4. Obsessive-compulsive disorders

5. Posttraumatic stress disorder (How does childhood sexual abuse relate to PTSD?)

III. D. Anxiety Disorders: Causes (p. 646)

➤ How does each of these theoretical perspectives explain the onset of anxiety disorders?

1. Biological

What is the preparedness hypothesis?

What effects do drugs have?

What does genetic evidence suggest?

2. Psychodynamic

3. Behavioral

4. Cognitive

III. E. Moods Disorders: Types (p. 648)

➤ Summarize the major symptoms of each mood disorder.

1. Unipolar depression

2. Bipolar disorder

III. F. Mood Disorders: Causes (p. 650)

➤ How does each of these theoretical perspectives explain the onset of anxiety disorders?

1. Biological

What role do neurotransmitters play?

What does genetic evidence suggest?

What is seasonal affective disorder and what is one way of treating it?

2. Psychodynamic

3. Behavioral

4. Cognitive

Summarize the theories of these scholars.

Aaron Beck:

Martin Seligman (mention the research findings on learned helplessness and explanatory style):

III. G. Sex Differences in Depression (p. 654)

➤ Summarize Susan Nolen-Hoeksema's explanation for sex differences in depression.

III. H. Depression and Suicide (p. 654)

➤ Summarize sex differences and racial differences with respect to attempted and successful suicides.

➤ What factors lead to particularly high suicide rates among adolescents?

➤ Why are Native Americans at particular risk for suicide?

IV. Schizophrenic Disorders (p. 656)

➤ What are the major symptoms of schizophrenic disorders?   Distinguish between hallucinations and delusions.

➤ Why does this disorder appear to be universal?

IV. A. Major Types of Schizophrenia (p. 657)

➤ Summarize the major symptoms of each type of schizophrenia.

1. Disorganized type

2. Catatonic type

3. Paranoid type (mention the different types of delusions)

4. Undifferentiated type

5. Residual type

➤ Summarize what each of these areas of research contributes to an understanding of the causes of schizophrenia.

1. Genetic approaches (include the diathesis-stress hypothesis)

2. Brain function and biological markers (include the dopamine hypothesis)

3. Family interaction and communication (include double binds)

4. Cognitive processes

Close-up: The Insanity Defense (p. 665)

➤ What is insanity? How did the legal system's first use of the concept of insanity arise?

➤ What standard was applied to John Hinckley? Under what circumstances will Hinckley be set free?

➤ How often does the insanity defense succeed?

V. A. The Problem of Objectivity (p. 664)

➤ Summarize the evidence that the definition of abnormality sometimes depends on the person making the judgment.

➤ What did David Rosenhan's research show?

➤ What is the view of Thomas Szasz?

➤ What is the view of R. D. Laing?

➤ What is the contextual or ecological model?

➤ Why does DSM-IV emphasize personal distress?

V. B. The Problem of Stigma (p. 667)

➤ Why should mental illness not be considered deviant?

➤ What is a stigma? How does the concept apply to mental illness?

➤ What consequences does bias toward the mentally ill have?

For Group Study

I. A. Deciding What is Abnormal
V. Judging People as Abnormal

The text gives a series of different examples of behavior that could be defined as abnormal. For each criterion, discuss examples from your own lives. This exercise should help you better understand what is meant by each criterion. It should also allow you to consider the ideas presented at the end of the chapter about how much abnormal behavior depends on context and who is making the judgment. How do you decide when behavior is abnormal in ways that begin to be problematic?

III. Major Types of Psychological Disorders

To master the material in this chapter, it may be a good idea for each member of the group to become an "expert" on one (or more, depending on the size of your group) of the disorders. Everyone should read the chapter, of course, but then one individual should be responsible for helping the other members learn the symptoms and causes of each major category of psychopathology. An alternative way to structure your study would be to have different group members be "experts" on the different categories of explanation (biological, psychodynamic, etc.). Studying in this way should prompt each of you to find the most efficient way to master a particular portion of the material.

III. G. Sex Differences in Depression
III. H. Depression and Suicide

Discuss the material in these two sections as it applies to your own lives. Because depression is so common, and because it can lead to suicide, it is particularly important that you discuss these topics in a context of social support.

IV. A. Major Types of Schizophrenia

How easy is it for you to understand the symptoms of different types of schizophrenia? As a group discuss what it might be like to live with each symptom of the disorder.

Close-up: The Insanity Defense

Discuss the insanity defense. Do group members think that some criminals really are "insane"? What criteria can be used to make that judgment?

1. In the aftermath of tragedies like the Oklahoma City bombing, psychologists are particularly careful to monitor people for symptoms of _____ disorders.

a. generalized anxiety
b. posttraumatic stress
c. obsessive-compulsive
d. panic

2. In _____ type schizophrenia, the patient is free from major positive symptoms but shows minor positive symptoms or negative symptoms such as flat emotion.

a. disorganized
b. paranoid
c. residual
d. catatonic

3. It may be a mistake to label psychological disorders as deviant because

a. many people who suffer from psychological disorders fully recover.
b. about 50% of young and middle-aged adults in the United States have suffered from some mental disorder.
c. many people have family members who are affected by mental illness.
d. personal distress is the most important indication of mental illness.

4. Lisa always has to be the center of attention. When she is not the center of attention, she will often do something overly dramatic or emotional to regain that spot. You might suspect that Lisa suffers from _____ personality disorder.

a. narcissistic
b. antisocial
c. paranoid
d. histrionic

5. Luis will not visit other people's homes because he fears that they may not have searched carefully enough to make sure there are no spiders on the premises. It sounds like Luis suffers from

a. a social phobia.
b. agoraphobia.
c. allurophobia.
d. a specific phobia.

6. You are sent the medical records for a women who has been admitted to a psychological treatment center. Unfortunately, the record fails to mention the diagnosis. You need to find the patient, so your first guess it to call the unit in which patients with _____ are treated.

a. bipolar disorder
b. schizophrenia
c. unipolar depression
d. dissociate identity disorder

7. The first scholar to create a comprehensive classification system for psychological disorders was

a. Philippe Pinel.
b. Franz Mesmer.
c. Jean Charcot.
d. Emil Kraepelin.

8. _____ theories suggest that phobias are maintained by the reduction in anxiety that occurs when a person withdraws from the feared situation.

a. Behavioral
b. Cognitive
c. Biological
d. Psychodynamic

9. The pattern of bipolar disorder among members of the Amish community in Pennsylvania suggests that _____ contribute(s) to the incidence of mood disorders.

a. social isolation
b. alcoholism
c. genetic factors
d. unconscious conflicts

10. Which of the following is NOT an appropriate conclusion from research on biological aspects of schizophrenia?

a. The brain's ventricles are enlarged in many individuals with schizophrenia.
b. Schizophrenia is associated with a relative excess of the neurotransmitter dopamine.
c. Many people with schizophrenia have an eye-movement dysfunction when they scan the visual field.
d. The risk of schizophrenia does not change when more than one parent has suffered from the disorder.

11. What evidence suggests that the families of people with schizophrenia can affect the course of the disorder?

a. Parents of children with schizophrenia learn to cope with double binds.
b. Parents of children with schizophrenia reinforce those children when they experience attention deficits.
c. Symptoms are reduced when parents are less critical and hostile toward a child with schizophrenia.
d. Symptoms are increased even when parents show greater responsiveness and sensitivity to their child.

12. Raphael has been unable to get a job because he is desperately afraid of job interviews. He is able to function just fine in non-interview settings. The criterion for abnormality that Raphael's behavior meets is

a. irrationality.
b. unpredictability.
c. violation of moral standards.
d. maladaptiveness.

13. People who suffer from schizophrenia often experience hallucinations or delusions. Hallucinations are _____ whereas delusions are _____.

a. false sensory experiences; irrational beliefs
b. irrational beliefs; distortions of emotions
c. false sensory experiences; distortions of emotions
d. irrational beliefs; false sensory experiences

14. You have been asked to give a lecture on Dissociative Identity Disorder (DID). One of the facts you are very likely to mention is that

a. DID is very similar to schizophrenia.
b. people who experience DID almost all report physical or sexual abuse.
c. multiple personalities serve no known function.
d. sufferers often experience their multiple personalities simultaneously.

15. Aaron Beck's cognitive triad of depression does NOT include negative views of

a. the future.
b. oneself.
c. ongoing experiences.
d. others.

16. After attempting to assassinate U.S. president Ronald Reagan, John Hinckley was found "not guilty by virtue of insanity." The jury believed that Hinckley

a. was incapable of controlling his behavior.
b. did not know that what he was doing was wrong.
c. was unaware that he was shooting a real gun.
d. had been cured by the time of the trial.

17. You have just heard a news story about the rate of suicide among adolescents in the United States. One fact you are likely to have heard is that

a. very few adolescents reveal their suicidal feelings before they take their lives.
b. African-American youths are less likely to commit suicide then are white youths.
c. men are more likely to attempt suicide than are women.
d. the suicide rate has gone down steadily since the mid-1970s.

18. In ancient times, mental illness was often interpreted as

a. possession by demons.
b. a gift from the gods.
c. poisoning by unclean substances.
d. a return to an animal state.

19. You are a clinician using the DSM-IV classification system. If one of your clients were mentally retarded, you would code that on

a. Axis I.
b. Axis II.
c. Axis IV.
d. Axis V.

20. In the contextual or ecological model, psychological disorders are viewed as

a. side-effects of toxic chemicals in the contemporary environment.
b. the products of dysfunctional family relationships.
c. mismatches between a person's abilities and the norms of society.
d. the consequences of neurotransmitter imbalances in the brain.

Practice Test ②

1. Dr. Simpson typifies the viewpoint of current researchers who are attempting to understand psychopathology. It is most likely that Dr. Simpson's perspective can be classified as

a. psychodynamic.
b. behavioral.
c. cognitive.
d. interactionist.

2. Traveling back once again in your time machine, you find yourself in a lecture hall listening to one of the first presentations by Sigmund Freud on the etiology of psychological disorders. You are one of the few people in the room who anticipates that Freud's suggestion that psychological disorders are the result of

a. negative self-attributions.
b. early childhood experiences.
c. interpersonal relationships.
d. social and cultural norms.

3. Dr. Dynamo believes that the psychodynamic model provides a convincing explanation for the etiology of anxiety disorders. You would expect that Dr. Dynamo would emphasize the importance of
a. unconscious conflict.
b. obsessive thoughts.
c. reinforcement.
d. genes.

4. Being aware of the importance of explanatory style in predicting depression, you have begun to listen to comments that your classmates make when they receive bad grades on tests. Which of the following explanations would be most likely to be associated with depression?

a. "I'm stupid and I'll never succeed at anything."
b. "These tests are so unfair nobody can expect to do well."
c. "The teacher gave me a bad grade because I ask questions in class."
d. "Next time maybe I'll try studying instead of partying."

5. Chip and Dale are identical twins, and Castor and Pollux are fraternal twins. If Castor and Chip are afflicted by a mood disorder, you can expect that, of the remaining twin pairs,

a. there is a better chance that Pollux will have a mood disorder.
b. there is a better chance that Dale will have a mood disorder.
c. there is an equal chance that Pollux and Dale will have mood disorders.
d. neither Pollux nor Dale is likely to have a mood disorder.

6. Cliff appears not to like people. He won't go to parties, doesn't eat out, absolutely will not use public transportation, and seems irrationally afraid of all of these situations. If you were to diagnose Cliff's problem, you would say that he has

a. posttraumatic stress disorder.
b. a social phobia.
c. obsessive-compulsive disorder.
d. a mood disorder.

7. Research on psychopathology from a cross-cultural perspective leads to the conclusion that schizophrenia

a. does not occur in primitive cultures that stress group goals and mutuality.
b. is a product of industrialization.
c. decreases in frequency as environmental and interpersonal stress increases.
d. occurs in all societies.

8. A complication in understanding what causes schizophrenia is that

a. the presence of hallucinations and delusions makes communicating with schizophrenics difficult.
b. schizophrenia may actually be a group of disorders, each with a distinct cause.
c. no factor has yet been directly linked with the presence of schizophrenia.
d. the DSM-IV does not present specific criteria for the diagnosis of schizophrenia.

9. In the context of the classification of psychological disorders, "DSM-IV" refers to the

a. federal law in which abnormal behavior is defined.
b. disorder known as sadomasochism, listed on the fourth level of the classification system.
c. widely accepted classification scheme developed by the American Psychiatric Association.
d. type of degree required by the national board that certifies practitioners.

10. According to the theory of _____, depressed people have three types of negative cognitions, which he or she calls the "cognitive triad" of depression.

a. Aaron Beck
b. Martin Seligman
c. Susan Nolen-Hoeksema
d. Edwin Shneidman

11. A man does not like the feel of clothing, so he typically walks around naked in his yard. His behavior upsets his neighbors and passersby. According to the criterion of _____, the man's behavior is "abnormal."

a. personal distress.
b. maladaptiveness.
c. unpredictability.
d. observer discomfort.

12. They know Sean well at the police station. Although only in his twenties, he has been arrested many times for a variety of unlawful behaviors. He usually denies any involvement, but eventually says that his victims are losers, and that their loss is his gain. Sean would most likely be classified with _____ disorder.

a. anxiety
b. posttraumatic stress
c. antisocial personality
d. histrionic personality

13. Susan Nolen-Hoeksema has suggested that the sex difference in the incidence of unipolar depression is related to

a. the economic and social disadvantages of being female.
b. biological differences between the sexes.
c. differences in the way men and women respond to negative moods.
d. bias in the diagnoses of male therapists.

14. In their explanations of the etiology of psychopathology, behavioral theorists are more likely than psychodynamic theorists to focus on

a. the present rather than the past.
b. internal psychological phenomena.
c. early childhood experiences.
d. hypothetical processes.

15. After feeling great yesterday, Tabitha feels really depressed today. She just found out that a distant relative is gravely ill, she got a bad grade on a test, and her boyfriend of two years has started dating someone else. If you were a psychologist, you would conclude that Tabitha probably has

a. normal depression.
b. bipolar disorder.
c. unipolar depression.
d. clinical depression.

16. Imagine that you are a behavioral psychologist. A person you know has such a fear of flying insects that she refuses to go outdoors in the summer. If asked to explain her phobia, you would most likely say that she

a. is being reinforced for not going outdoors with a reduction in anxiety.
b. believes that flying insects are symbolic of freedom from dependency.
c. clearly has a neurological disorder that is causing her symptoms.
d. needs to be shown that her perception that flying insects are dangerous is distorted.

17. Popularized in books and movies, and sometimes known as "split personality," _____ is a disorder in which two or more distinct personalities exist within the same individual.

a. dissociative amnesia
b. schizophrenia
c. bipolar disorder
d. dissociative identity disorder

18. One of the findings of the National Comorbidity Study was that

a. the number of individuals suffering from a psychological disorder has been steadily declining.
b. people who have experienced one disorder often experience others in their lifetimes.
c. the system of classification of psychological disorders should be revised on an annual basis.
d. there is no available information on the prevalence of different disorders.

19. Although she finds them repugnant, a patient of Dr. Strange is plagued by unwanted and uncontrollable sexual thoughts and images. This is an example of a(n)

a. compulsion.
b. hallucination.
c. delusion.
d. obsession.

20. Suppose that someone you know has been talking to you about committing suicide. He seems distressed, and has written to his friends about his intentions. It would make most sense if you

a. take him seriously and try to get immediate professional help.
b. try to determine if he is the "suicidal type."
c. act cheerfully, as though nothing is happening.
d. ignore the person, as suicide threats are rarely carried out.

Answers, Practice Test ①

1. b (p. 645)

2. c (p. 659)

3. b (p. 668)

4. d (p. 639)

5. d (p. 644)

6. c (pp. 648 and 654) Unipolar depression is the most common form of psychopathology among women. Therefore, it's your best first guess.

7. d (p. 632)

8. a (p. 647)

9. c (p. 650)

10. d (pp. 659-662) People are more likely to suffer from schizophrenia if both parents have, rather than if just one parent has.

11. c (p. 663)

12. d (p. 629)

13. a (pp. 656-657)

14. b (p. 641)

15. d (p. 653)

16. a (p. 665)

17. b (p. 655)

18. a (p. 630)

19. b (pp. 636-637)

20. c (p. 667)

Answers, Practice Test ②

1. d (p. 635)

2. b (p. 634) In the psychodynamic model, early childhood experiences shape both normal and abnormal behavior.

3. a (p. 646)

4. a (p. 653)

5. b (p. 650) Studies of twins show that when one twin is afflicted by a mood disorder, the chances are much greater that the second twin will have the disorder if the twins are identical than if the twins are fraternal.

6. b (p. 643)

7. d (p. 657)

8. b (p. 664)

9. c (p. 636)

10. a (pp. 652-653)

11. d (pp. 629-630)

12. c (p. 639)

13. c (p. 654)

14. a (p. 634) Behavioral theorists focus on the current behavior and the current conditions or reinforcements that sustain behavior.

15. a (pp. 648-649)

16. a (p. 647)

17. d (p. 640)

18. b (p. 638)

19. d (p. 644) Obsessions are thoughts, images, or impulses that recur or persist despite a person's efforts to suppress them.

20. a (p. 655)

🗒 Chapter Outline

Section	What you need to know

I. The Therapeutic Context

    A. Goals and Major Therapies   What are the goals of the major categories of therapies?

    B. Entering Therapy   Why do people enter therapy?

    C. Therapists and Therapeutic Settings   In what settings would you find different types of therapists?

    D. Historical and Cultural Contexts   How did contemporary treatment of mental illness evolve?

        1. History of Western treatment
        2. Cultural symbols and rituals of curing

II. Psychodynamic Therapies

    A. Freudian Psychoanalysis   What therapeutic procedures did Freud devise?

        1. The origins of the talking cure
        2. Free association and catharsis
        3. Resistance

Section	What you need to know

4. Dream analysis
    5. Transference and
       countertransference	

B. Neo-Freudian Therapies	What did Freud's followers add to his practices?
III. Behavior Therapies	
A. Counterconditioning	How can a maladaptive behavior be replaced?

1. Systematic desensitization
       and other
       exposure therapies
    2. Aversion therapy	

B. Contingency Management	How can behavior be changed by modifying its consequences?
1. Positive reinforcement strategies	
2. Extinction strategies	
C. Social-Learning Therapy	How are models used to promote therapeutic change?
1. Imitation of models 2. Social-skills training	
D. Generalization Techniques	How can changes be made that extend to real-life settings?
IV. Cognitive Therapies	
A. Cognitive Behavior Modification	How can therapy change thoughts about life experiences?

Section	What you need to know
B. Changing False Beliefs	How can therapy change interpretations of life events?

    1. Cognitive therapy for depression
    2. Rational-emotive therapy

V. Existential-Humanistic Therapies

A. Person-Centered Therapy	How do clients direct their own course of therapy?
B. Group Therapies	What are the advantages of group therapies?

    1. Gestalt therapy
    2. Community support groups

C. Marital and Family Therapy	How are couples and families aided by therapy?
Close-up: Therapy for Drinking Problems	How can alcoholics best be helped?

VI. Biomedical Therapies

A. Psychosurgery and Electroconvulsive Therapy	What types of biomedical therapies do not involve drugs?
B. Drug Therapy	How is the brain affected by psychoactive drugs?

    1. Antipsychotic drugs
    2. Antidepressant drugs
    3. Antianxiety drugs
    4. When is drug therapy necessary?

VII. Does Therapy Work?

Section	What you need to know
A. Evaluating Therapeutic Effectiveness	How can researchers determine whether therapies have been successful?
B. Depression Treatment Evaluations	What have comparisons between depression treatments demonstrated?
C. Building Better Therapies	How do researchers devise new therapies?
D. Prevention Strategies	How might some mental illnesses be prevented?

VIII. A Personal Endnote

Guided Study

☞ ☞ ☞ ☞

I. A. Goals and Major Therapies (p. 672)

➤ List and explain the four goals of therapy.

1.

2.

3.

4.

➤ What are the major categories of therapy? (Note that this section is a preview for the rest of the chapter.)

I. B. Entering Therapy (p. 673)

➤ Why do people go into therapy? Why *don't* people go into therapy as soon as they should?

➤ Which therapists use "patient" and which use "client"?

I. C. Therapists and Therapeutic Settings (p. 674)

Summarize the approaches and settings for each of these types of therapists.

Counseling psychologists:

Clinical social workers:

Pastoral counselors:

Clinical psychologists:

Psychiatrists:

Psychoanalysts:

1. Summarize the history of Western treatment. What roles did Philippe Pinel, J. C. Heinroth, and Clifford Beers play?

2. How do non-Western views contrast with Western views of treatment?

What is shamanism?

What are ritual healing ceremonies?

➤ Of what importance is repression?

➤ Why is psychodynamic therapy called insight therapy?

1. In what context did Joseph Breuer develop the talking cure?

What was the fate of Bertha Pappenheim (Anna O.)?

2. Explain free association and catharsis.

3. Why is resistance so important in psychoanalysis?

4. What roles do manifest and latent content play in dream analysis?

5. What is the significance of transference and countertransference?

II. B. Neo-Freudian Therapies (p. 681)

➤ Summarize the ideas of these neo-Freudian thinkers.

Harry Stack Sullivan:

Karen Horney:

Heinz Kohut:

III. Behavior Therapies (p. 682)

➤ Does behavior therapy lead to symptom substitution?

III. A. Counterconditioning (p. 682)

➤ What is counterconditioning? Summarize Mary Cover Jones's early use of this logic.

1. What was Joseph Wolpe's theory of reciprocal inhibition?

What are the three steps of systematic desensitization?

What is implosion therapy? Give examples.

What is flooding therapy? Give examples.

What common element is shared by these therapies? How can such therapies be applied to obsessive-compulsive disorders?

Summarize the technique of eye movement desensitization and reprocessing.

2. How does aversion therapy work? Give an example.

III. B. Contingency Management (p. 686)

1. How is positive reinforcement used to change behaviors? Give examples.

2. How is extinction used to change behaviors? Give examples.

III. C. Social-Learning Therapy (p. 687)

1. How are models used to bring about behavior change?

Contrast participant modeling therapy and symbolic modeling therapy.

2. What is the goal of social-skills training? Why is this an important goal?

What is behavioral rehearsal?

Has social skills training been effective?

III. D. *Generalization Techniques (p. 690)*

➤ Why is generalization important?

➤ Give examples of generalization techniques at work.

IV. *Cognitive Therapies (p. 691)*

➤ What is the goal of cognitive therapy?

IV. A. *Cognitive Behavior Modification (p. 692)*

➤ Why are self-statements central to cognitive behavior modification?

➤ How does this type of therapy work to change self-statements?

➤ How does this therapy affect self-efficacy?

IV. B. Changing False Beliefs (p. 693)

➤ What are three basic types of faulty thinking?

1. Summarize the main tactics of Aaron Beck's cognitive therapy for depression.

2. How does rational-emotive therapy attack "musturbatory" thinking?

V. Existential-Humanistic Therapies (p. 694)

➤ Why is the humanistic movement referred to as a third force in psychology?

➤ What are existential crises? What is existentialism?

➤ What accompanies the freedom to choose?

➤ What is the phenomenological view?

➤ What is the human potential movement?

V. A. Person-Centered Therapy (p. 695)

➤ What are the major assumptions of Carl Roger's therapy?

➤ What are important attributes of the therapist's approach?

V. B. Group Therapies (p. 696)

➤ What are the general advantages of group therapy?

1.

2.

3.

4.

5.

1. What therapy did Fritz Perls invent? What is its focus?

2. How did self-help groups develop and what kinds of problems do they deal with?

🖎 *Close-up: Therapy for Drinking Problems (p. 698)*

➤ Contrast the abstinence approach and the controlled drinking approach.

➤ What approaches have been effective? For what drinkers?

V. C. Marital and Family Therapy (p. 699)

➤ What makes couples counseling effective?

➤ What makes family therapy effective?

VI. A. Psychosurgery and Electroconvulsive Therapy (p. 700)

➤ What is the purpose of prefrontal lobotomies? Are they common in contemporary times?

➤ How is electroconvulsive therapy (ECT) administered? What effect does it have?

➤ Why is ECT controversial? What research results answer some of the criticisms?

VI. B. Drug Therapy (p. 702)

➤ What is psychopharmacology?

➤ Why did psychoactive drugs have such a large effect on the treatment of the mentally ill?

➤ For each group, summarize why each type of drug has the effect it does. Are there problems with the treatments?

1. Antipsychotic drugs

2. Antidepressant drugs

3. Antianxiety drugs

4. When is drug therapy necessary?

VII. A. *Evaluating Therapeutic Effectiveness (p. 705)*

➤ What challenge did Hans Eysenck issue?

➤ What is the spontaneous-remission effect? How can it be controlled for?

➤ What is placebo therapy? How can it be controlled for?

➤ What is a meta-analysis? What have meta-analyses shown about the effectiveness of psychotherapy?

VII. B. *Depression Treatment Evaluations (p. 706)*

➤ Summarize the methodology used to contrast depression treatments.

➤ What were the major results of this study?

VII. C. Building Better Therapies (p. 708)

➤ How are new therapies developed? What concerns give rise to new therapies?

VII. D. Prevention Strategies (p. 709)

➤ Define these types of prevention.

Primary prevention:

Secondary prevention:

Tertiary prevention:

➤ What is clinical ecology? In what ways has mental health care shifted its focus?

For Group Study

I. A. Goals and Major Therapies

This is another chapter for which it makes sense to have each group member become an expert on one of the major forms of therapy. Try to learn the material in each section, but also challenge your friends to create and analyze new examples.

I. B. Entering Therapy

Are you willing to discuss the circumstances in your own life that might lead you to seek therapy? Why is "entering therapy" such a big step for many people? What could be done to make it easier? Discuss the ways in which the contents of Chapter 17 and this one has changed your view about mental illness and therapy.

II. A. Freudian Psychoanalysis
III. Behavior Therapies

Table 18.2 provides a point-by-point comparison of Psychoanalytic and Behavioristic Approaches to Psychotherapy. Use this table to have a mini-debate. Choose different types of problems that affect people in real life and try to understand them with respect to both of these programs of therapy. Discuss the merits of each.

V. B. 2. Community support groups

In what sense is your study group a support group? How can participation in this sort of group enhance your mental health?

VIII. A Personal Endnote

The authors of the text express the hope that you will further pursue your interest in psychology. Discuss the types of things each of you would like to know more about. Try to come up with a list of your group's "great unanswered questions." You can approach your professor to find out what other courses are most likely to answer those questions for you. Or perhaps the time will have come to begin your own program of research. Are you ready?

1. Generalization procedures are important because they ensure that

a. clients will lose their fear of all members of a phobic category.
b. patients will extend their emotional catharses to other repressed memories.
c. self-statements will be applied to other people as well.
d. behavioral changes will endure after therapy has been terminated.

2. One of the major differences between Western and non-Western treatment of individuals with psychological disorders is that many

a. Western cultures use ritual healing ceremonies.
b. non-Western cultures attribute mental illnesses to the stresses of city living.
c. non-Western cultures do not remove mentally ill individuals from society.
d. non-Western cultures believe in the use of asylums.

3. Research with young monkeys demonstrated that they acquired a fear of snakes

a. to the greatest extent when they watched their parents showing fear.
b. to the greatest extent when they watched strangers showing fear.
c. only when they themselves interacted directly with the snakes.
d. when they interacted with real snakes, but not with toy snakes.

4. Antipsychotic drugs work by reducing the activity of the neurotransmitter _____ in the brain.

a. serotonin
b. dopamine
c. norepinephrine
d. GABA

5. Marge and Joan are sisters. If Marge is an alcoholic then the probability that Joan is also an alcoholic is

a. no higher than if Marge weren't an alcoholic.
b. highest if they are identical twins.
c. highest if they are fraternal twins.
d. lower if they also have a third sister.

6. The National Institute of Mental Health project that compared the effectiveness of different therapies for depression found that

a. the drug therapy was the least effective.
b. the placebo treatment was better than psychodynamic therapy.
c. psychodynamic and cognitive therapies were about equally effective.
d. the drug therapy was only better than the psychodynamic therapy.

7. One of the main advantages of electroconvulsive therapy over drug therapies for depression is that

a. treatment only lasts for one day.
b. it works more quickly.
c. the reasons for its effectiveness are well-understood.
d. it never produces any memory deficits.

8. Part of the recovery that patients experience when they go into therapy arises from their own expectations of healing. This is known as

a. catharsis.
b. the placebo effect.
c. spontaneous remission.
d. self-efficacy.

9. You have been trained as a family therapist. You are most likely to

a. treat each family member apart from the others.
b. focus on the one individual within the family who is most disruptive.
c. assume that family difficulties are situational rather than dispositional.
d. let family members work out their problems with minimal intervention from you.

10. Suppose you were in therapy with a psychoanalyst and he asked you to free associate. He would treat the free associations as if they were

a. random words, intended only to start you talking.
b. predetermined, with the superego providing most of the content.
c. random words, with the id providing most of the content.
d. predetermined, with important patterns lying below the surface.

11. You are setting up a mental health program in a rural community. Your goal is to identify people who are suffering from psychological disorders and try to limit the duration and severity of the disorder. Your program provides _____ prevention services.

a. primary
b. tertiary
c. rational
d. secondary

12. The theorist who rejected Freud's emphasis on the phallus and suggested that men suffer from envy of pregnancy, motherhood, breasts, and suckling was _____.

a. Heinz Kohut
b. Mary Cover Jones
c. Karen Horney
d. Bertha Pappenheim

13. One day in therapy, Willem bursts out with, "Stop treating me like a child! You're always treating me like I'm a little boy!" If the therapist has not, in fact, been treating Willem in this way, you might suspect that this is a case of

a. countertransference.
b. musturbatory thought.
c. transference.
d. resistance.

14. Suzanne is a therapist. When she offers a prognosis to a new patient she

a. identifies the probable origins of the disorder.
b. estimates the course the problem will take with and without treatment.
c. outlines the treatment she will use.
d. makes a determination of the disorder that is affecting the patient.

15. You are introduced to Sonia, who identifies herself as a type of therapist. She goes on to explain that she is particularly sensitive to the social context of people's problems. You guess that Sonia is a

a. clinical social worker.
b. pastoral counselor.
c. psychiatrist.
d. counseling psychologist.

16. In _____ therapy, therapists strive to be nondirective; they do not interpret or instruct the client.

a. insight
b. existential
c. rational-emotive
d. person-centered

17. Luis would like to be rid of his phobia for spiders. Which type of therapy is likely to put him in contact with an actual spider earliest in the course of treatment?

a. systematic desensitization
b. aversion therapy
c. implosion therapy
d. flooding

18. Which of these statements would most likely be the focus of discussion in cognitive behavior modification?

a. "I'm the worst employee at my company."
b. "I was very close to my mother when I was a child."
c. "When I think about snakes, I start to feel sick."
d. "People should treat me more fairly."

19. People may benefit more from group than from individual therapy for all of the following reasons except that group therapy does NOT

a. allow people to practice being an authoritarian figure with respect to the group.
b. allow group processes to be used to influence individual maladaptive behavior.
c. provide people with opportunities to observe and practice interpersonal skills within the therapy session.
d. provide an analogue of the primary family group, which enables corrective emotional experiences to take place.

20. A behavioral contract is an explicit agreement that

a. requires negative behaviors to be punished immediately.
b. specifies the code of ethics for therapists' behavior.
c. relates changes in behavior to positive reinforcement.
d. spells out the hierarchy of fears for a patient with a phobia.

471

Practice Test ②

1. Since the professor is presenting the topic of therapy to a group of computer science students, he decides to use a computer analogy. He says that if we think of the brain as a computer, _____ therapies focus on changing the hardware (mechanisms that run the central nervous system), and _____ therapies focus on changing the software (behaviors).

a. psychological; biomedical
b. biomedical; psychological
c. psychodynamic; behavior
d. behavior; psychodynamic

2. Looking back at the mental hygiene movement in the United States in the 1900s, what was the role of the mental asylum?

a. Its purpose has always been to offer treatment to those who could not help themselves.
b. It evolved from having the goal of rehabilitation to the more practical goal of containment.
c. Initially, it was looked upon as a money-making instrument of the state.
d. It was developed to contain the poor, criminals, and the mentally disturbed.

3. "Tiny" is seeing a behavior therapist because he feels compelled to eat a gallon of ice cream each night before he goes to sleep. His therapist is likely to describe the problem in terms of Tiny's

a. current relationships with his parents.
b. early childhood experiences.
c. eating behavior.
d. unconscious motivations.

4. Dorcas is depressed and Nancy is narcissistic. According to a new clinical version of existential psychology, the syndromes exhibited by Dorcas and Nancy are the result of

a. their lack of ability to find satisfaction in their careers.
b. how they reacted to the realities of modern life.
c. the relationships they have with "significant others."
d. random factors in the universe.

472

5. A researcher would like to determine if Dr. Charisma's new form of therapy is more effective than a placebo therapy. The researcher will compare Dr. Charisma's therapy to

a. each of the major forms of therapy.
b. only those therapies that have previously been shown to be effective.
c. the effects obtained through the spontaneous-remission effect.
d. a neutral therapy that just creates expectations of healing.

6. Which of the following is out of place?

a. the "talking cure"
b. participant modeling
c. Joseph Breuer
d. Anna O.

7. The humanistic movement has been called a "third force in psychology" because

a. it grew out of a reaction to psychoanalytic theory and behaviorism.
b. the approach is the least favored of the three major perspectives on behavior.
c. it has been embraced by the nations of the "third world."
d. it followed close on the heels of structuralism and functionalism.

8. Jessica tells her psychoanalyst about a dream in which she and her husband went to an amusement park. While on the merry-go-round she became very hungry and had a craving for a hot dog, but her husband wouldn't buy her one. The psychoanalyst would be most interested in determining

a. the latent content of the dream.
b. the manifest content of the dream.
c. why Jessica's husband was so cheap.
d. whether Jessica had ever been to an amusement park.

9. Which of the following suggests that catharsis has occurred?

a. Tom remembered how much he liked the little girl who sat next to him in the first grade.
b. Henry didn't want to tell his therapist how he felt about his brother.
c. Sally felt better after she had a good cry.
d. Mary's idea of success is owning lots of jewelry.

10. The Addams family is seeing a family therapist. The therapist is most likely to

a. focus attention on the cognitions of the most maladjusted individuals in the family.
b. focus attention on the behaviors of the most maladjusted individuals in the family.
c. view family problems as being caused by dispositional aspects of family members.
d. view each family member as a part of the whole family system.

11. Lionel loves showing his son things, like how to set up the train set and construct the village out of blocks. Lionel is engaged in what Albert Bandura would call

a. social skills training.
b. behavioral rehearsal.
c. contingency management.
d. participant modeling.

12. Charles and Diana are experiencing marital difficulties. If they go to couples counseling, the therapist is likely to emphasize their

a. sexual practices.
b. communication patterns.
c. ethical and moral values.
d. psychopathology.

13. Edgar is terrified of being in a confined space from which he cannot escape. He avoids airplanes, and can only ride buses if they stop frequently. Today, he and his therapist will be riding in an elevator that the therapist has arranged to get stuck between floors. This is an example of the technique called

a. flooding.
b. implosion therapy.
c. reciprocal inhibition.
d. eye movement desensitization.

14. Tardive dyskinesia and agranulocytosis are

a. two major forms of schizophrenia.
b. recently developed antidepressant drugs.
c. side effects caused by certain antipsychotic drugs.
d. side effects of electroconvulsive therapy.

15. Unreasonable attitudes, false premises, and rigid rules are aspects of what cognitive psychologists call

a. faulty thinking.
b. rational-emotive thinking.
c. unconditional positive regard.
d. tardive dyskinesia.

16. Someone might choose a clinical psychologist over a psychiatrist if they wanted a therapist who

a. had completed their medical school training.
b. had a broader background in psychology, assessment, and research.
c. was most trained in the biomedical base of psychological problems.
d. could prescribe drugs.

17. In a classroom exercise, you are to role-play a person-centered therapist. When your client sobs, "My life is so hopeless, what should I do?" you should respond

a. "Why not get a job and stop moping?"
b. "You sound unhappy and uncertain."
c. "Hopelessness often symbolizes sexual inadequacy."
d. "The reason you feel hopeless is because you feel guilty."

18. The observation that patients who suffered both from schizophrenia and epilepsy showed improvement in their schizophrenic symptoms after epileptic seizures led to the development of

a. electroconvulsive therapy.
b. prefrontal lobotomies.
c. psychosurgery.
d. drug therapy.

19. Buffy is plagued by a lack of assertiveness. A social learning therapist would be most likely to recommend

a. cognitive behavior modification.
b. behavioral rehearsal.
c. rational-emotive therapy.
d. person-centered therapy.

20. Boris and Natasha are discussing their behavior therapy programs. The therapy that Boris is getting uses a positive reinforcement strategy, and Natasha's is based on an extinction strategy. It sounds as though Boris and Natasha have therapists who are using

a. aversion therapy.
b. contingency management.
c. person-centered therapy.
d. cognitive behavior modification.

Answers, Practice Test ①

1. d (p. 690)

2. c (p. 677)

3. a (p. 688)

4. b (p. 703)

5. b (p. 698)

6. c (p. 707)

7. b (p. 701)

8. b (p. 706)

9. c (p. 699)

10. d (pp. 679-680)

11. d (p. 709) This is secondary prevention because your main effort is not to prevent disorders (primary prevention) but to limit their duration.

12. c (p. 681)

13. c (p. 680) It's possible that Willem has transferred his relationship with his mother onto the therapist.

14. b (p. 672)

15. a (p. 675)

16. d (p. 695)

17. d (p. 684)

18. a (p. 692) This is a negative self-statement.

19. a (p. 696)

20. c (p. 686)

Answers, Practice Test ②

1. b (p. 673)

2. b (p. 676)

3. c (p. 682) For a behavior therapist, the symptom itself is the problem.

4. b (p. 695)

5. d (pp. 705-706)

6. b (p. 679)

7. a (p. 694)

8. a (p. 680)

9. c (p. 680) Catharsis involves an emotional release.

10. d (p. 699)

11. d (p. 689)

12. b (p. 699) Couples counseling for marital problems seeks to clarify the typical communication patterns of the partners and then to improve the quality of their interaction.

13. a (p. 684)

14. c (p. 703)

15. a (p. 693)

16. b (p. 675)

17. b (p. 695) The client-centered therapist reflects and at times restates the client's evaluative statements and feelings.

18. a (p. 702)

19. b (p. 689)

20. b (p. 686) Contingency management refers to the general treatment strategy of changing behavior by modifying its consequences.

EXPERIMENTS AND DEMONSTRATIONS

Strategies for Discussion Sections:
Experiments and Demonstrations

➡This section is designed to be used only with the direction of your teacher.

Becoming directly involved in research is one of the best ways to put life into psychology. Toward that goal, we have prepared a set of research projects to be conducted in class. They are designed to sample different areas of psychology, to illustrate various methodological approaches and important issues, and to offer a range of activities that can engage the entire class.

Ideally, participating in these demonstration research projects should enable you to get a feeling for the exciting process of analyzing complex psychological problems, generating quantitative and qualitative data, and drawing conclusions. Indeed, it is precisely by experiencing this process of discovery that you may come to appreciate the products of psychological investigation that are presented in the text and lectures.

When this experience works as intended, your outlook is transformed from the passive: *"What* do I *need* to know?" into the active mode: *"How* can I find out what I'd *like* to know?" Such a change in thinking will fire your intellectual curiosity to go beyond acquiring what is given or required to challenging the given and seeking the knowledge desired. If this happens, even "ordinary students" may become scholars and scientists who make extraordinary contributions to society.

Some introductory psychology courses include a laboratory or discussion section component that supplements the basic lecture class. We have designed a set of research projects that accompany this edition of *Psychology* for use in those courses. If your teacher plans to use some or all of our research projects, then **you should bring this Study Guide and Workbook to your class meetings.** It contains the materials necessary for carrying out the research projects, such as instructions, stimulus materials, tables and charts for tabulating your data, and so forth. The research demonstrations include the following:

Domain	*Title*	*Begins on*
Social Perception	Impression Management and Formation	p. 484
Sensory Perception	Being Temporarily Blind	p. 486
Methodology	Reaction Times Can Be Revealing	p. 487
Conditioning	Salivating for Pavlov	p. 488
Memory and Cognition	Strategies for Enhancing Memory	p. 489
Motivation and Assessment	Detecting Guilt and Deception	p. 497
Psychopathology	Suicide: Intentions and Acts	p. 498
Ethics and Research	Evaluation of Research Ethics	p. 502
Psychotherapy	Clinical Interventions	p. 509

IMPRESSION MANAGEMENT AND FORMATION

Materials
a. Impression formation tally sheet
b. Chart for outlining a taxonomy of self-presentational styles

Impression Formation Tally Sheet

As each of your fellow students introduces himself or herself, use this sheet to record your impressions of each of them by listing up to five adjectives that you think are characteristic of each person.

STUDENT NAME	DOMINANT CHARACTERISTICS AND PRIMARY DESCRIPTIVE ADJECTIVES
1	
2	
3	
4	
5	
6	
7	
8	
9	
10	
11	
12	

INSTRUCTOR'S THREE DOMINANT CHARACTERISTICS:	EVIDENCE FOR THOSE CHARACTERISTICS:
1	
2	
3	

* Check those you think he or she is unaware of, and note why you infer this.

A Taxonomy of Self-Presentation Styles

Style	Emotion to Be Aroused (Goal)	Positive Attributions Sought	Prototypical Actions	Negative Attributions Risked
1. Ingratiation				
2. Intimidation				
3. Self-promotion				
5. Supplication				

From Jones & Pittman, 1982

BEING TEMPORARILY BLIND

Materials

Table for comparison of anticipated and actual reactions to being temporarily blind

Comparison of Anticipated and Actual Reactions to Being Blind for a Day

	Anticipated Date: _____ Time: _____	After Experience Date: _____ Time: _____ Total Blind Time: _____
1. Most difficult motor skill or response to make		
2. Sense you will rely upon most		
3. How long it will take to adjust to the situation to function appropriately		

4. What, if any, will be the major problem or difficulty in:
   a) dressing
   b) eating
   c) attending class
   d) engaging in a hobby or favorite recreation
   e) social relations		

5. Sources of anxiety		
6. Sources of gratification		

REACTION TIMES CAN BE REVEALING

Materials

This page is available for you to record the reaction times of males and females, and to write your conclusions regarding the experiment.

REACTION TIMES

Trial	Male	Female	Trial	Male	Female
1	_____	_____	6	_____	_____
2	_____	_____	7	_____	_____
3	_____	_____	8	_____	_____
4	_____	_____	9	_____	_____
5	_____	_____	10	_____	_____

My conclusions are:

_____

_____

_____

_____

_____

_____

Experiments and Demonstrations

SALIVATING FOR PAVLOV

Materials

Sheet for recording your responses and reactions to the stimulus

TEST TRIAL	PERCENT SALIVATING	TEST TRIAL	PERCENT SALIVATING	TEST TRIAL	PERCENT SALIVATING
1	_____	6	_____	11	_____
2	_____	7	_____	12	_____
3	_____	8	_____	13	_____
4	_____	9	_____	14	_____
5	_____	10	_____	15	_____

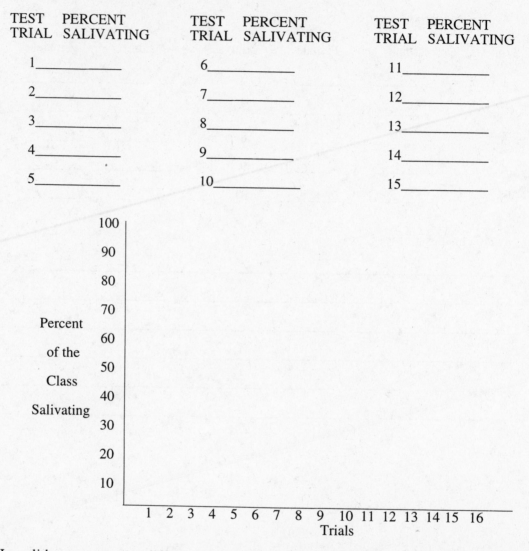

How did your response differ on the various trials? (taste, physical and cognitive responses, etc.)

_____

_____

_____

STRATEGIES FOR ENHANCING MEMORY

Materials

a. Blank sheet for recall test

b. Blank sheet for delayed recall test

c. Recognition test

d. Answer key for immediate recall test

e. Answer key for delayed recall test

f. Answer key for recognition test

g. Data tabulation sheet

Experiments and Demonstrations
RECALL TEST

A.
(Practice) _____

B.
(Practice _____

1. _____

2. _____

3. _____

4. _____

5. _____

6. _____

7. _____

8. _____

9. _____

10. _____

Do *not* turn to the next page until you are instructed to do so.

DELAYED RECALL TEST

_____	_____
_____	_____
_____	_____
_____	_____
_____	_____
_____	_____
_____	_____
_____	_____
_____	_____
_____	_____
_____	_____
_____	_____
_____	_____
_____	_____
_____	_____
_____	_____
_____	_____
_____	_____
_____	_____
_____	_____
_____	_____
_____	_____
_____	_____

Do *not* turn to the next page until you are instructed to do so.

Experiments and Demonstrations

Recognition Test

Circle each word if it was on a list that you heard and saw.

1. iron	soil	chair	doctor	lake
2. crane	rain	garden	shoes	star
3. machine	heap	green	book	button
4. ketchup	almond	lamp	moat	car
5. market	party	square	train	roast
6. house	business	lip	ram	horse
7. spit	boy	dam	shore	railroad
8. sea	illness	hall	harness	hand
9. film	shout	dirt	box	rock
10. mortar	sprain	loan	sugar	prison
11. river	door	picture	golf	ball
12. sip	water	mountain	map	sheet
13. guest	juice	meat	judge	couch
14. home	skin	stone	television	village
15. priest	gold	cat	weapon	kangaroo
16. wind	cannon	sled	city	valley
17. spoon	bird	mast	pickax	spell
18. seat	steeple	letter	sky	corn
19. vehicle	money	fox	wax	lily
20. tree	body	game	girl	camp

Do *not* turn the page until instructed to do so.

Answer Key Immediate Recall Test

A. (Practice)		B. (Practice)	
	apple		flower
	fire		queen
	storm		army
	ship		kiss
	king		street

1.		2.	
	river		body
	garden		letter
	lake		girl
	sugar		rock
	bird		tree

3.		4.	
	lip		shoes
	book		machine
	seat		boy
	gold		village
	valley		green

5.		6.	
	water		weapon
	hall		home
	market		skin
	camp		meat
	shore		car

7.		8.	
	cat		soil
	sky		city
	horse		mountain
	vehicle		house
	money		prison

9.		10.	
	iron		picture
	party		judge
	doctor		star
	railroad		door
	square		sea

Totals

Correct R: _____   Correct H: _____

Do *not* turn to the next page until instructed to do so.

Repeat Words	*Hello Words*
river	body
garden	letter
lake	girl
sugar	rock
bird	tree
lip	shoes
book	machine
seat	boy
gold	village
valley	green
water	weapon
hall	home
market	skin
camp	meat
shore	car
cat	soil
sky	city
horse	mountain
vehicle	house
money	prison
iron	picture
party	judge
doctor	star
railroad	door
square	sea

Totals

Correct R: _____   Correct H: _____

Do not turn the page until you are instructed to do so.

Answer Key Recognition Test

1. +9 iron (+8) soil — +9 doctor + 1 lake
2. — — +1 garden (+4) shoes (+10) star
3. (+4) machine — (+4) green +3 book —
4. — — — — (+6) car
5. +5 market +9 party +9 square — —
6. (+8) house — +3 lip — +7 horse
7. — (+4) boy — +5 shore +9 r a i l - road
8. (+10) sea — +5 hall — —
9. — — — — (+2) rock
10. — — — +1 sugar (+8) prison
11. +1 river (+10) door (+10) picture — —
12. — +5 water (+8) mountain — —
13. — — (+6) meat (+10) judge —
14. (+6) home (+6) skin — — (+4) village
15. — +3 gold +7 cat (+6) weapon —
16. — — — (+8) city +3 valley
17. — +1 bird — — —
18. +3 seat — (+2) letter +7 sky —
19. +7 vehicle +7 money — — —
20. (+2) tree (+2) body — (+2) girl +5 camp

[ ] Circled numbers are the list numbers of "Hello" words (even-numbered lists)
[ ] Uncircled numbers are the list numbers of "Repeat" words (odd-numbered lists)
[ ] —are false positives, words you thought were on a list but were not

Total Correct R: _____

Total Correct H: _____

Total False Positives: _____

Experiments and Demonstrations

DATA TABULATION SHEET

Name:_____

Record frequency of scores under each of the following conditions.

	Memory Measure		
Experimental Condition	Immediate Recall	Delayed Recall	Delayed Recognition
Repeat (Repetition)			
Hello (Depth-of-processing)			
Totals			
			False Positives

Conclusions: What is the effect of the experimental conditions on

      (a) immediate recall

      (b) delayed recall

      (c) delayed recognition

Plot these data on a bar graph. Use different shaded bars for the two experimental conditions.

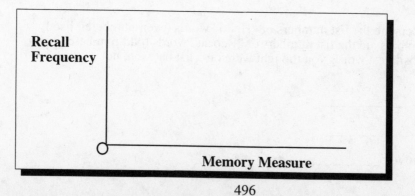

Memory Measure
DETECTING GUILT AND DECEPTION

Materials

a. Data tally sheet of reactions to each of 30 stimulus words

b. Expressive Behavior Encoding Guide and table for summarizing data for each of two subjects

c. Table of word association norms

d. Reaction Time summary table

e. Verdict slip

Data Sheet

Stimulus Word	Suspect 1			Suspect 2		
	Response Word	Reaction Time	Expressive Behavior	Response Word	Reaction Time	Expressive Behavior
1. school						
2. music						
3. orange						
4. black						
5. buy						
6. country						
7. letter						
8. tree						
9. boy						
10. bat						
11. lake						
12. crushed						
13. street						
14. pay						
15. heaven						
16. spot						
17. miss						
18. smooth						
19. finger						
20. water						
21. whistle						
22. red						
23. light						
24. dream						
25. work						
26. burn						
27. three						
28. tattoo						
29. ashes						
30. trash						

Expressive Behavior Encoding Guide

Code Letter	Expressive Behavior
S	Speech-disturbance behavior, such as stuttering, answering in an especially low or loud voice, clears throat often, coughs, signs, and so forth
P	Physical movements, such as shifting in one's seat, crossing and uncrossing one's legs, twisting, wringing hands, fidgeting with things, and so forth
F	Facial expressions, such as excessive smiling or frowning, wetting of the lips, shifting of eyes, closing of eyes, and so forth
O	Other unusual behavior you might notice and want to record that doesn't fall into the other categories

Expressive Behavior. Tally the instances of expressive behavior in the following table.

Categories	Suspect 1				Suspect 2			
	S	P	F	O	S	P	F	O
Critical Words								
Neutral Words								

Is there a difference in frequency of expressive behavior for critical and neutral words for the two suspects? Conclusion regarding expressive behavior:

Verbal Responses: Some word association norms for a selected set of words are given below for comparative purposes. They were collected from a sample of 1000 respondents (Kent-Rosanoff norms[1]).

Word	Associations (by percentage)
dream	sleep (45), night (9), nightmare (5)
light	dark (65), lamp (8), bright (3)
boy	girl (77), man (4), scout (4)
street	avenue (19), road (13), cars (1)
music	song(s) (18), note(s) (17), sound (12)
black	white (75), dark (5), cat (3)
smooth	rough (33), soft (21), hard (14)
whistle	stop (13), train (9), noise (7)
red	white (22), blue (20), black (12), blood (3)

[1] Kent, G. H., & Rosanoff, A. J. (1910). A study of association in insanity. *American Journal of Insanity, 67,* 37-96, 317-390. For a more recent discussion of these norms, see Woodworth, R. S., & Schlosberg, H. (1954). *Experimental psychology* (rev. ed.). New York: Holt.

Experiments and Demonstrations

Judged by these norms, how common or unusual and idiosyncratic were the word associations given by the suspects? Is there a difference in the quality of their responses to the critical versus neutral words? Do the differences give you clues to who is guilty? How?

Conclusion regarding verbal responses:

Reaction Time. Compute the mean RTs in the following table.

Categories	Suspect 1	Suspect 2
Premeasured neutral words		
All neutral words		
All critical words		
Critical words in common		

Do the suspects' mean reaction times give you clues as to which one is guilty? Are there any extreme RTs for individual words? Do you see any differences on particular critical words that might indicate guilt?

Conclusion regarding reaction times:

- -

Verdict

I believe the guilty person is _____

My confidence in this judgment is _____

(on a scale from 0-100 where   0 = no confidence,
50 = moderate confidence, and
100 = complete confidence)

- -

SUICIDE: INTENTIONS AND ACTS

Materials

A 10-item Suicide Quiz

How Much Do You Know About Suicide?

Circle the letter that indicates whether the following statements are true or false.

T   F   1. Men *attempt* suicide more often than women.

T   F   2. Women *commit* suicide more often than men.

T   F   3. Poisoning, by either pills or gas, is the most common form of suicide.

T   F   4. Minorities commit suicide more often than whites.

T   F   5. The higher the socioeconomic level, the lower the suicide rate.

T   F   6. After about 60 years of age, the suicide rate begins to decline continuously.

T   F   7. Suicide rates for college students reached an all-time peak in the 1960s and have declined somewhat since then.

T   F   8. Suicide rates are lower for people who are terminally ill than for people who have illnesses with no end in sight.

T   F   9. Those people who never mention suicide are more likely to actually commit the act than individuals who occasionally discuss it.

T   F   10. One of the difficulties in predicting suicides is that they are often committed without warning.

EVALUATION OF RESEARCH ETHICS

Materials

a. Four research proposals

b. University request form for institutional review/approval

c. Research proposal format and a guide to review-evaluation-analysis

Proposal 1

Title: Resolution of Social Conflicts
Department: Social Anthropology

Proposal: Many groups face social conflicts that, without adequate means of resolution, erupt into group hostility and destructive behavior. On the basis of previous research by M. Sherif, we believe that the critical variable in the conflict resolution process is the availability of superordinate goals, that is, common goals or objectives that can be fulfilled only via cooperative rather than competitive strategies.

Subjects will be housed in an environment that is new to them (a summer camp) with others who are strangers. This is to control for extraneous influences and prior group formation. The subjects will be divided into two groups each of which will be housed separately, and led by a team of adult supervisors-observers. There will be four phases to our study: (a) development of strong within-group cohesion and solidarity in each of the two camp groups; (b) creation of the opportunity for conflict between the two groups; (c) introduction of a common problem (e.g., breakdown in water supply to the camp) facing both groups; (d) observation of strategies of resolution.

The duration of each phase will be: Phase 1-five days; Phase 2-three days; Phrase 3-one day; Phase 4-five days—a total of two weeks.

Trained observers will record all interactions that occur during meals, sports, recreation, and at other times.

Subjects: 60 lower-class children whose parents agree to send them to this experimental summer camp for two weeks. There will be no fees at all for transportation, food, tuition, etc., in return for the use of the children as subjects. The children will not be informed of the experimental nature of the camp, but parents will sign an informal consent form (submitted to this committee separately). All parents will receive a report of the study in which children's identity will be confidential. There will be adequate medical and health supervision at all times during this study.

Remarks: It is expected that we will learn some important principles to help in the design of environments to promote cooperation and minimize competition. Such "social engineering" may remove conflicts not only in gangs but also between ethnic and racial groups and be of value even at the political-international level (witness cooperation among oil-deprived nations).

Proposal 2

Title: Low-Pressure Determinants of Compliance
Department: Psychology

Proposal: Research done in the mid-1960s by Freedman and Fraser demonstrated that compliance with a small request greatly increased the probability of future compliance with a large request, even when the large request was made two weeks after the small request. The large request made in this research required the subjects to allow their home property to be used in specific ways. It was thus a request for acquiescence.

Our study will replicate the Freedman and Fraser investigation, except that the large request will call upon subjects to actively carry out a rather time-consuming task.

The subjects will be householders in a suburban middle-class community. They will be contacted in their homes, in person, and treated in one of three ways: (a) informed about a new effort to persuade the city council to enact an ordinance prohibiting research and development of antipersonnel weapons in the city limits (FAMILIARIZATION CONDITION); (b) asked to sign a petition to the city council advocating such an ordinance (SMALL REQUEST CONDITION); (c) agree to sign a petition when approached to do so later (AGREEMENT CONDITION). Half the subjects in each of these three conditions will later be approached and asked to invite their neighbors to a coffee meeting in their homes to generate support and raise funds for this effort. The other half will be approached and asked to hold a similar meeting to generate support and raise funds for an effort to enact new pollution control ordinances.

The study therefore includes a control group that is merely contacted, a group that agrees to a small request, and a group that actually carries out the small request. Subjects from all three groups are then asked to carry out major requests that are either related or unrelated to their previous experience.

Remarks: Events of the past few years have caused great concern among Americans about political manipulation and commercial exploitation of the public. In politics, "dirty tricks" has become a household phrase. Advertising through the media is widely believed to influence consumer preferences. We believe that understanding of the subtle tactics political organizers and salespeople attempt to use can enable private individuals to behave in a more independent fashion. Our interest focuses on low-pressure techniques precisely because many people are sensitized to high-pressure tactics and can presumably defend themselves against those tactics to some extent. Low-pressure tactics, on the other hand, may go unrecognized by the target population and thus render them more susceptible to insidious influence attempts.

Proposal 3

Title: Obedience in Response to Authority
Department: Educational Psychology

Proposal: This study will replicate and extend research by Milgram and by Sheridan and King on the conditions under which adults will administer painful or potentially lethal punishment to a victim in obedience to the instructions of an authority figure. Male and female subjects will be asked to serve as the "teacher" in a study of the effects of punishment on learning. A fluffy, attractive puppy in a cage with an electrifiable grid floor will be presented as the learner attempting to learn to discriminate steady lights from lights flickering at rates near the Critical Fusion Frequency for dogs. The subject's task is to administer a series of increasingly intense shocks to the puppy, increasing the shock level after each error. The panel of switches on the shock generator will be marked to indicate a range of 15 to 450 volts, increasing in 15-volt steps.

In fact, the shocks the puppy experiences will be restricted to levels insufficiently intense to produce tissue damage. For half the subjects of each sex a small amount of anesthetic gas will be introduced into the dog's cage so that the animal appears to slump into unresponsiveness as a result of the shocks.

Dependent measures in this study will include: (a) the maximum shock administered by the subject; (b) the duration of shocks administered; (c) subject's verbal and expressive behavior during the experiment.

Remarks: History is tragically rich in examples of atrocities carried out by people whose principal motivation is responsiveness to instructions issued by an authority figure. Thus, ordinary German citizens participated in the torture and massacre of Jews, American aviators dropped atomic bombs on Japanese cities, and flesh-shredding antipersonnel weapons are currently being used in Indochina by technicians whose remote control devices prevent them from even seeing the results of their actions.

It is vital that we understand the conditions under which people will and will not carry out instructions leading to inhumane acts, so that adequate legal and social safeguards against the abuse of authority may be instituted without delay. The subversion of the American political process revealed through the Watergate investigations only highlights the urgency of research in this area.

The puppy victims will experience some distress in the course of each session. While the investigators do not consider an animal's suffering something to be treated casually, it is felt that this research design is compatible with the traditional requirement that animal suffering be justified by the human benefits of the resulting knowledge. Variations on the design will include creating a "compliance hierarchy" with a series of subjects passing orders down the line to the final executor.

Proposal 4

Title: Interpersonal Dynamics in a Simulated Prison
Department: Sociology

Proposal: The institution of prison is of special interest for social scientists because of the unique character of the social relations and interactions which occur there. Several years ago, research by Zimbardo and his colleagues demonstrated that prison behavior could be scientifically studied under the control conditions of a "simulated" laboratory environment. They found that behavioral syndromes associated with prison life (for example, guard brutality, prisoner disintegration) could be reliably elicited in an experimental milieu, with little loss in the authenticity of reactions, and within a relatively convenient time period.

In our modest proposal, we will attempt to extend this early research in several crucial directions. Generalization from the Zimbardo study to social behavior in real prisons is limited by the fact that it employed normal, healthy, middle-class college students—precisely the kind of people least likely to enter a real prison. In our study we propose to utilize a subject population of lower-class, preferably minority, persons as prisoners, and a group of working-class white males as guard personnel. In this way we will be better able to draw inferences about the parameters which control the behavior in actual prison populations. In addition, our study will employ much larger groups of prisoners and guards than the 20 used in the original study, since it is only in this way that statistically reliable results may be obtained and valid conclusions drawn about prison behavior. Finally, we propose increasing the length of the study to several months (depending upon budgetary constraints) in order to investigate the more important effects of long-term imprisonment, rather than simply short-term adjustment. We will also study, in a second phase of the research, whether female guards and prisoners act as the males do, and whether different types of training of the guards yield more "positive" outcomes.

Because our simulated prison environment will be designed to maximize experimenter surveillance and data collection, we are confident that all deleterious effects will be carefully monitored and recorded.

Experiments and Demonstrations

Administrative Panel for Human Subjects in Behavioral Science Research

PROTOCOL_____
(Leave blank)

Request for Institutional Review/Approval

Regular Review ☐ Expedited Review ☐ _____ *

Date_____

Principal Investigator(s)_____
_____

Faculty_____ Student_____ (check one)
If student, please indicate faculty
sponsor:_____/_____
         (name)   Extension

Department_____

Phone/extension where you may be contacted_____

_____
(Faculty Sponsor Signature)

Title of Research Proposal_____

_____

For Sponsored Projects *(Funding by outside agency):*

New
Proposal ☐   Continuation ☐   Competing Renewal ☐   Project is under an existing grant ☐

For Unsponsored Projects:
New ☐   Renewal ☐

Funding Agency_____ _____

Proposed start date:

Grant/Contract No._____
(Include P.I. name if other than one given above)

_____

*Proposed Start Date*_____
Approval certification (HHS Form 596) to be sent to: _____

_____
(Name & Agency if available)

For Renewal of Approval *(whether sponsored or unsponsored)*

(Please submit at least 30 days PRIOR to expiration date of previous approval)
Date of previous approval_____Protocol No. (if known)_____

In addition to a copy of original protocol, please provide a brief progress report of the previous year's activity which includes:

     1. Number of subjects involved
     2. Problems or complications (if any)
     3. Description of results to date
     4. Any changes or modifications since original approval was given
     5. Project plans for the coming year (for which approval is being requested)
     6. A copy of the consent form you are using for this study

Name and address to which human subject approval memo should be sent (if other than investigator and department indicated above):

*Give paragraph # which qualifies protocol for expedited review (see reverse side)

*Give paragraph # which qualifies protocol for expedited review (see reverse side)

Instructions

A short (1-3 pages) summary of the project is needed for review by the Human Subjects Panel; this should include a description of the purpose of the study, the procedures which will involve human subjects, the length of their involvement, and the means for ensuring confidentiality of data regarding the subjects. *Please avoid any technical terms not readily understood by individuals outside your discipline. You do not need to include a copy of your complete proposal, but please do include copies of any questionnaire or structured interviews (if any).*

Some specific points to be included in the summary are the following:

1. Risk or Benefit to the Subject

This is a major concern of the Panel—please detail any deception, possible psychological or physical risk to the subject, and benefit (if any). *(Benefit does not include any compensation the subject may be given for participation.)*

Projects involving deception raise certain ethical problems often best dealt with by debriefing subjects after their participation. Please describe your debriefing procedures. If you choose not to debrief, this decision must be justified in your summary. In addition, for your protection as well, it is advisable to have a second consent form after the subject is debriefed, reaffirming permission to release information received from the subject during the study.

2. Description of Sample Population

This should include where the study will take place, age of subjects, the number of subjects and the length of involvement time, and must identify precisely the type of subjects if other than normal.

3. Description of the Disclosure of Information and Consent

A consent form must describe the project in nontechnical language; it must clearly indicate that participation is voluntary, that the subject is free to withdraw his/her consent and discontinue participation at any time, and that individual privacy will be maintained in publication of any data resulting from the study.

In addition, the consent form must include the name and telephone number of the researcher as a contact if further information is sought by the subject, and also the following statement (although not necessarily this wording): "If I have any concerns or dissatisfaction with any aspect of this program at any time, I may report grievances—anonymously, if desired—to the Human Subjects Coordinator, Sponsored Projects Office, Stanford, CA 94305." A copy of the consent form should be given to the subject.

Projects involving children often require a consent form for the child (especially those from upper elementary and high school levels) as well as the parent.

Include copies of consent form(s).

TO REQUEST REVIEW OF YOUR PROTOCOL, PLEASE SEND EIGHT COPIES OF THIS APPLICATION AND ALL ATTACHMENTS TO:

_____

_____

_____

Research Proposal Format

All proposals must follow the following outlined format.

Please answer the questions, identifying each by number. Please *type* all responses.

1. Describe the purpose of your study and the procedures that human subjects will undergo in your research design. What are the risks and possible consequences of these procedures?
2. Please write, using layman's terms, a description of what is disclosed to a subject concerning the purpose of the research and its possible risks.
3. Describe your subject population and your method for obtaining the subjects' informed consent. Please attach a sample of a written consent. Also indicate briefly where and how these consent forms will be filed. University policy dictates that they be retained for a period of three years after the conclusion of the project.
4. If personality tests, questionnaires, or inventories are to be administered, describe the reason for their use, the manner in which they will be given, and the information to be given to the subjects about obtained scores. How will you ensure confidentiality of the findings from this research?
5. If your response to any of the following is affirmative, please explain.
   a. Will deception be used in any aspect of the subjects relation to the research? YES____ NO____
   b. Will any stimulus or other conditions be imposed on subjects, or any response be required of them, that could possibly pose a physical risk? YES____ NO____
   c. Will any personality tests, questionnaires, or inventories be administered? YES____ NO____

Note: The proposals already submitted for student reviewers to evaluate are not in that format but will be accepted for review here because they were prepared prior to this memo.

A Guide to Review-Evaluation Analysis

1. For each proposal, decide whether it should be
   a. approved as is;
   b. approved with minor changes (noted);
   c. denied approval until major changes are made in the design and procedure;
   d. denied approval pending pilot study evaluation on following questionable issues;
   e. rejected in principle.

2. Detail specific benefits/risks, gains/losses if each study is conducted or refused permission.

CLINICAL INTERVENTIONS

Materials

Therapeutic Intervention Coding Form

Therapeutic Intervention Coding Form

Disorder:_____   Disorder:_____

	Positive	Negative
Behavioristic		

	Positive	Negative
Past		
Present		
Future		

	Positive	Negative
Pschodynamic		

	Positive	Negative
Past		
Present		
Future		

	Positive	Negative
Humanistic		

	Positive	Negative
Past		
Present		
Future		

Tell us what YOU want!

We need your reactions and ideas about this study guide so that we can give you even more of what you want in the future. What did you like best and least? What would you have more or less of? Could it have been better organized? Please jot down your suggestions, cut out this page, fold and tape it, then mail it to us, postage free.
Thanks!

HarperCollins Supplements Department

Date:_____ Sex: ☐ Male ☐ Female Age:_____ Major:_____
School:_____ Title of course:_____
Title and author of textbook:_____

Did you buy this study guide... ☐ New? ☐ Used?
Why did you buy this study guide? ☐ Teacher recommended it
    ☐ Other student recommended it ☐ Mid-term coming, needed to review
    ☐ I needed extra help ☐ Teacher required it
    ☐ It caught my eye ☐ Other_____
How many of your classmates also use the study guide?
    ☐ 0% ☐ 5% ☐ 15% ☐ 50% ☐ 100% ☐ Don't know ☐ Other_____
Do you prefer answers to the questions... ☐ All together in the back of the book
    ☐ At the end of each chapter ☐ Right below the question
Do you like text page references where you can find the correct answer? ☐ Yes ☐ No
Do you like the answers briefly explained? ☐ Yes ☐ No
How did you find out about the study guide?
    ☐ My professor ☐ Bookstore ☐ Other_____
Did you use any of the study guide exercises in class as group? ☐ Yes ☐ No
Did your professor give you required assignments in the study guide? ☐ Yes ☐ No
How much did you pay for your study guide?_____
Did you feel that you paid a fair price? ☐ Yes ☐ No
If not, what would you consider to be a fair price?_____

Do you feel that this study guide helped your final grade in the course?_____
Do you feel that the study guide accurately reflected the material in the parent text?_____
_____
What did you like best/least about the study guide?_____
_____
What elements would you add or delete?_____
_____
Was the study guide too long, too short, or just right?_____

Would you be interested in reviewing study guides and textbooks for us? If so, please give us your name, permanent mailing address, and subject areas of interest.

HarperCollins*Publishers*

Attn: Evie Owens, Manager of Supplements Development
College Division—Fourth Floor
10 East 53rd Street
New York, NY 10022

- -

Fold along dotted line

Please tape along this edge. Do not staple.

- -

Fold along dotted line